# Beverly Hills
### Anatomy of a Nightclub Fire

Robert G. Lawson

# Beverly Hills
## Anatomy of a Nightclub Fire

Commonwealth Book Company
—— St. Martin, Ohio ——
2016

© 1984 by Robert G. Lawson
New material © 2016 by Commonwealth Book Company, Inc.
All rights reserved. Published 2016
Printed in the United States of America

ISBN: 978-0-9905351-6-4

Front cover photograph courtesy Kenton County Historical Society.

# Contents

| | | |
|---|---|---|
| Preface | | VII |
| 1. | The Seeds of Tragedy | 1 |
| 2. | The Making of a Firetrap | 27 |
| 3. | The Calm Before the Storm | 57 |
| 4. | Discovery & Notification of the Fire | 87 |
| 5. | Escape From the Front | 123 |
| 6. | Escape From the Showroom | 161 |
| 7. | Rescue and Recovery | 201 |
| 8. | The Aftermath | 237 |
| Conclusion | | 277 |
| Epilogue | | 287 |
| Notes | | 295 |
| About the Author | | 299 |

# Preface

Southgate is a small municipality in the greater Cincinnati area on the Kentucky side of the Ohio River. On Saturday, May 28, 1977, it was the scene of the second worst nightclub fire in the history of the United States. An unknown number of people suffered serious and permanent injuries in the fire; 165 lost their lives. Only the Cocoanut Grove fire of November 28, 1942, was worse. It resulted in the death of almost 500 people.

The Southgate fire occurred in the Beverly Hills Supper Club. Billed by its owners as "The Showplace of the Nation," Beverly Hills was a lavish nightclub by almost any standard of measurement, perhaps even extravagant. Virtually from end to end it was beautifully and tastefully decorated, with an appearance appropriate to an elegant showplace. The floors were covered with plush carpeting, the walls and windows were decorated with expensive paneling and drapes, and the ceilings were hung throughout with huge, attractive chandeliers. The country's most popular entertainers appeared in the club's showroom before crowds that frequently numbered near a thousand.

Most of the major features of the building—at least those important to a description of the tragedy—were captured on some drawings prepared after the fire from construction plans and on-site inspections. One such drawing (see Diagram No. 1 on page ix) shows the internal design and layout of the first and second floors of the building. It also shows the relative sizes of the various rooms, their locations and configurations, and the means of ingress and egress for each. Another drawing (see Diagram No. 2 on page x) shows the size and location of the second story of the building in relation to the first. It also shows the large garden area that existed at the back of the club as well as the two smaller structures that were not physically attached to the main building. With ground level dimensions of approximately 240 feet by 260 feet the big nightclub had sufficient square footage on the first floor alone to cover an area the size of a football field.

Literally the entire structure shown in these drawings was destroyed by the fire that struck the club on May 28, 1977. But only three parts of the club played a crucial role in the tragedy. The first was near the front of the building (at the bottom of Diagram No. 1) to the right of the Main Bar. At that location there was a small L-shaped area called the Zebra Room. There is no doubt that the fire started in this small room while it was unoccupied and spread rapidly to other parts of the building. The second was the club's main corridor which began near the Zebra Room and ran north toward the rear of the building. The fire traveled down this corridor with astonishing speed to the place where most of the deaths occurred. The third was the large showroom located on the northeast corner of the club (at the top right of Diagram No. 1). This area, called the Cabaret Room, was heavily occupied by patrons and employees when fire erupted in the front part of the building. All but two of the 165 people who died in the fire were in this room at the time.

Following the Beverly Hills fire the state of Kentucky, with assistance from federal agencies and the National Fire Protection Association, conducted an investigation that lasted several months. An overwhelming mass of information about the fire and the physical facility where it occurred was produced. A comprehensive report of the circumstances surrounding the fire was prepared by a team of investigators named by the governor of Kentucky. A second report was prepared by a fire analysis specialist of the National Fire

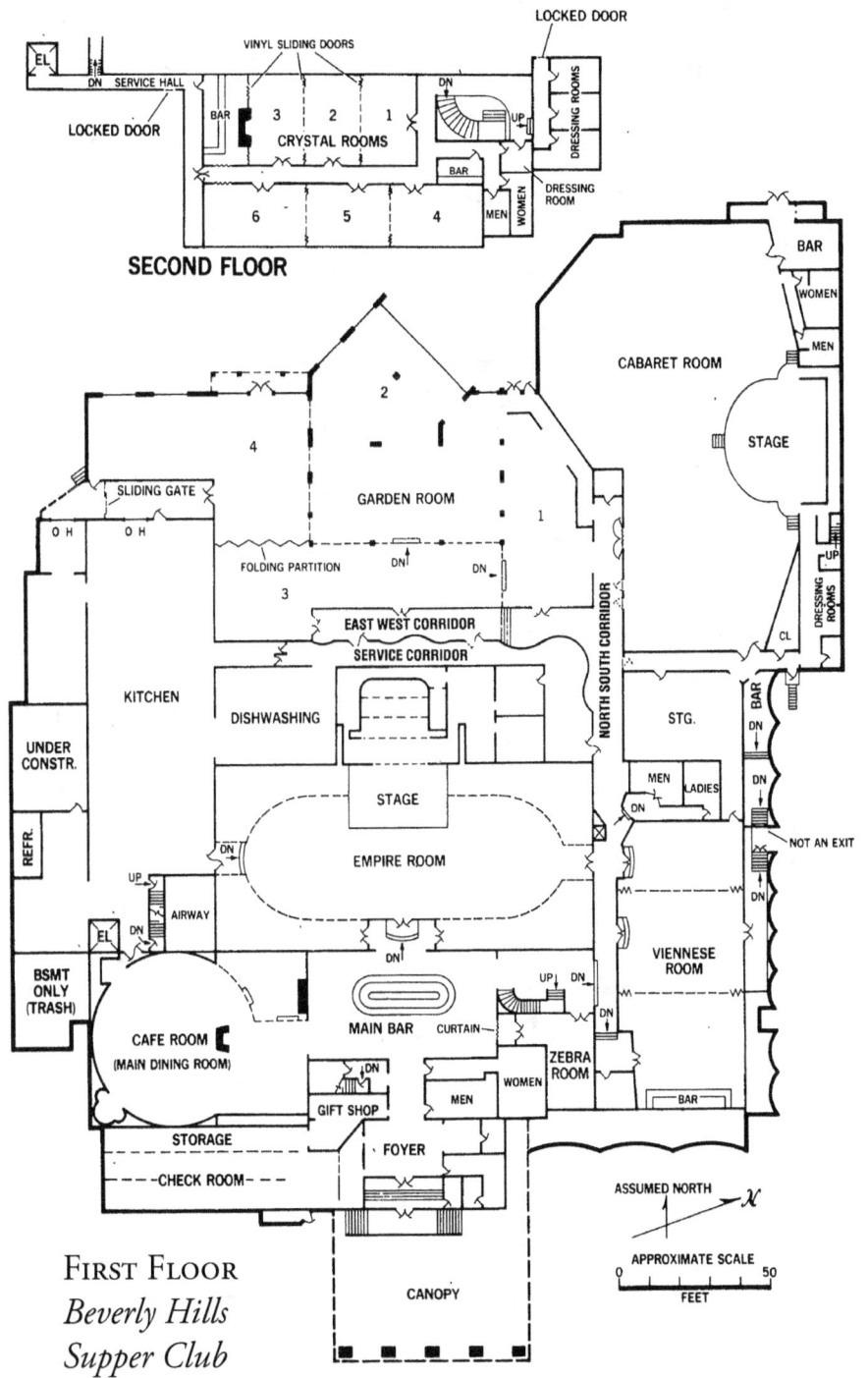

Diagram No. 1

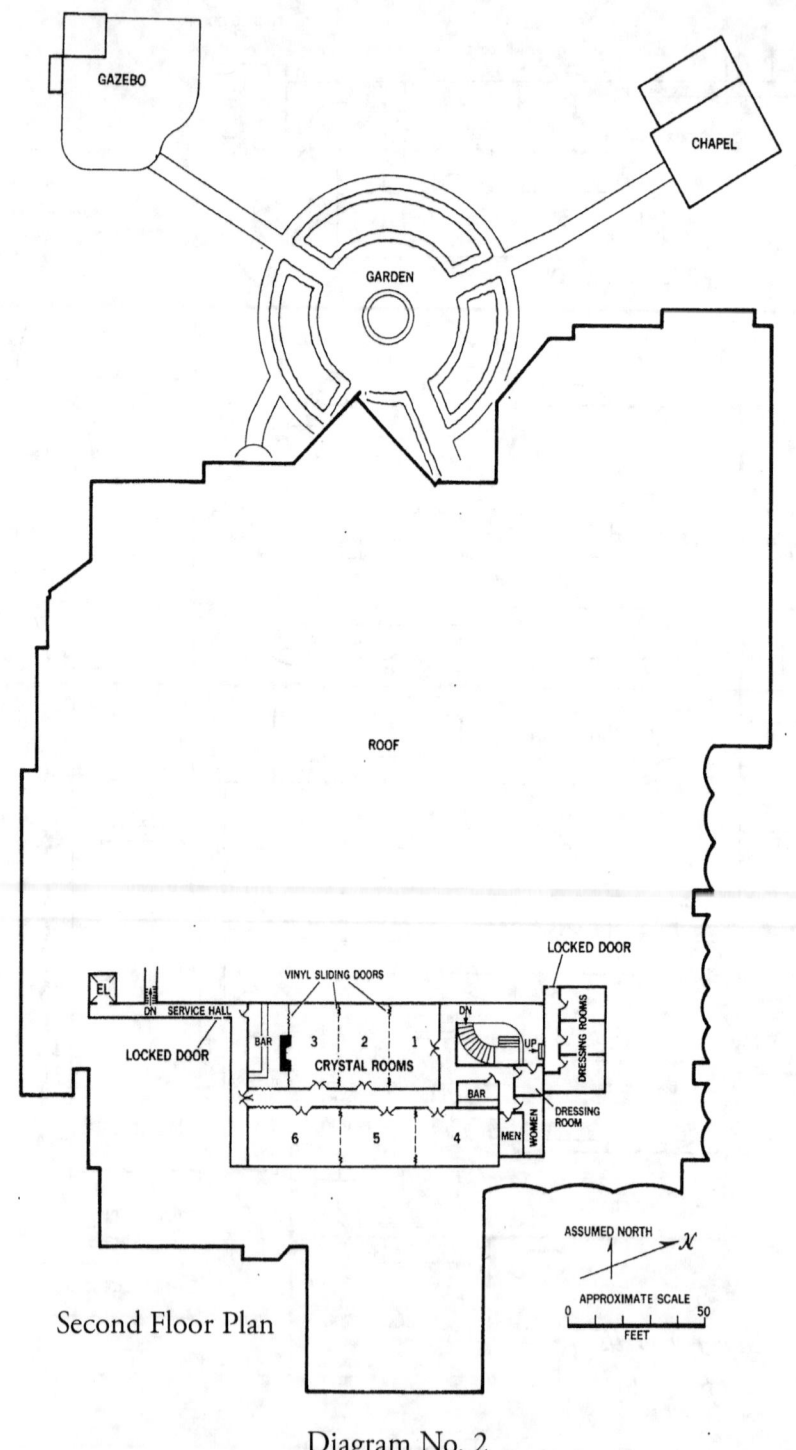

Second Floor Plan

Diagram No. 2

· x ·

Protection Association. In each of those reports the big nightclub was portrayed as a firetrap of major proportions that had come into existence through scores of acts committed in disregard of the law.

All of the information gathered through this investigation, along with those reports, was submitted to a grand jury near the end of February 1978. The grand jury conducted an independent investigation that lasted five months and then reported that it was unable to find sufficient evidence to pursue criminal charges in connection with the fire. The governor of Kentucky initiated action shortly thereafter to secure the appointment of a special prosecutor to review the action of the grand jury and determine if further steps to enforce the criminal laws should be taken. The special prosecutor conducted a third investigation of the fire only to report in February 1979 that further action was not warranted. The report of the special prosecutor was accepted by state authorities, and the criminal prosecution was terminated without a public trial.

Civil litigation over the fire progressed at a slightly slower pace. Damage claims were filed against an almost endless list of individuals, corporations, and governmental entities. The most significant suits were filed against the owners of the club, the state of Kentucky and some of its employees, and the public utility that had supplied electricity for the building. A trial of any one of these actions would have resulted in a complete development and public presentation of the circumstances surrounding the fire.

In early 1979 the suits against the owners of the building and the public utility were settled out of court. At about the same time the one against the state and its employees terminated with a pretrial dismissal on the ground that the defendants had an immunity under the law against all damage claims based on negligent enforcement of the state's safety codes. These two developments, in conjunction with the termination of the criminal prosecution, served to ensure that the Beverly Hills fire would never be subjected to a full-fledged public trial. They also served to ensure that important parts of the historical record surrounding the tragedy would not be publicly known.

This book is an effort to minimize the loss of this historical record. The raw materials from which it was produced are those that would have been used in a public trial over the fire—thousands of pages of sworn statements taken from survivors of the fire, sworn testimony of scores of witnesses given in depositions, official and quasi-official reports about the fire, public and private records that have been obtained through the various investigations of the fire, and face-to-face interviews with persons prominently connected with the fire or some aspect of its investigation. The objective of the book is singular: to provide an accurate historical record of the pertinent events and circumstances that preceded, accompanied, and followed the tragedy that resulted in the deaths of 165 people.

# One

## THE SEEDS OF TRAGEDY

I

Dick Schilling started in business for himself before World War II as a small ice cream vendor. After the war he ran an in-house cafeteria for a large northern Kentucky corporation, which he left after several years, and bought his first nightclub while still a young man. Subsequently he built and operated a sizable restaurant on a major highway, developed an industrial catering business, and built and operated a motel. In the 1960s he sold them all and bought an established restaurant and nightspot called the Lookout House. He remodeled the building in which this business operated and ran it simultaneously with another restaurant in the same general area. In late 1969 he discovered that the doors of the "old" Beverly Hills Supper Club had been closed for lack of business.

The old club had a shady history. It had been built in 1937 at a modest cost and had been operated for a couple of decades as a prosperous nightclub and dining facility. During part of this time it had been known to allow more than a little gambling activity to occur in violation of the law. In the 1950s, partly because of stricter enforcement of gambling prohibitions, it had lost its prosperity.

In the early 1960s it had closed down. In October of 1969 it had reopened for business as a supper club only to fail once again, this time very quickly. Two months later—December 30, 1969, to be exact—the building and surrounding acres were deeded to an enterprise called the 4-R Corporation. The four Rs were a father and three sons: Richard, Sr., Richard, Jr., Ronald, and Raymond.

To Dick Schilling, the Beverly Hills purchase was a hope for the future. His oldest sons, Rick and Ron, were in college at the time but were already highly experienced in the restaurant business. They had been under the watchful eye of their father at the Lookout House and had worked at various jobs in a major restaurant by the time Beverly Hills became available. Only Raymond (better known as "Scott") was too young at this time to contribute significantly to the operation of a new business; he was thirteen years old. But even he was ready, his father thought, to begin acquiring the necessary skills for productive work. So, in a sense, the old club offered for Dick Schilling an opportunity of a lifetime: *I intended to purchase it, redecorate it, and turn it over to my sons. It was my intention to be there with them for a while and see if they could run it.*

2

In 1969 the Beverly Hills Supper Club was a two story structure with a partial basement. With respect to the basement and second story it was not too different from the facility that would sit on the hilltop outside Southgate on May 28, 1977. But the first floor of the building—the main body of the club—was nothing like the one where 165 lives were lost on the night of the fire. Against an outline that shows the configuration and size the club would ultimately achieve, the "old club" is shown on Diagram No. 3, (see p. 4). The location and size of its major rooms, the Empire Room, the Main Bar, the Foyer, and the Viennese Room, are correctly represented on the drawing. The physical space for the Main Dining Room and the Zebra Room existed at this time but not the rooms themselves. The southwest portion of the building (identified on the drawing as the Cafe Room) was used as the club's original kitchen and the space that would one day become the Zebra Room was an unfinished area used only for storage.

Dick Schilling wanted his club to be special, to have a unique look, to be a showplace. But he had no grandiose plans for Beverly Hills at this moment and no thoughts of adding to the building. It was his intention merely to refurbish and redecorate the old club and to do so as much as possible through his efforts and those of his two older sons. He knew enough about the construction of buildings, he thought, to formulate plans for the renovation and remodeling of his acquisition and to implement those plans with a limited amount of professional assistance. In any event he had little choice, for he had invested his entire life's savings ("every dime I had") in the purchase of the building. So he borrowed as much money as possible after taking possession of the property and set to work on his project.

He promptly acquired the services of a professional to redesign the interior of the club and hired a man experienced in construction to help with necessary remodeling. He bought the most expensive wallpaper, drapes, and carpeting available and purchased high-quality furniture and furnishings for the banquet and party rooms. From cities in Europe he ordered chandeliers that cost thousands of dollars and belonged only in an extravagant showplace. And he took his interior designer to clubs in other parts of the country to get just the right ideas for Beverly Hills. He was determined to beautify the interior of his building, to furnish it as tastefully as possible, and to spare no effort or expense in doing so.

Through the winter and early spring of 1970 he and his sons worked long and hard to prepare the building. They redecorated and refurnished the entire first floor of the old club and converted all of the second floor from office space to dining area. During this period nothing of major consequence was done without his prior approval. Almost no detail of the renovation was too small to escape his attention.

The demands on his time and energy were enormous. On most days he came to the building early and left late. He was eager to open for business as soon as possible and worked tirelessly toward

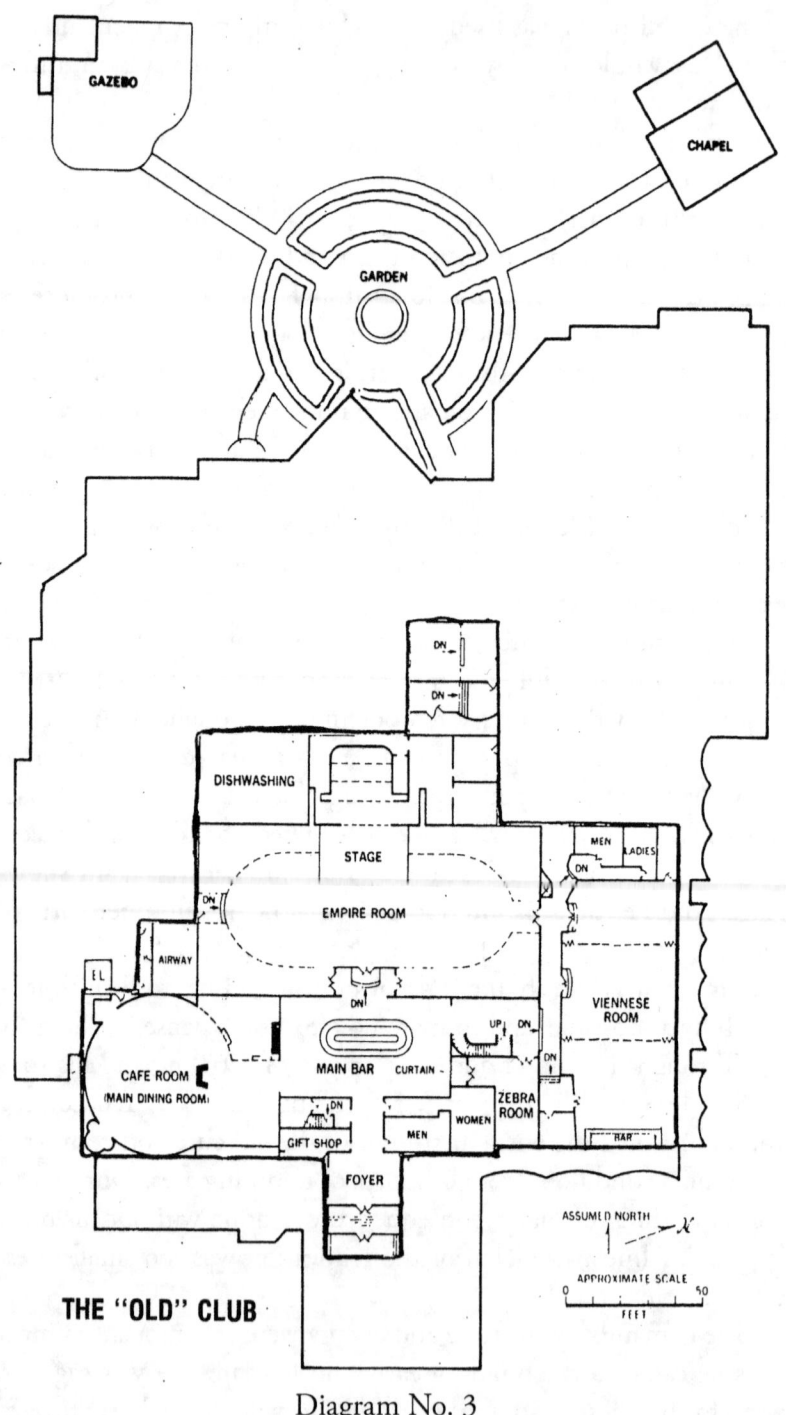

Diagram No. 3

that end. Never did his enthusiasm for the club waver. Never did his confidence in success wane in the slightest. By the time he was halfway through the renovation effort he was so sure of his ability to do something special with the club that he had begun to contemplate enlargement of the building.

### 3

Some years earlier, well before Dick Schilling entertained his first thoughts about the purchase of Beverly Hills, the city of Southgate found itself without a building inspector. The year was 1964. At this time, in small towns across Kentucky, the building inspector was not regarded by the average citizen as a significant public official. His responsibilities were thought to be those of issuing permits for new construction and keeping the community reasonably free of rats, debris, and dilapidated buildings. Hardly anyone viewed him as a person with major responsibility for the enforcement of laws designed to guard against fire hazards in public buildings. In the eyes of nearly everyone he was little more than a petty bureaucrat.

The city of Southgate was typical of these small towns. It imposed on the building inspector through its ordinances enormously important and burdensome responsibilities.

> 1. *It shall be the duty of the building inspector to enforce all laws relating to the construction, alteration, repair, removal, and demolition of buildings and structures.*[1]

> 2. *The building inspector shall inspect all buildings or structures during construction to ascertain that the provisions of law are complied with and that such construction is prosecuted safely.*[2]

And then it gave him a status in government that virtually assured his failure to perform the duties of his office. He was provided with no staff, not even a secretary, no transportation with which to move about the city in performance of his duties, and no expense allowance for the use of his own automobile toward that end. He was allowed to retain the fees charged for the issuance of building permits but got no compensation from the city for his work. In an average year he could reasonably expect to earn for his efforts approximately $200. For all practical purposes he was a volunteer worker.

The city council of Southgate was not overwhelmed on this occasion with applicants for the vacant office. For a time there was but one—an elderly man who had worked in building construction before reaching the age of retirement. A little later, because of efforts of the council to dredge up additional applications, there was a second—a younger man from the community who worked in the area as a journeyman bricklayer. With no other applicants and a need to fill the position, the council decided that the retired contractor was the man for the job. Unfortunately his appointment did very little to solve the city's problem. He died a couple of months later and left the office vacant once again.

By this time the bricklayer, still available and still willing to serve, looked much better to members of the council. He possessed at least some knowledge of building construction, had lived in the area for most of his life, and knew the city of Southgate well. He had a high school education and by reputation the qualities of a highly responsible man. He was only thirty-seven, and energetic. And perhaps most importantly, unlike the only other applicant for the vacant position, he was not a retired shoe salesman. An appointment was made by the council. A second important figure in the tragedy entered the picture.

The new building inspector was not installed in his office with ceremony or fanfare. An official of the city placed in his hands two complex legal documents, The National Building Code and the Kentucky Standards of Safety, and told him that the construction and remodeling of buildings within the territorial boundaries of the city had to conform to their contents. No one introduced him to the responsibilities of the office or provided him with even minimal instruction on the contents of the laws he was obligated to enforce. He was simply accepted for the job, handed the baton of office, and sent on his way: *I was just given whatever records they had accumulated. And that was it.*

4

In early spring of 1970 Dick Schilling left Southgate and crossed the Ohio River for a business engagement in Cincinnati. He had a set of architectural drawings of his club and some firm ideas for expansion of his building. His renovation project was on schedule but he was no longer thinking only in terms of redecoration. Foremost in his thoughts at the moment was a new showroom of sufficient size and quality to attract top nightclub entertainment to Southgate. His destination was the offices of a man in whose hands he was about to place his hope for something special at Beverly Hills.

His engagement in Cincinnati on this occasion was brief. He delivered the drawings of his existing club, explained what he thought were his needs, and asked for the preparation of plans and drawings for a major addition to his building. The man to whom he made his request was heavily involved at the time in the construction business. He was a graduate architect but had no license to practice architecture in either the state of Ohio or the state of Kentucky. He had no official seal of office and no legal authority to prepare plans and drawings for the construction of a public building on the Kentucky side of the Ohio River. Dick Schilling believed him to be a competent professional with good architectural tastes. For the moment nothing more seemed important. He left Cincinnati with a promise for the prompt delivery of plans and drawings for the expansion of his building. This action was sure to do no more than keep him barely inside the boundaries of the law.

5

After six years the bricklayer was an experienced building inspector. Few in the state were any better, by most indications, but he was still seriously handicapped by the fundamental flaws of his office. He had no independent means of livelihood, a family to support, and no alternative to treating his uncompensated official duties as a sideline. He had received no instruction from the city of Southgate on fire and safety codes and through his own efforts had acquired knowledge of only the most basic requirements of the law.

He knew that no structure inside the city limits could be enlarged or altered without a permit from his office, that no permit could be issued without the prior submission of plans and drawings of the proposed construction, and that plans and drawings submitted to his office had to contain the seal of an architect licensed to practice in the state of Kentucky. But he knew virtually nothing about the technical requirements of the state's standards of safety and, without that knowledge, was left to perform the duties of his office almost exclusively on the basis of common sense. He was indeed an experienced building inspector by the spring of 1970. But he was not at all equipped for his first official encounter with Dick Schilling and the Beverly Hills Supper Club.

Near the middle of April the unlicensed architect from Cincinnati finished some of the plans and drawings sought by Schilling. The owner of the club visited the building inspector and made application for a construction permit. The building inspector probably informed the owner of a need for the services of a licensed architect. He even may have obtained assurances that such services would be promptly acquired. But he did not send the owner on his way empty-handed, as he could have done. He did not reject the application. He glanced at the plans and drawings in Schilling's possession, made a feeble attempt to evaluate them technically, and issued a permit for the construction of an addition to the building—a new kitchen on the west side of the club and additional dining space across the back.

The date was April 17, 1970. The fire was still seven years down the road. But the first seeds of tragedy had been planted. The plans and drawings for the first major expansion of the old club—cost estimate of $170,000—had not been checked against the building and safety codes of the state of Kentucky. Neither the owner of the facility nor the building inspector knew that those plans and drawings failed in highly significant ways to conform to the safety requirements of the law.

6

Exactly two months later, Dick Schilling made a second call on the Southgate building inspector. Once again he had a set of plans and drawings prepared by the unlicensed Cincinnati architect and now, a firm commitment for additional expansion of the building. This time he sought approval for construction of the showroom that he considered so essential to the success of his club. The project was much smaller than the first—only $31,000 by cost estimate—but no less important to the owner of the building and no less significant to the development of the tragedy.

The building inspector reacted to the request as he had done before. By force of habit he glanced at the plans and drawings for the new construction, reviewed these as superficially as the others, perhaps put the owner of the building under an obligation to acquire the services of a licensed architect, but promptly issued a second building permit for the construction of an addition to the club. Once again no one inside or outside government had checked the plans and drawings against the building and safety codes of the state of Kentucky.

The date was June 17, 1970. The showroom authorized for construction was not the Cabaret Room where 163 would die in 1977. In fact it was nothing at all like the big room that would exist at the back of the building in seven years. Nonetheless a crucial first step had been taken. No longer did a showroom for the big nightclub in Southgate exist only as an idea in the mind of the owner. The predecessor of the Cabaret Room, routinely and inconspicuously, had slipped into being.

The principal owner of the building could hardly have been happier. His pursuit of the special showplace that he wanted for himself and his sons was in its sixth month. He had not yet opened the doors of his club to a single patron, booked his first banquet, or staged his first performance. He had reason to be a little weary. But his creation had begun to take shape, and he could see his dream moving steadily toward reality. He was filled with enthusiasm and hope when he left the building inspector on this late spring day with authorization to commence the construction of his showroom. He was totally unprepared for the week ahead.

## 7

On June 21, 1970, just four days later, a phone rang in the home of the Southgate fire chief at three o'clock in the morning. The chief lifted himself out of bed, anticipating emergency, and grabbed a receiver that was essentially an extension of the fire department telephone. The caller did not identify himself. The conversation that ensued did not reach the intelligible level. It was gibberish and ended quickly, with the phone back on the hook, the chief back in bed, and the call stored momentarily in his memory as a false alert. Perhaps it was. But in fifteen minutes the chief was back on his feet. An alarm had sounded in the Southgate fire station and in the homes of local firefighters to announce the existence of fire in the Beverly Hills Supper Club. This time the alert was not false.

All units of the fire department responded to the alarm immediately. Within four minutes the lead vehicle arrived on the hill outside the front of the building. Not even a night watchman was on hand to direct the firefighters to the site of the blaze. But under the circumstances no such directions were needed. The fire had been burning for a considerable period of time and was clearly visible against the night sky.

It was located toward what was then the back of the building with practically all of the Empire Room engulfed in flames. It was obvious to the first arrivals that the fire had already outdistanced the fighting capacity of the Southgate department. The fire chief sounded a second alarm that filled the station-houses of fire departments across a wide area of northern Kentucky. In a matter of minutes pumpers and firefighters from cities and towns on all sides of Southgate were on the way to Beverly Hills.

For nine years the fire department had known that the water system at Beverly Hills was insufficient to fight a major fire. There was only a single hydrant at the top of the hill near the building and it was short on both volume and pressure. At the bottom of the hill near the highway, more than 2,000 feet from the location of the fire, there was a second hydrant connected to a main water line. In another direction about 1,000 feet from the building was a small lake from which water could be pumped. The firefighters hooked their lines to the hydrants as quickly as possible and simultaneously positioned a couple of pumpers near the lake. From these sources they poured water on the burning building for the remainder of the night. By morning they had the situation under control but had suffered a substantial defeat at the hands of the fire. Much of the building was ruined.

Rumors about the character of the fire surfaced even before the smoldering stopped. A number of things about the blaze suggested the possibility of something other than accidental ignition. In the early stages of their operation, firefighters had encountered four separate fires going at the same time in the barroom. They found unusual burn patterns in parts of the building and near the suspected point of ignition, they discovered exterior doors that seemed to have been opened by force. Most significantly, they found in the debris left by the fire a couple of five-gallon fuel oil cans that no workman or employee could explain or identify. In a post-mortem report the chief expressed an opinion shared by many of those who had battled the fire: *My personal belief is that the fire was the work of an arsonist.*[3] Officers of the Kentucky State Police conducted an arson investigation that proved inconclusive. They could never provide a satisfactory explanation for the cause of the fire.

8

In the early morning light of June 21, 1970, Dick Schilling stood in silence on the grounds outside his club and gazed painfully at the devastation caused by the fire. He could plainly see that substantially more of the building had been destroyed than saved. The extreme front end of the club (the part located south of the Main Bar on Diagram No. 3) had suffered only minor damage. The basement and the kitchen had survived intact and the area on the east side of the building (where the Viennese Rooms were located) had not been significantly impaired. But very little was left of the rest.

The second floor had been gutted from end to end and the roof over that part of the club had been ruined. Heavy damage had been inflicted on the Main Bar. The Empire Room, the largest area in the building by far, had been all but destroyed. The rear wall of the club had partially fallen and most of the roof had collapsed. The building looked far more like a nightmare to Dick Schilling than a dream. He had invested the fruits of a lifetime of work in the old club. In little more than a flash it had been reduced to a heap of ashes and rubble. But left standing was Schilling's dogged determination to make something special of the old supper club: *I had every dime I'd ever made tied up in it. I had put up $100,000 to buy the place, and had just enough money and credit to remodel it. I had to go back.* And go back he did. Quickly. Within three days after the fire he was back on the hill chasing his dream with renewed enthusiasm. He needed to rebuild practically the whole structure but his plans for the club had neither changed nor moderated. He still wanted something special and unique for himself and his sons, a place he might someday feel comfortable in billing as "the showplace of the nation." The way to accomplish that, he thought, was to rebuild and restore the old structure and complete the expansions planned and underway at the time of the fire. So he started once again on a dream that was destined to end in even greater disaster.

9

For the next six months there was non-stop demolition, remodeling, and construction activity at Beverly Hills. Dick Schilling visited nightclubs in Las Vegas and elsewhere to get new ideas for use in his club and, as before, spared neither effort nor expense in implementing the ones he liked. Once again he purchased the most expensive wallpaper, drapes and carpeting available, and ordered the highest quality furniture and furnishings for his banquet and party rooms. During the period of construction he received the expensive chandeliers ordered from Europe and installed them in the most attractive parts of his building. One such fixture for the Main Dining Room was so huge and so perfectly balanced that it took half a day for five men to hang it from the ceiling and more than a full day for two employees to attach the prisms.

By late fall the construction and restoration of the building began to wind down. The building was a long way from finished but it began to assume that special look that Schilling wanted. It was to be much bigger than the one purchased almost a year earlier (as indicated on Diagram No. 4 on following page) and substantially more adaptable to multiple uses than the old building. It would have dining and party rooms of all sizes and shapes when finished and, most importantly, the facilities necessary to attract top quality nightclub entertainment to Southgate. It looked good to the principal owner long before it was ready for finishing touches. He could hardly wait to open the doors of his club to his first patrons.

At some point during this period of time, though he rarely did anything but work on his building, he turned his attention to a problem that predated the fire. The plans and drawings under which the new construction was being done were those prepared by the unlicensed architect. The building inspector had put the owner under an obligation to obtain plans and drawings containing a seal of an architect licensed by the state of Kentucky. He had retained sufficient leverage to force compliance with this requirement of the law, and Schilling knew it. Without a certificate of occupancy from the city of Southgate he would not be able to open his club to the public for business. He had no choice but to satisfy the building inspector. He had to acquire the necessary professional services to get his plans and drawings properly sealed.

A few years earlier, at a time when he owned a much smaller club, Schilling had needed the services of an architect. The man he had employed on that occasion had a Kentucky license. He had practiced his profession for a number of years in the northern part of the state, had designed buildings for use by the general public, and had even written a building code for a small city in the area. The job he had done for Schilling was small. But he had done it well. So his name naturally came up after the 1970 fire.

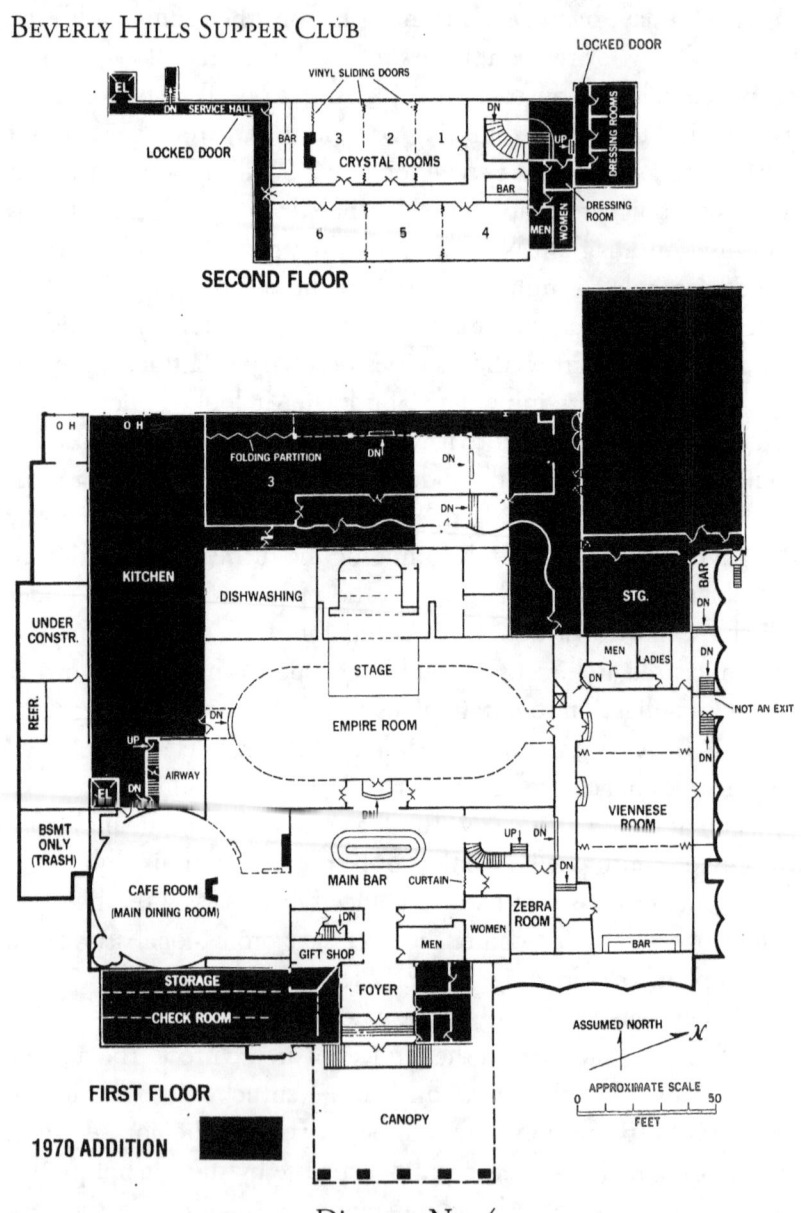

Diagram No. 4

The owner of Beverly Hills had no easy time finding his former architect. He probably expected the difficulty, for the man he sought had long suffered the changing fortunes of profession mixed with alcohol. And by the time of Schilling's need for his services, those fortunes had bottomed out. His professional life was in shambles. He had no office and no secretary. He had no means of transportation and was living alone in a farm shack somewhere in the countryside of northern Kentucky. He had isolated himself from society by choice and had no particular desire to reestablish contact with former clientele. Schilling managed nonetheless to find him and to place in his hands the plans and drawings that had been prepared by the unlicensed architect from Ohio.

Of course Schilling sought little more through this effort than access to a seal of office. What he got, as things turned out, was something quite different. The new architect made a few minor modifications of the drawings placed in his hands, combined them with a set of drawings of the old club, and delivered the finished product to his employer. What he did not deliver, however, was the one thing that the owner of the building needed. Four years earlier he had allowed his professional license to lapse and he had no seal of office to attach to the drawings. Schilling promptly supplied him with sufficient funds for a renewal of his license and the acquisition of a current seal of office. But in the end he had no time to wait for action on the application. A third architect entered the picture.

The contribution of the third architect to the construction project of 1970 is a cloudy issue despite years of investigation. It is clear that he took possession of the plans and drawings prepared by the unlicensed Ohio architect and modified slightly by the unlicensed Kentucky architect. It is clear that he returned to the owner of the building a set of plans and drawings with a proper seal of office attached. It is clear that those plans and drawings were submitted to the building inspector of Southgate and accepted in satisfaction of the owner's obligation. And it is clear that once this occurred Schilling was satisfied that he had solved his problem. Perhaps he had. At least he no longer had reason to fear that the city would refuse him a certificate of occupancy once the building was ready for public use.

## 10

The building inspector of Southgate visited Beverly Hills at least once a week during the entire period of construction and restoration. He made himself as visible as possible to the laborers, the subcontractors, and even the owner, believing that his presence exerted a positive influence on the quality of the construction. He examined the materials being used in the construction, checked the workmanship for quality, and acquainted himself with the reputations of suppliers and subcontractors. He made a conscientious attempt to carry out the responsibilities of his office and to protect the public against the hazards of fire. But he did so under handicaps that virtually assured a failure of his effort.

In 1964 the city council had provided him with copies of appropriate building and fire codes. Since that time both the state and the city had adopted new codes for use in the construction and restoration of buildings. No one yet had provided him with copies of the new ones or even informed him that the old ones had been changed. So he conducted all of his inspections of Beverly Hills without knowing that the building and fire codes in his possession were obsolete. More significantly, he conducted those inspections in near total ignorance of the technical requirements for exits, stairways, corridors, and other critical features of a place of public assembly. He relied almost entirely on common sense and common judgment in his struggle to make the building safe. And under the circumstances that was simply not enough.

By late fall of 1970 the big nightclub was loaded with fire hazards. Some were more crucial than others and all were well concealed in the design of the building. Near the front of the club, corridors had been finished with materials that would facilitate rather than impede the spread of fire through the building. The main stairway between the first and second floors had not been enclosed to prevent the movement of fire from one level of the club to another. The second floor had not a single exit sufficient by design to satisfy the requirements of the law. And the avenues of escape from the front of the building were in serious violation of standards of safety and critically insufficient to accommodate a rapid evacuation of a full house. Already the club was predisposed to disaster, and it was yet to be finished.

## 11

In the city of Southgate, as in most other small towns across the state, the fire department of 1970 was not a well-financed or highly professional organization. It had a stationhouse, only a modest supply of equipment, and no professional firefighters. It was an association of volunteers serving the public without the benefit of compensation. And yet it had the same onerous responsibilities for the safety of public buildings as those imposed by law on the fire departments of major cities. Specifically it had a duty to inspect all places of public assembly "as often as practicable" and to enforce with respect to such places all applicable building and fire codes.[4]

In the fall of 1970 the department had a chief who spent most of his time working as a beer distributor. In many ways he was a carbon copy of the city's building inspector. He received no compensation for his public service, worked at regular employment out of necessity, and performed his offical duties at night and on weekends: He had never received from the state or the city copies of applicable building and fire codes and knew almost nothing about the standards of safety for public buildings. He had no real understanding of the scope of his inspection responsibilities and even less competence than the building inspector to evaluate the safety of construction: *I don't know one piece of plywood from another, or one wire from another, or how much voltage you can throw through this wire or that.* He performed the duties of his office conscientiously. But he had no chance of finding fire hazards hidden away in the design of a building.

He made several trips to Beverly Hills during the period of construction and restoration. He examined the firefighting facilities at the club and ordered some modifications. A road was cut to the small lake on the property. A bigger water line was laid up the hill from the highway, and an additional fire plug was installed at the top of the hill near the building. He inspected the interior of the unfinished structure but found no fault with the exits, the stairways, or the corridors. He did not think that the building would be unfit for occupancy when it was ready to open.

At some point toward the end of construction, however, he began to entertain some nagging concerns about the safety of the club. Perhaps it was only because the early morning fire of June 21 was still a fresh memory. Toward the end of November he placed a call to the fire marshal's office in the state capitol to seek information. His concerns about the safety of the building lingered. He made arrangements for a meeting with the building inspector and at the end of that meeting decided to make a call on the city's mayor.

The mayor wanted to know if plans and drawings for the building expansion and restoration had been submitted to proper authorities as required by law. The building inspector reported that plans and drawings had been received by his office and that the owner had given assurances that approval for the construction had been obtained from the state fire marshal's office. But neither he nor the fire chief could assure the mayor that such approval in fact had been obtained. Both thought an official inquiry necessary.

On November 23, 1970, the mayor wrote and mailed a letter to the state capitol. He reported that the Schilling property had been severely damaged by fire in the spring of the year and that extensive remodeling and expansion was underway. He inquired of the fire marshal about the submission of plans and drawings and about approval for construction. At the end of his letter he removed all doubt about the reason for the inquiry: *Our concern is about fire hazards.*

On December 2, 1970, the mayor got a reply to his letter. It was short and to the point: *Please be advised that this office has not received plans and specifications for renovation or additions to the Beverly Hills Country Club; therefore no approval has been given.*

## 12

In the fire marshal's office at this time there was a high level employee who carried the title of "plans and specifications specialist." It was the responsibility of this employee to review all plans and drawings for building construction requiring the approval of the fire marshal and to check them against building codes and other laws enacted to protect the public against the hazards of fire. It was a responsibility of supreme importance that he shared with no one. When plans and drawings for construction arrived in the office they were routinely routed to him for review. A secretary or clerk would assign a log number to the plans and drawings upon receipt, open a file on the building in question if none existed, and make delivery of the documents to his office. In the course of an average year no less than 6,000 sets of plans and drawings would pass through his hands in this fashion.

But on the morning of December 7, 1970, he sat down to pore over some plans and drawings that had not reached his desk in routine fashion. They had arrived without a log number (meaning that submission to the fire marshal's office had occurred through unusual channels) and without the involvement of a secretary or clerk. The head of the agency, the Fire Marshal himself, had delivered them to the specialist to ask for prompt review. Though this had not occurred before, the specialist made no inquiry about the departure from normal procedures: *He was the Fire Marshal. He gave me instructions to do something. I didn't question it.* He accepted the assignment, assumed it to be special if not sensitive, and went to work. The plans and drawings in his hands were those for the Beverly Hills Supper Club.

Very quickly he discovered that the documents were not sufficient to satisfy the requirements of the law. The safety and adequacy of the exits from the building could not be ascertained from the drawings. Stairways required to be enclosed with fire resistant materials to prevent the spread of fire from one level of the building to another had been designed to be open. The flame spread potential of the interior finish of the club, a matter strictly regulated by law for public buildings like Beverly Hills, could not be determined without more information. The list of important deficiencies discovered by the specialist inched ever upward as he plodded through the review. By the time he had finished, the list had grown to ten.

A building known to be free of fire hazards could not have been constructed under the plans and drawings delivered to the fire marshal. The man who had checked them against the state's standards of safety entertained no doubt: *The building shouldn't have gone forward.* Under ordinary circumstances he would have rejected the plans and drawings as inadequate. The architect who had prepared them would have been contacted and given an opportunity to offer corrections and modifications. Only upon receipt of such corrections and modifications would the required approval for construction have been granted. But the circumstances in this instance were anything but ordinary. Never before had the Fire Marshal himself delivered a set of plans and drawings to the specialist for review.

So the specialist did nothing to reject the plans and drawings for the construction and restoration of the Southgate club. He made no effort to contact the architect who had put his seal of office on them. He chose instead to follow the instructions of his superior to the letter. He prepared a memorandum[5] listing the deficiencies he had discovered through his review, placed that memorandum along with the plans and drawings in the hands of the Fire Marshal, and terminated his involvement in the matter without initiating action to halt the construction underway at Beverly Hills. By this time, of course, there was little construction left to be done. The building was all but finished despite the fact that the fire marshal's office had yet to authorize the commencement of construction.

13

On December 8, 1970, one day after the memorandum of deficiencies had been written, a field inspector from the fire marshal's office visited Beverly Hills for an on-site inspection of the construction. While there he located the principal owner of the building, placed in his hands a copy of the memorandum of deficiencies, and talked some with him about the safety of the building. At the end of his visit he prepared a report for the Fire Marshal that summarized the results of his effort: *I have discussed the ten items listed in your memo of Dec. 7, 1970 with Schilling and he assures me that all will be complied with in the completion of the building. He will let us know prior to completion so that we can make a final inspection.*

The arrival of this report in the state capitol caused barely a ripple of activity. It served only to establish for all time that Beverly Hills would not be a priority item for the state fire marshal's office. No consideration was given to halting the work at the club for failure of the owner to submit proper plans and drawings. No contact was made with the architect who had satisfied Schilling's need for a seal of office, and no attempt was made to acquire the necessary corrections and modifications to the plans and drawings. No thought was given to the possibility of issuing a belated disapproval for the commencement of construction. Apparently the officials of this office thought it adequate under the circumstances to leave the safety of the building to the good faith and judgment of the owner. On December 10, 1970, the Fire Marshal responded to the concerns of the Southgate officials about the possibility of fire hazards at Beverly Hills. He wrote and addressed a letter to both the building inspector and the fire chief:

> *After finally receiving plans for Beverly Hills I immediately sent an inspector to the site. The inspector carried a list of recommendations to be complied with that were accumulated after reviewing the plans.*
>
> *I received my inspector's report on said building and after visual inspection and discussion of these corrections with Mr. Schilling, I have been assured that the corrections under discussion will be taken care of. My inspector was also assured that the parties responsible for construction of this building will notify this office prior to occupying so that a final inspection can be made by this office.*

No copy of the memorandum of deficiencies was attached to the letter. Neither the building inspector nor the chief was ever told of its existence and neither of the two made inquiry about the kind of corrections ordered to be made in the building.

They accepted the fire marshal's letter at face value. For them that meant but one thing of importance. The state fire marshal's office was on top of the situation. The building inspector promptly communicated with the mayor and the city council. He intended to dispel their fears about the safety of the building: *The state fire marshal's office is involved in the construction at Beverly Hills. All controversy surrounding the expansion and restoration of the facility has been satisfactorily settled.*

14

The owner of the building pushed ahead with his construction and restoration. But in at least two ways he made an effort to deal with the matters presented to him earlier by the marshal's field inspector. For the benefit of state officials, he provided manufacturers' certificates showing the spread ratings of at least some of the interior finish and decorations. And on the second floor of the club he installed fire rated doors with automatic door closers at each opening between the dining rooms and the upstairs corridor, apparently having been told by the inspector that such installation would substitute adequately for the required enclosure of the open stairway between the two floors.

In doing so the principal owner decided to deal with the memorandum of deficiencies without professional assistance. He submitted his plans and drawings to no one for modification and made no substantial changes in the design of his building. During this period he got the benefit of frequent inspections by the city's building inspector. But no one from the fire marshal's office returned to the club to check on the construction. The last part of 1970 and the first month of 1971 slipped away, with work still to be done to complete the building. But in early February Dick Schilling scheduled an opening night and informed the city of Southgate of his need for a certificate of occupancy.

The field inspector from the fire marshal's office, at the direction of his superiors, returned to the site of the construction for an inspection. Whether or not he had the memorandum of deficiencies in his possession at the time is unknown. He finished his inspection routinely, without ever seeing the principal owner, and left the building. He communicated with at least one local official about the condition of the club and prepared a written report of his findings for his superiors. He made no mention in his report of the finish materials in the corridors, the open stairway between the first and second floors, the exits from the upper level, or the avenues of escape from the front of the building. He said absolutely nothing that might have served to arouse concern about the fundamental safety of the club.

An opportunity to prevent a disaster at Beverly Hills vanished on this day, for there was now no one left to declare the facility unfit for use. Among those with official responsibility for the safety of the building there was none who believed it unsafe. So at the end of the state's inspection the city of Southgate issued a certificate of occupancy authorizing Dick Schilling to open his club to the public. Less than twenty-four hours later the first patron walked through the doors of the new club. The date was February 10, 1971.

15

Doubts about safety did exist. A newspaper reporter from north of the Ohio River traveled to the fire marshal's office in the state capitol to inquire about the safety of the building. The still unexplained and destructive fire of June 21, 1970, was on his mind. In that office he examined the records available to him, recorded some opinions of an assistant to the fire marshal, and on the following day provided Dick Schilling a highly unpleasant surprise. The headlines in his newspaper, the Cincinnati Enquirer, captured the owner's undiluted attention: BEVERLY HILLS SUPPER CLUB A SAFETY RISK, SAYS STATE.[6]

In the story underneath the headlines the reporter told his readers that no final inspection of the building had been done by the state and that no approval had been given by the fire marshal's office for occupancy. He mentioned in general terms most of the crucial deficiencies still hidden away in the design of the building—"stairway enclosures," "interior furnishings," and "exits." And then he restored at least a breath of life to the memorandum of deficiencies: *Records in the Kentucky State Fire Marshal's office indicated that the posh Beverly Hills Supper Club in Southgate opened two weeks ago without remedying ten major safety defects outlined by the state.*[7]

In the days that followed the story, additional concerns about Beverly Hills were exposed. A degree of public controversy over the safety of the building materialized, threatened to grow, and then dissipated before anyone could hear the warning that had been sounded. In no small way local and state officials were responsible.

The assistant fire marshal declared that his earlier opinions about the building had been mistakenly based on partial records. The building inspector reported that he had been given assurances by Schilling that all fire hazards had been eliminated. The fire chief told a reporter that the owner was "doing his damnedest" to comply with all standards of safety.[8] And then the Fire Marshal himself killed the issue: *Somehow everything was blown way out of proportions. It still doesn't cease to amaze me that this became such a big issue.*[9] He spoke in the past tense. The controversy was dead.

16

Within a month of Schilling's opening night a local judge sat in a courtroom not too far from the site of the club. A grand jury was seated in the jury box waiting to receive instructions from the court. The safety of Schilling's building weighed on the mind of the judge. He reminded the grand jury of the recent controversy about the property, expressed some concerns of his own, and instructed the jurors to conduct an investigation of Beverly Hills "to prevent a holocaust at the club."

Like all grand juries this one worked behind closed doors. A little is known about how it started. A little is known about how it finished. All else is hidden from public view by the mantle of secrecy inherent to the proceedings. It is known that several witnesses were called to present testimony—the building inspector, the fire chief, the state fire marshal, and of course the principal owner of the building. It is known that Dick Schilling was asked about the condition of his club and that he told the jury—because he believed it so—that his building was very, very safe.

Eight days after being impaneled the jurors communicated their thoughts to the judge:

> *We heard testimony from state and local fire officials and are satisfied that Beverly Hills has complied with all fire and safety regulations. Frequent visits to this establishment are made by the Southgate Fire Department. We have been informed that the operators of Beverly Hills will train their employees in fire prevention and fire fighting in order to have its own "fire brigade," as soon as the employment situation stabilizes.*[10]

Of course their communication was released for public consumption. It comforted the community, silenced the press, and calmed the waters of controversy. It contributed to a growing sense of security about the building and to a tragedy that was now all but inevitable.

# Two

## The Making of a Firetrap

I

In the first few months after the opening, Dick Schilling completed the work on his building. No one from the fire marshal's office ever came back to the facility for a final inspection. And no one from the city of Southgate ever inquired or complained about that failure. No major fire hazard was added to the building during the final phase of construction, but none of those already there was eliminated. The finished structure was no safer for occupancy than the one that existed on opening night. But it was not a firetrap of rare magnitude; that condition was yet to be created.

Through the last half of 1971 and the first few months of 1972, the principal owner found every day in the building a little busier than the day before. The plan devised for the operation of the club had proved to be a masterpiece. Top quality entertainment in the showroom was attracting people to the facility in large numbers. The charm and beauty of the place and the exquisite touch of the owner were bringing them back again and again. By the time of its first anniversary, the club was an unqualified success.

Schilling's oldest son Rick had joined him full time in the business; his second son Ron was heavily involved in the operation while trying to finish college. Neither of the two was permitted to believe that he was yet anything special to the operation. They carried trays from the dining areas to the dishwashers, worked in the kitchen preparing food for diners, and even helped clean the building. They dressed in formal attire to cultivate their father's clientele and began to assume some responsibility for the supervision of the club's employees. But never did they entertain any doubt that the management of the business was in the hands of their father. He was on top of everything.

At this point the future of the club could hardly have looked brighter. Bigger banquets and more dinner parties were being booked for the facility every month. The showroom was prospering beyond anyone's expectations, and the regular clientele of the club was expanding at a steady rate. The public controversy over the safety of the building had slipped quietly and conveniently out of sight. Dick Schilling had begun to think of bigger and better things for Beverly Hills.

## 2

In the late spring of 1972 he left the club one day, retraced some steps he had taken almost two years earlier, and ended up on a farm in an adjoining county. The architect he had rescued from self-imposed isolation in 1970 had once again abandoned his professional career. He had permitted his architectural license to lapse for a second time and had returned to the secluded existence he had known before. When Schilling found him on this occasion, he was sustaining himself by building fences across the farm on which he lived. He was not displeased to see his former employer.

Schilling wanted his former architect to accompany him to Las Vegas to get some ideas for use at Beverly Hills and afterwards to prepare plans and drawings for a facade that would give the exterior of the building a new look. He got what he wanted quickly and without difficulty. The architect discarded his tools, bought some new clothes with money provided by Schilling, and headed across the country to see Las Vegas. In no more than a few hours he had ceased to be a builder of farm fences in rural Kentucky and had become a student and critic of the architecture of Caesar's Palace and other landmarks in the city of casinos.

On his return from Las Vegas the architect prepared plans and drawings for a facade at Beverly Hills that would extend from roof to ground across half the front and most of the east side of the building. He delivered those plans and drawings to the owner, accepted a modest fee for his services, and slipped quietly out of sight once again. Dick Schilling took his plans and drawings to the building inspector of Southgate and without difficulty obtained a permit authorizing new construction at his club. The date was July 10, 1972.

In due course Schilling used the permit to move a step closer to his dream for a club that he could comfortably call the showplace of the nation. The facade across the front and side of the club was built; Beverly Hills assumed a "Vegas look," and the exterior of the building became almost as attractive as the interior. The owner added no major fire hazards to the facility during this construction, but neither did he change in any respect the pattern of behavior that headed him toward disaster.

The man he employed to prepare plans and drawings on this occasion may have possessed professional skills and competence surpassed by none. He may have been as familiar with building and fire codes as an architect could possibly be. But Schilling could hardly have surmised that from the circumstances. The architect was not at the time engaged in professional practice. He was not licensed and had no seal of office. He could engage in the practice of architecture in the state of Kentucky only in violation of the law. There was undoubtedly a degree of risk involved in the use of his professional services. But the principal owner, who believed his architect to be competent, saw none of it.

Nor did he see the risk involved in a potentially more dangerous development. He proceeded with construction in this instance, as he had done in the past, without submitting plans and drawings to appropriate state officials. But this time no one from the city of

Southgate alerted the state fire marshal's office to the existence of new construction. No one from that office ever reviewed the plans and drawings for the facade, and no one familiar with the contents of building and fire codes ever conducted an inspection of the new addition. The overall safety of the building was not seriously affected by these failures, but subsequent failures would not be so inconsequential.

3

Not too many months after construction of the facade, Dick Schilling crossed the Ohio River once again to conduct some business in Cincinnati. His operation at Beverly Hills was still expanding, and the prosperity of the club was better than ever. He intended to see the unlicensed architect who had prepared the plans and drawings for the original expansion and restoration of his building to acquire professional services needed to correct a growing inadequacy of his facility. His particular concern was again that part of the building which he considered so essential to the success of his operation.

As always he had very definite ideas about what he wanted from the architect. In his mind the configuration and layout of his showroom left a lot to be desired. He wanted to move the stage to a more central location in the room and to tier the floor space so that his patrons could better see the performers. He wanted to add rest room facilities and a service bar to this part of the building and to improve substantially the lighting and electrical equipment for the stage. But most of all he wanted additional space. In the existing showroom he could seat no more than 350 people. He wanted space in the new room for more than one thousand seats and particularly stressed this objective in his discussion with the architect.

The task was a formidable one. Nothing less than major construction was required. The north wall of the existing room would have to be removed, and new walls for the expansion would have to be constructed. Heavy steel beams and girders would have to be erected to support a new roof of bar joists and metal decking.

Substantial excavation inside the expanded room would be needed to provide for the multiple levels of floor space requested by the owner around his relocated stage. A new and expanded electrical system and other interior facilities would have to be designed and built. In total cost estimate, the job looked like one that would exceed $100,000.

The architect had in his employ at this moment an architectural student from the University of Cincinnati who occupied the position of draftsman, a technician who assisted with the preparation of blueprints. Soon after Schilling's visit he handed the student a copy of the plans and drawings for the existing showroom at Beverly Hills, told him of the owner's objectives, and gave him some highly generalized instructions: *Expand the room, resolve the lighting problems, and increase the number of people he can seat.* He said nothing about building and fire codes and nothing about the need to comply with the requirements of Kentucky law.

The student accepted the assignment and began to prepare the necessary plans and drawings. From time to time he delivered preliminary sketches to his employer who in turn presented them to Schilling for approval. Never once did he talk directly with the owner about the expansion, and never once did he permit building and fire codes to play very much of a role in his work: *I did not design the addition. I was only the draftsman drawing it. I did not do any calculations.* He produced the drawings that Schilling wanted in about a month and turned his attention to other matters. He had no idea that he had put into the owner's hands a blueprint for catastrophe.

4

Dick Schilling had gone to Cincinnati for the principal purpose of expanding his showroom. He had asked his architect for sufficient space to seat one thousand people and thought the new plans and drawings would accomplish that objective and more. He intended to build and furnish his showroom for that number and to fill it to capacity as often as possible.

The occupancy load for a place of public assembly is strictly limited by building and fire codes. The maximum capacity of such a facility is a function of two factors: square footage of floor space and the use to be made of that space.[11] The capacity of the new showroom designed for Schilling, if measured against appropriate standards of safety, was nowhere near a thousand. It was barely half that much—511 to be exact—and at such odds with the owner's impression that hardly anything more was needed to create the necessary conditions for inevitable disaster. But there was more, whether needed or not. In the plans and drawings delivered to Schilling there were flaws of immense importance concerning the exits.

The exit requirements for a public building are partly a function of a technical concept called exit unit.[12] An exit unit is defined by building and fire codes as twenty-two inches of unobstructed width in an exit doorway. Every place of assembly and every individual room in such a place are required by law to have sufficient exit units to allow for the prompt escape of a crowd equal to the occupancy load of that place or that room. For purposes of this requirement a unit of exit width that opens to the outside at or near grade level can be calculated to serve no more than one hundred people. One that opens above or below grade level to a set of stairs or steps can be calculated to serve no more than seventy-five people.[13]

The new showroom at Beverly Hills had been designed for an occupancy load of more than a thousand, at least as the owner of the building intended to use it. Consequently he needed no less than eleven units of exit width to satisfy the requirements of the law. In the plans and drawings prepared for him without careful attention to the contents of building and fire codes there was provision for a total of only five units. He had in the design of his new showroom not quite half enough exit capacity to allow for the prompt escape of a capacity crowd, and he had on top of this yet another problem with the exits.

In any place of public assembly there is an obvious and substantial risk that fire may block avenues of escape to safety. To minimize that risk, building and fire codes require that there be in places designed for one thousand or more people at least four separate exits as remote from each other as practicable. But in the plans and drawings prepared for Schilling in Cincinnati there was provision for only three—one on each side of the relocated stage and one at the back of the room opposite the stage. So he had in his plans and drawings for a new showroom the most lethal combination of fire hazards that can exist in a public building—over-occupancy, inadequate exit capacity, and perhaps most importantly, a missing exit.

5

On July 8, 1974, he took his plans and drawings to the building inspector of Southgate and applied for a construction permit. On the face of those plans and drawings there was no seal of office of a licensed architect. The owner of the building had no reason to believe that this technicality would prove to be a barrier. He was right. The building inspector accepted the documents, assumed they had been prepared by a competent professional, and issued a building permit authorizing construction. In so doing he scribbled on the blueprints for the new showroom the name of the unlicensed Cincinnati architect and a reminder that was far more crucial than he imagined: "Check with architect about another exit door."

Schilling intended once again to be personally and heavily involved in the work on his building. He had a local firm lined up to provide and erect the steel for the addition and an experienced man in his employ to help with the supervision of construction. He intended to hire bricklayers, carpenters, and laborers to do as much of the work as possible and to find subcontractors to do the rest. He intended to go forward without a general contractor and to waste no time in getting started.

Within a week after the building permit had been issued, the footers for the new room were in the ground, construction on the hill outside Southgate was in full swing, and the state law had suffered another serious defeat. Neither the owner of the club nor anyone from the city had done anything yet to inform the state fire marshal's office of the plan to enlarge the building. And of course no one from that office had yet been given an opportunity to scrutinize the plans and drawings prepared by the unlicensed architect and his draftsman.

Even at this time, the building inspector was not much better equipped to protect the public against the hazards of fire than he had been earlier. He was still no more than superficially familiar with the building and fire codes in his possession and not even faintly aware that newer versions of those codes had rendered the ones in his hands partially obsolete. He had not gained a full appreciation of the magnitude of his responsibilities nor of the importance of his office. He was a bricklayer who just happened to be occupying the office of building inspector, and never before had this simple truth been so crucial. For at this moment he was the only public official in a position to prevent the construction of a firetrap at Beverly Hills.

6

For several weeks he watched the construction of the new showroom without concern. About halfway through the project, during the second month of work, he traveled to the site one afternoon for a routine inspection. By this time the shell for the expanded showroom was practically finished. The roof was on, the exterior walls in place, and the characteristics of the interior fairly well defined. Though much work was left to be done the construction revealed for the first time what the new showroom would look like when finished.

Once inside the building, the inspector stood opposite the stage and took his first good look at the design of the new room. Before long his attention focused on the exits. The concern he had earlier noted on the subject entered his thoughts once again. He could plainly see that the new showroom was to be substantially bigger than the old one—floor space doubled and occupancy load tripled. He could also plainly see that the exit facilities that had existed in the old showroom were not to be substantially improved—no new exits added and no apparent increase in exit capacity.

Regarding exits, he knew almost nothing about the specific requirements of the law. Consequently his thoughts were neither profound nor technical. His assessment of the situation was grounded entirely in common sense and instinct. A substantially bigger showroom with a substantially greater occupancy load surely meant the need for additional exits. It was that simple for him: *I just felt that there should have been another exit there.*

During this inspection Dick Schilling was in the building. So the building inspector collared him for an important discussion. He was direct in the expression of his concern but not forceful: *I'd like to have another door in the showroom.* The owner had accepted some earlier suggestions of the inspector but did not share his concern about the sufficiency of the exits. He had confidence in the architect who had designed the addition and no reason to believe that another exit was required by law. He felt comfortable with the safety of his new showroom and was in no frame of mind for unnecessary changes. So he balked.

The date was August 23, 1974. Another opportunity to steer a different course for Beverly Hills had slipped away. The building inspector, despite instincts to the contrary, failed to push his point. He left the building determined to pursue the matter on another occasion but with no firm intention of ever forcing the issue over the showroom exits. At the end of the day, in recording the results of his inspection, he scribbled an entry in his log that reflected both his concern and his hope: *One outside door still in question.*

7

In the weeks that followed, the owner moved steadily toward the completion of his project. The building inspector returned to the site of the construction for occasional inspections. He lost none of his doubt about the adequacy of the showroom exits and found nothing to improve his ability to do something about it. Never once did he think to turn to the building and fire codes for a better understanding of the requirements of the law. Nor did he ever consider using the power of his office to get his way on this important issue. He did what he had done before: *I still kept after Mr. Schilling for another exit in the Cabaret Room. Even though I didn't believe that there was any violation, I just felt sure that if he had another exit in there it would be better for him and for the club.*

Toward late fall most of the construction at the back of the building ended. The new showroom was all but finished and the owner was beginning to anticipate the opening of his expanded facility. The building inspector arrived on the hill one afternoon for his seventh inspection of the new addition. He walked through the showroom as he had done before, discussed his concerns with the owner briefly, and left the building to think once again about the need for an additional exit. At the end of the day he used a familiar line to log a familiar thought: "One exit still in question." The date of this entry was October 29, 1974.

Schilling moved quickly to complete the work on his showroom. He made final arrangements for an opening night and officially requested a certificate of occupancy. On any one of several grounds the building inspector could have balked. He had plans and drawings that had never been sealed by a licensed architect. He could not have known of state approval for the construction, for none had been given. He had an uneasy feeling in his gut about the safety of the exits. But the one thing he needed, determination to take a firm stand on the issue of exits, he did not have. So he issued a certificate of occupancy for the new showroom and recorded in his log the only entry that mattered for the moment: "Final approval."

The showroom at Beverly Hills had been called the Cabaret Room since 1971. But the new version provided the owner with much more of what he had long wanted. It was very large (as shown on Diagram Nos. 5 and 6, see pages 38-39), with two service bars, dressing rooms off stage, and restrooms for patrons and employees. It was only one story high but had four separate levels of floor space facing a centrally located stage. It had a ramp on each side of the stage to facilitate movement from one level of floor space to another, and, of course, three exits—one in the corner of the room on each side of the stage and a third at the back of the room opposite the stage. It was destined, without a doubt, to become the feature attraction at Beverly Hills.

It had come into existence in disregard of nearly every safeguard offered by the law against the construction of a firetrap. The plans and drawings used for construction had not been prepared or reviewed by a licensed architect. They had not been examined by anyone known to be familiar with the building and fire codes of the state of Kentucky. The building permit that authorized the commencement of construction had been illegally issued. No one from the state fire marshal's office had ever received plans and drawings for the new room. No one from that office had gone to the site of construction for an inspection of the work. And no one from the state had ever issued approval for construction. During this period of activity, the owner of the building had little more than luck on his side. That was most clearly not enough.

On November 11, 1974, he opened the doors of the Cabaret Room to the public. The big showroom at the back of the building was two entirely different creatures. It was a beautiful showplace, tastefully decorated from wall to wall, and every bit as classy as the elegant place that Dick Schilling had long wanted for himself and his sons. But it was at the same time something else. In the true sense of the word, it was a firetrap of enormous magnitude.

8

In early April of 1975, in an office in the state capitol, a file on the Beverly Hills Supper Club was lifted from a cabinet and laid on a table. A few days earlier someone from the city of Southgate had contacted the fire marshal's office to express some new concern about the safety of the big nightclub. The fire marshal or one of his chief deputies leafed through the correspondence in the file and extracted a copy of the memorandum of deficiencies that had served in 1971 as the focus of public controversy over the safety of the building. He (or his chief deputy) handed the memorandum to a subordinate, provided a brief description of its history, and with a few simple words issued a very tall order: "Bring the building into compliance with the law."

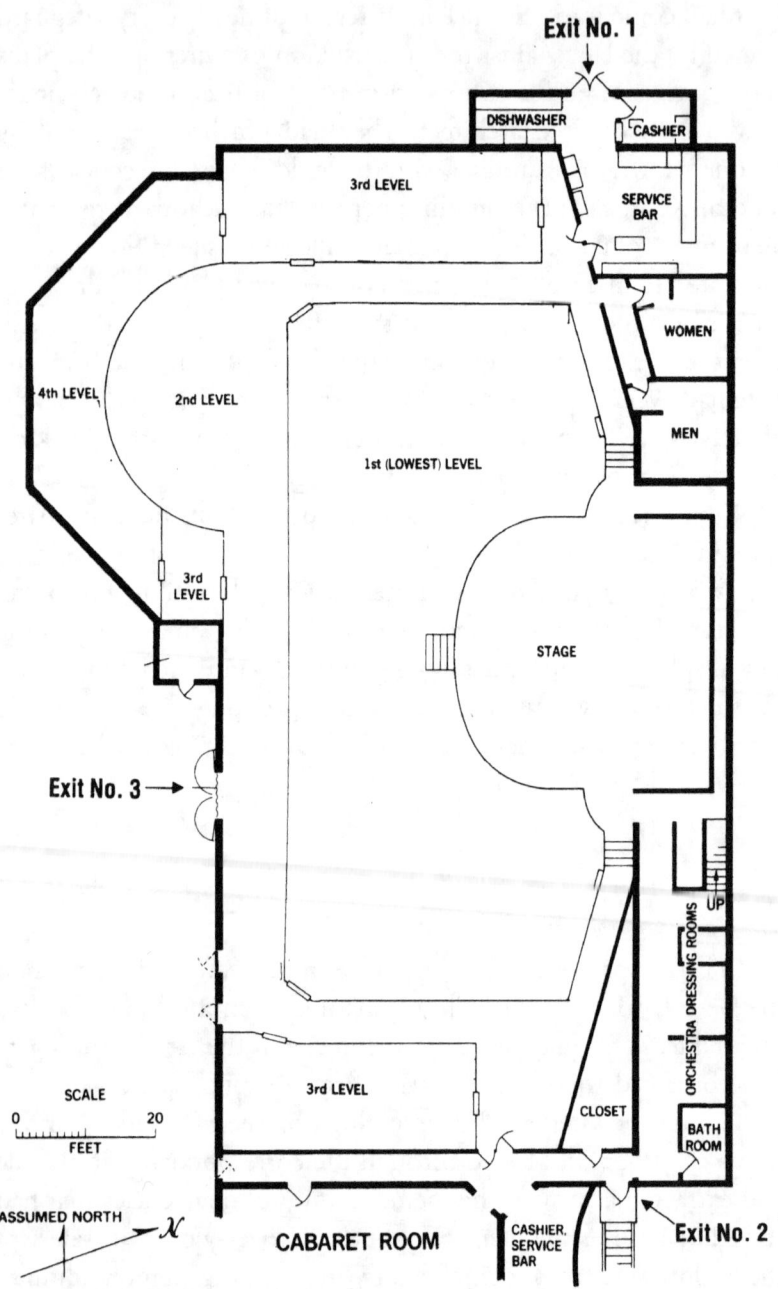

**Diagram No. 5**

# The Making of a Firetrap

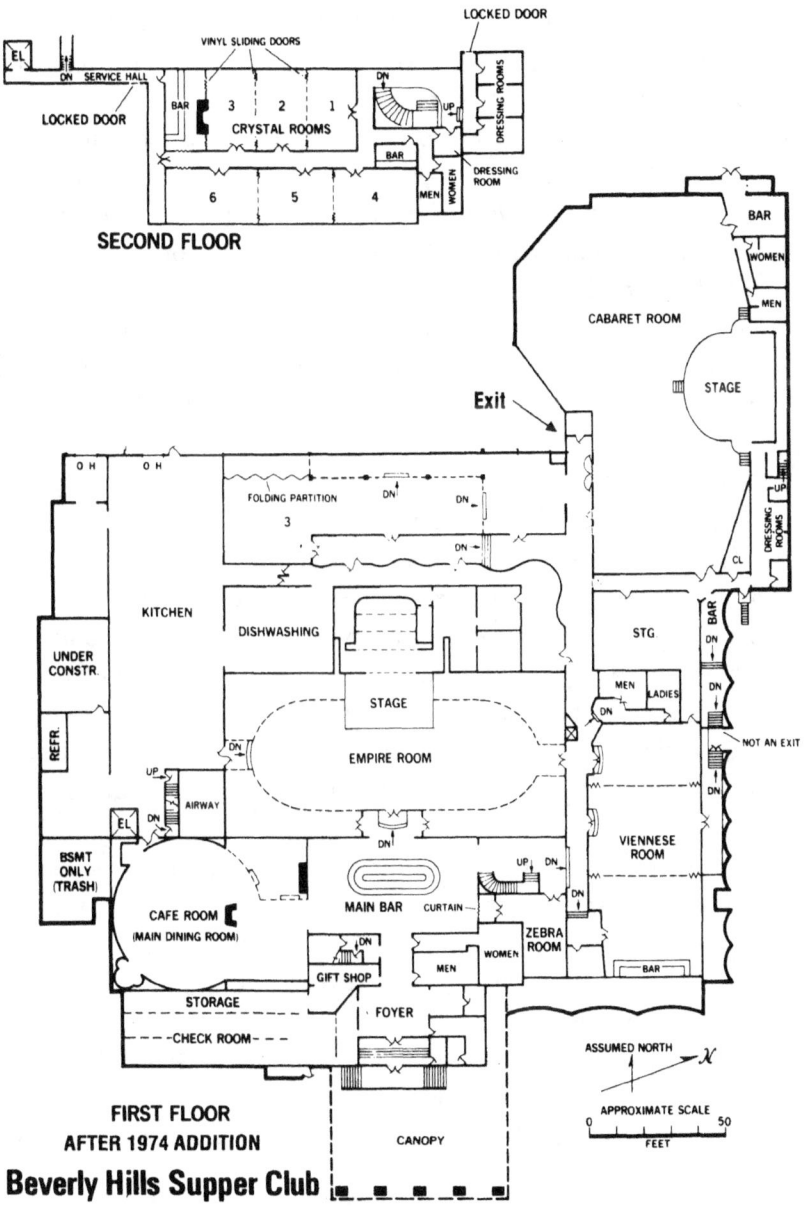

**Diagram No. 6**

An important new phase of the tragedy was about to be initiated through the actions of an important new character. The subordinate to whom the fire marshal had delivered the fate of Beverly Hills, like others caught in the web of the tragedy, was not a particularly remarkable individual. He was about fifty years old, had only eight years of formal education, and had learned what he knew about buildings through personal experience. He had worked for twenty-two years as a professional firefighter for a major fire department, had retired after advancing to the position of captain of inspection, and had joined the fire marshal's staff to serve as field inspector for the part of the state that included Southgate. He had lived much of his life just a short distance from Beverly Hills, had been there but once, and knew almost nothing about the history of the club.

About a week after his trip to the state capital he went to Beverly Hills in pursuit of the new assignment. The memorandum in his possession at the time contained a list of items calculated to alert him to most of the major hazards then existing in the building. It provided him with a rare opportunity to change the course for the big nightclub in Southgate, though he couldn't have known that none better would ever again appear. He located the principal owner of the club after arriving on the hill, and together they started through the building checking the items on the memorandum one by one.

At the top of the list was an item concerning unenclosed stairways. Near the front of the building was a beautiful open stairway that spiraled upward from the first to the second floor (see Diagram No. 1, page ix, just to the right of the Main Bar). It was one of the club's most charming features and at the same time one of its most obvious and dangerous hazards. The inspector moved to that part of the building, examined the open stairwell with some care, and entered a question mark beside the first item on the memorandum:

Q. *What was the question mark to indicate?*
A. *That I wasn't sure if it was even a required exit at that time.*
Q. *Well, it doesn't have to be an exit in order to have to be enclosed, does it?*
A. *No, no. I was in doubt about the stairway all the way.*

> Q. So really you knew that it should have been enclosed, didn't you?
> A. I felt that it should have been, yes.
> Q. And did you make a report to your superiors, or anyone, that the stairway should have been enclosed?
> A. I don't think I did. I don't think I did.
> Q. And do you know why you did not?
> A. No, I don't.

Through the beauty and charm of the open stairway he saw the violation of law. But he did not see the threat to human life embodied in that violation: *I wasn't concerned with the spiral staircase because I didn't feel that it created a problem. This was my opinion.*

Near the open stairway was another dangerous condition that was the subject of an item in the memorandum of deficiencies. In violation of law, the corridors in this part of the club had been finished with materials that would facilitate rather than impede the spread of fire. But neither the danger in that condition nor the violation of law was visible to the naked eye. Only through an examination of certificates provided by manufacturers could this threat to life have been discovered. The field inspector asked the owner about the certificates and was told that the fire marshal's office had received them long ago:

> Q. How did you satisfy yourself that those certificates had been sent to Frankfort and received?
> A. I took Mr. Schilling's word for it as a gentleman.

He scribbled the letters "O.K." beside the item on interior finish, dismissed the possibility of fire spread as a major concern, and turned his attention to other matters.

Ultimately he worked his way to the most important item on the agenda, the avenues of escape from the building. In both the front of the club and in the Cabaret Room, he spent considerable time examining the exits and their capacity to facilitate a rapid evacuation of the club in the event of an emergency. The memorandum of deficiencies alerted him to the possibility of a problem with the exits but did nothing to pinpoint or identify specific weaknesses. In only one way could he have discovered that occupants might experience difficulty in getting out of the building in the event of fire. He needed to measure the widths of the exits, ascertain the dimensions and occupancy loads of the various rooms, and apply the results of his efforts to the requirements of the law:

> Q. Did you go to each exit and...determine whether or not they met the requirements of the Kentucky Standards of Safety?
> A. I don't believe I went to all the exits, no...
> Q. Well, if you didn't go to all the exits, you really couldn't have determined that the exits were sufficient for the size of the rooms then, could you?
> A. Not at that point I couldn't.
> Q. Did you ever go to those exits and look at them and measure them?
> A. Not all of them, no.
> Q. And you didn't measure the rooms?
> A, No, I didn't.
> Q. And you, therefore, could not make a conclusion as to whether the exit facilities were appropriate?
> A. That's correct.

He completed his evaluation of the club's avenues of escape with no concern about the safety of the exits and no awareness of their insufficiency

He left the building at the end of his inspection with nothing of supreme importance to report to his superiors in the state capitol. He had been told to bring the building into compliance with the law and had directed his efforts toward that objective. He had discovered some minor deficiencies in the facility and had instructed the owner to make some corrections. He had contributed modestly to the overall safety of the club but had done almost nothing to change its fundamental flaws.

## 9

A few months later Dick Schilling found himself in need of additional floor space once again. Inside the existing structure, at a choice location, he had a room that was being used for storage. Though small in comparison to other rooms in the building, it was perfectly suited for many of the minor functions accommodated by the club. So he decided to convert the area into a party room and to do so quickly. Within three weeks he had in place of the old storage room one of the most beautiful spots in the whole building.

The new room was located off the Main Bar, underneath the spiral stairway, and near a junction of two of the building's main corridors (see Diagram No. 1). Called the Zebra Room, it was truly a creation of the principal owner. He had designed it without professional help, had purchased the materials for its construction, and had arranged for the labor needed to complete the job. For the remodeling, he had used the construction man who had worked on most of his other projects and the electrician who had wired the Cabaret Room. He had carefully supervised the work of both men. At the end of the construction he had exactly what he wanted in the old storage area. He also had a new and extremely dangerous fire hazard.

Inside the concealed spaces of this small room (between the walls and above the suspended ceiling) there was a supply of combustible materials sufficient to fuel a sizeable fire. In addition there was enough electrical wire for eight to ten ceiling lights, two chandeliers, and several wall outlets. And, most importantly, there was a flaw in the electrical system that was as dangerous as could be in a place of public assembly. All of the wire for the system had been strung through the concealed spaces of the small room protected only by the insulation that had come on the wire from the manufacturer.

The electrician, in clear violation of the state's electrical code, had failed to provide the necessary metallic conduit for the system:

> *Q. And what type of wire did you run to the Zebra Room?*
> *A. There was 12 Romex with ground copper.*
> *Q. Was that placed in conduit?*

A. *No sir.*
Q. *Would you normally have placed that type of run in conduit?*
A. *Yes sir.*
Q. *Why did you not at that time?*
A. *Well, the same reason I hadn't in the Cabaret Room.*
Q. *And what was that reason?*
A. *Mr. Schilling didn't want it in conduit.*

Under ordinary circumstances the work of the electrician would have been examined by an independent electrical inspector. The flaw would have been detected and eliminated perhaps. But the circumstances under which the Zebra Room had come into existence were not ordinary.

The owner of the building had obtained no construction permit from the building inspector. He had done nothing to inform the state fire marshal's office of his intention to alter the club. He had opened the doors of his new room to the public without a certificate of occupancy from the city of Southgate. No one with responsibility for the enforcement of the state's standards of safety had entered the building for an inspection. In other words, every official act that might have served to prevent the installation of a fire hazard during the new construction had been circumvented.

The electrical system inside the Zebra Room was flawed. That system would one day provide the source of energy needed to ignite a fire. Whether or not its flaws would contribute to that ignition would develop into a post-fire controversy without any clear-cut resolution. But with respect to the construction that occurred in the Zebra Room, one thing would never become a subject of doubt. Once it was completed, the big nightclub in Southgate had what would prove to be the last ingredient necessary for the disaster of May 28, 1977.

10

The Zebra Room was completed in December of 1975. It did very little to alleviate the space problem generated by the success of the expanded showroom. A month or so later, Dick Schilling contacted the architectural student who had prepared the plans and drawings for the Cabaret Room and asked him to come to the club. By this time the student had completed the work necessary for a degree in architecture but had not taken the examination for a license. He came to Southgate for a meeting with the principal owner and left the club a little later with an obligation to provide additional plans and drawings for Schilling.

Within a few weeks he returned to the club with a set of blueprints for an addition to an existing part of the building then being called the Garden Room. In his preparation of those prints he had made almost no attempt to conform to the appropriate requirements of the law: *I did not refer directly to the state of Kentucky building code. I referred to the state of Ohio Code.* Like his earlier work on the Cabaret Room, he had relinquished that responsibility to others: *I believed at the time that Dick Schilling was going to get a licensed architect to look at the plans and make sure everything was in compliance with the code.* He delivered the plans and drawings to the owner of the building and dropped out of the picture.

Schilling's intentions were no different on this occasion. He was more confident than ever of his ability to turn a set of plans and drawings into a finished product with a minimum of professional assistance. He had at his disposal the construction man who had done much of the work on his other additions and the electrician who had wired the Cabaret and Zebra rooms. He intended to use them extensively on the new project, to engage subcontractors to the extent necessary, and to complete the construction without the benefit of a general contractor.

11

In April of 1976, before Schilling began his new construction, a member of the Southgate volunteer fire department entered the big nightclub for what he thought to be a routine inspection. Because of his regular occupation as a public school teacher, he was acutely aware of the danger of fire in a public building, and he was about as serious and conscientious as anyone could be about safety inspections. At his own expense he had taken night courses at a local college on fire prevention. He had advanced to the position of captain of inspection in the fire department and was undoubtedly one of the city's best inspectors. But on the occasion of this inspection he entered the building handicapped.

Neither the state nor the city had ever provided his department with copies of applicable building and fire codes. He was barely familiar with the state's standards of safety and had even less understanding of the true scope of his inspection responsibilities. He assumed that the building had been constructed under the watchful eye of competent professionals (architects, building inspectors, and fire marshals), and that it was structurally safe. He had so narrowed the focus of his own efforts that his inspection was predestined for superficiality and unqualified failure.

His own words, given to investigators after the 1977 fire, provide a complete explanation:

> *I was under the impression that the number of exits, things like that, would have been checked downstate when they approved the plans. The same with interior finish. As far as interior finish of a room I couldn't tell you what it is by looking at a wall. I have no idea, none whatever.*
>
> • • •
>
> *I was the fire inspector. But the things I didn't know and still don't know were so enormous. For example, the spiral staircase, I really had no idea that was a fire violation.*
>
> • • •
>
> *It boils down to the simple fact that I was probably a most incompetent fire inspector, out of ignorance. But I don't see how I could have learned any more. I believed I was doing the best job that I could.*

During his inspection, he did not overlook even a small corner of the big building. He visited the basement and every room on the two main floors. He checked all the fire extinguishers, the corridors and exit doors, the boilers, the electrical system, and the housekeeping. He made a conscientious effort to do his job.

In so doing he brushed against every major fire hazard then existing in the building, but he saw no serious threat to the safety of the building or its occupants: *I felt Beverly Hills was in the best shape it had ever been in.* He ended his inspection routinely and left the building without concern.

Other fire department members had done the same on earlier occasions. But this effort was an uncommon one. The firefighters of Southgate had once had an abundance of opportunity to protect the public against the hazards of fire at Beverly Hills. But now they had none left. Never again would anyone from the department have a chance to discover the firetrap in Schilling's club. The captain of inspection had expended the last.

12

Toward the end of April 1976 the police chief of Southgate sought out the building inspector to initiate a conversation that went something like this:

*Are you aware of the new construction at Beverly Hills?*
*No. Where is it?*
*At the back of the building, and it's substantial.*
*I've issued no permit. I'll check.*

On the heels of this conversation the building inspector visited the club and found footers in the ground for a large addition to the back of the building. He looked unsuccessfully for Dick Schilling, cornered the man who seemed to be in charge to express concern about the unauthorized construction, and left word for the owner to call.

On the following day he went back to the construction site for another check. His inquiry of the day before had done nothing to stop activity at the back of the building. He located the owner without difficulty this time and promptly asked about the plans and drawings for the new addition. Schilling produced the blueprints for the construction of the Garden Room, and the building inspector quickly noticed the one thing that meant something to him. The architect who had prepared the drawings had done so without a license and without a seal of office. The owner had not taken them to a licensed architect. They had no seal.

The proper course of action for the building inspector was clearly defined by the law—no architect's seal, no building permit. No building permit, no construction. He had the authority to bring the construction at the back of the building to a halt, but he was not accustomed to using that authority in the performance of his duties. In particular he was not accustomed to insisting on strict adherence to the law at Beverly Hills. So he asked for proper plans and drawings for the new addition, withheld the issuance of a building permit, but verbally authorized the owner to continue with the construction.

## 13

Less than a month later the state fire marshal's office dispatched its local field inspector to Beverly Hills for a routine inspection. No plans and drawings for the new addition had been submitted yet to state officials. No building permit had been issued yet by the city of Southgate. Quite by accident the inspector came upon the construction at the back of the building. He sought out the owner for an explanation:

*What are you doing here?*
*We're building a new addition to the club.*
*You have submitted plans to the fire marshal's office, haven't you?*
*No, we haven't.*
*You realize we have to know about these things. Send us a set of complete drawings signed by a registered architect.*
*I'll take care of it.*

Of course the field inspector also had the authority to terminate the construction. Like his counterpart with the city of Southgate, he chose not to exercise it. He reported his discovery to superiors in the state capitol, told them of the owner's promise, and made one of his own: "I'll recheck."

In about a week he returned to Beverly Hills for additional conversation with the owner. The plans and drawings for the Garden Room had not arrived in the fire marshal's office. He was asked by the owner to contact the man who had prepared the blueprints for the new construction and did so promptly. He informed the unlicensed architect of the requirements of the law and warned that a stop-work order would be obtained unless plans and drawings with a proper seal were received promptly. He reported to the fire marshal's office on the results of his effort: "Expect to receive plans on above project very soon." But he did nothing to hinder the activity of the owner. The work at the back of the building moved ahead at a normal pace.

In the meantime Schilling's architect turned his attention to the matter of a seal. He contacted the manufacturer who had supplied the steel for the new addition and asked for help. He got an agreement from an employee of that firm who had a Kentucky license to put his seal on the plans and drawings in question. But he took more time to solve the problem than the officials of the fire marshal's office were prepared to tolerate.

The field inspector returned to the site of the construction believing that the owner had no intention of sending drawings to the state. A brief confrontation with Dick Schilling ended with a threat and a promise:

*I'll be back!*
*Where are you going?*
*I'm going to the courthouse to get a stop-work order.*
*Don't do that I'll get the plans.*

Within a couple of days the field inspector received a letter from the unlicensed architect informing him that the plans and drawings had been sent to the fire marshal's office in the state capitol. It was July 15, 1976. The work on the Garden Room addition was three months old. The state had not yet authorized the commencement of construction.

14

By this time the building inspector of Southgate was visiting the club regularly to inspect the new construction. An old concern about the safety of the building had reentered his thoughts. Almost two years had passed since he had attempted to persuade the owner of the club to add an exit to the Cabaret Room. The showroom still had only three avenues of escape. Four were needed to satisfy the state's standards of safety. The inspector had yielded to the owner in 1974, not knowing the minimum requirements of the law, but his anxiety about the safety of the big showroom had survived intact. And now, for very good reason, it had resurfaced with even greater intensity.

At the beginning of the new construction, the main corridor of the building ran north from near the Zebra Room all the way to the back of the club (see Diagram No. 6). Near the end of the corridor, in close promixity to the exit at the back of the showroom, there was an exterior door. To reach safety via this avenue of escape one had to travel a distance of only a few feet. There were no turns to make or obstacles to clear to reach the garden area behind the building. The exit at this location, both technically and functionally, was undoubtedly the showroom's best. It was obviously indispensable.

But in the plans and drawings for the new addition, it was being treated otherwise. The exterior door so essential to this avenue of escape was to be eliminated. The exterior wall at the rear of the building was to be moved approximately fifty feet farther north. The corridor outside the back of the showroom was scheduled to become a dead end upon completion of the construction, and, most importantly, the exit in question was scheduled to lose its direct access to the safety of the grounds at the back of the building. In other words, the Cabaret Room which was already short one required exit was about to lose another one.

This time the building inspector decided to seek help. He contacted the field inspector for the fire marshal's office, described his concern for the safety of the Cabaret Room, and asked for assistance. In a couple of days the two men conducted an inspection of the new construction and rather quickly agreed that something had to be done to preserve the integrity of the exit at the back of the showroom. They decided on a course of corrective action and went to Dick Schilling with a proposal: *The corridor outside the showroom will have to be extended on through the building to the garden. An exterior door will have to be installed at the end of the corridor to serve the occupants of the showroom in the event of an emergency.* The owner agreed. The plans and drawings for the new addition were amended.

The building inspector and the fire marshal's field inspector were satisfied. They had reduced the impairment of the exit in question to an acceptable level and had preserved for the showroom an avenue of escape. They had done very little to change the fundamental character of the Cabaret Room. It was still a firetrap. But it was a firetrap with three exits to safety rather than two. The difference was crucial. The night of May 28, 1977, would leave no doubt.

15

In early August a letter addressed to Dick Schilling arrived in Southgate from the office of the state fire marshal. It was brief and to the point: *We regret we cannot approve the plans submitted for the above captioned project [the Garden Room addition]. The plans will have to have a seal of an architect registered in Kentucky.* The drawings sent to the state capitol by Schilling's unlicensed architect had contained the seal of office of a registered engineer rather than that of a registered architect. The owner was still in violation of the law.

The problem was not an unfamiliar one to Schilling. Nor was the solution he sought. Living in a small town in another state was the architect to whom Schilling had turned for help with similar problems on earlier occasions. He had left the farm on which he had earlier isolated himself but had not returned to a productive professional life. Though not engaged in the practice of architecture he had a valid Kentucky license, a seal of office that was current, and a willingness to put that seal on architectural prints prepared by someone else.

A few days after a telephone conversation between Schilling and his old friend, a set of plans and drawings with a proper seal arrived in the fire marshal's office in the state capitol. Promptly thereafter an official of that office communicated with the owner of Beverly Hills by mail: *We are pleased to inform you that plans and specifications submitted for the above captioned project have been approved for the commencement of construction.* The date on the letter was September 2, 1976. The new addition to the building was almost finished.

## 16

In a few weeks the field inspector from the fire marshal's office returned to Beverly Hills for an appraisal of the new addition. He completed that assignment quickly and routinely but decided while he was there to conduct an inspection of the whole building. He examined all of the exit facilities, the corridors leading to the exits, and the stairways connecting the first and second floors. He entered the Cabaret Room for an evaluation of the avenues of escape from there. He visited all three floors of the structure and entered every room on every floor. Along the way he saw all of the club's important features. He brushed against all of its major fire hazards.

His inspection this time was similar in character to his earlier ones: he did not measure the width of any exits; he did not ascertain the occupancy load of any rooms; and he did not calculate the square footage of floor space in any part of the building. In his effort to protect the public against the hazards of fire, he relied more on instinct and common sense than on the technical requirements of the law. He found a few code violations to report but none significant enough to cause much concern about the safety of the building. He ended his inspection as he had ended earlier ones, without feeling that the big nightclub seriously threatened human life.

The date was October 25, 1976. He prepared a report of his findings before the end of the day and mailed it to the state capitol. In that report he noted that the new addition was now complete and that the construction was in compliance with the requirements of law. Then he provided his superiors in the fire marshal's office with a description of his general feelings about the building as a whole: *It is my opinion that as of now this project is probably as good as we can expect, although it does not come into complete compliance.*

In a few days his report arrived and was delivered to the desk of the fire marshal's chief deputy. It could hardly have fallen into more knowledgeable hands. For almost six years the chief deputy had been heavily involved in the state's effort to make the club safe. While in another job in the fire marshal's office he had prepared the memorandum of deficiencies that had played such a big role at an earlier time. He surely knew enough about the history of the building to exercise a degree of caution on a matter of such importance.

For a couple of weeks he sat on the report from the field. He had been asked by the field inspector to approve his evaluation of the case or provide additional direction. On November 16, 1976, he made a decision that all but ended any chance to avert disaster at Beverly Hills. He put his signature to a letter that surely served to reinforce a belief long entertained by the owner of the club that his building was free of fire hazards:

*Dear Mr. Schilling:*

*Final inspection has been made of the above captioned project [the Beverly Hills club].*

*Our field representative's report states that the above captioned project was constructed in substantial compliance with minimum fire safety regulations.*

*If we can be of any further assistance, please feel free to call upon us.*

## 17

Toward the end of December 1976 a young man who served in the state senate of Kentucky entered the fire marshal's office in the state capitol. He was looking for the fire marshal but found instead a deputy with whom he was acquainted. He opened the following conversation:

> *Sen: Are you familiar with the Beverly Hills Supper Club?*
> *Dep: No. Why do you ask?*
> *Sen: Well, there's a problem in that building.*
> *Dep: What do you mean?*
> *Sen: I was there for a show the other night. It took me more than twenty minutes to get out of the showroom at the end of the performance, and another ten to fifteen minutes to get through the main corridor to the front of the building. There's a shortage of exits in that place.*

The senator wanted an inspection of the building but the deputy with whom he spoke had no power to issue such an order. So he made arrangements to see higher authority.

In a few days he returned to the office for a conversation with the fire marshal. He repeated the story of his experience in the showroom and main corridor at Beverly Hills and suggested once again the need for an inspection of the building. He later recalled the fire marshal's reaction: *I thought I would mention to him how dangerous I thought the facility was, and that something bad might happen up there. Lo and behold, he already knew about it He said they knew it was dangerous—a fire hazard—and that they had done what they could do to correct it.*

Following the senator's visit, the fire marshal issued an order for a new inspection of the building. On January 27, 1977—just four months before the catastrophe—the field inspector returned to Beverly Hills to carry out the assignment. He did on this occasion much of what he had done just a few weeks earlier. He climbed the stairway to the second floor, walked corridors with which he was now thoroughly familiar, and examined exits that he had seen on several occasions. He made no effort to ascertain the occupancy load of the Cabaret Room and took no measurements for the purpose of evaluating exit capacity. He formed all of his impressions about the safety of the building while it was almost totally unoccupied.

He finished the inspection and left the building to record what would turn out to be the last official thought about the club before the fire. It was addressed to his superiors in the state fire marshal's office and was calculated to settle the issue raised by the state senator. It contained an opinion that patrons leaving the front of the building following a showroom performance might encounter congestion while waiting for their automobiles. It ended with a conclusion that served in remarkable fashion to set the stage for the events of May 28, 1977:

> *But in case of emergency, evacuation should be no problem with existing exits.*

*Cabaret Room in 1977, not long before the fire. Courtesy Wayne Dammert*

## *Three*

## THE CALM BEFORE THE STORM

I

May 28, 1977, arrived on Saturday. Dick Schilling was in Florida recuperating from recent surgery. The club was in the hands of his sons and his chef. The day was warm and beautiful in the Cincinnati area, and the night was expected to follow suit. Dick's oldest son Rick arrived on the hill outside the club at about eleven o'clock in the morning. He had been away for only a few hours. John Davidson, a well-known singer and performer, had been on stage in the Cabaret Room the night before. The front door to the building had not been locked until well past midnight.

Davidson was a regular at Beverly Hills and always a big attraction. The crowds for his performances in the Cabaret Room were invariably large and never a disappointment to the owners of the club. He was nearing the end of a ten-night engagement and on Friday had filled the showroom to the rafters for two performances. Every chair that could be squeezed in had been occupied. For at least one show, patrons had been admitted for standing room only, and the crowd near the stage had been so compact that Davidson had found it necessary to alter his routine. On other evenings he had left the stage to do a number in the audience. But on Friday night, with the house full, he had not ventured off stage during either performance.

Rick Schilling knew that Saturday night would be just as good and perhaps better. He also knew that such good fortune for the club was not without its problems for those in charge. The people at Beverly Hills, owners and employees alike, were not adept at denying their patrons access to the showroom. They had a system for booking advance reservations for most performances. And the reservationists worked under a standing order—issued by both Rick and his brother Ron—to book no more than 900 for the Cabaret Room. But in many instances they found it difficult to live with the limit. That would surely be true on a Saturday night with John Davidson.

Earlier in the week Rick had reviewed the reservation sheets with one of the employees. Already the reservationists had overbooked for Saturday night. An effort had been made in advance to deal with the problem: *We called people for days, telling them we were overbooked. We told them we would be unable to get them into the show.* But success had been limited. Very few of those called had accepted the disappointment graciously. Some had pretended to be important people. Others had claimed personal friendship with the owners. Many had indicated a willingness to accept any available accommodation: *You can put me on the ceiling, just as long as I can get in. I don't care where I sit.* And some had decided to take a chance on entry to the showroom without reservations. Undoubtedly the thought of offering money to employees for access to the Cabaret Room had crossed some minds. Such offers were not uncommon at the club. And some were sure to be made before the end of the day.

## 2

By this time the number of employees at Beverly Hills had grown to 160. Some had worked for Dick Schilling for many years. A few were close enough to him for personal contact on a regular basis. But on the very eve of the tragedy most of those who worked in the club barely knew the principal owner: *I've only met the man four or five times in all the years I've worked for him.* And yet they generally harbored warm feelings toward him as a person and a boss: *Dick Schilling is a hard man to work for. He demands a lot; if you give it to him, he treats you well. He's a nice person, hard to work for, but personally a very nice man.*

The sons of Dick Schilling had not done quite as well with the employees. The youngest, perhaps only because he had not yet assumed the role of a manager, had fared the best. Older employees on the staff had watched him grow up at Beverly Hills and still thought of him as just a boy, although he had now reached the age of twenty. The younger employees identified with him in a closer and more personal way, for he had shown special interest in their contributions to the business and had occasionally associated with them away from the club. He was disliked by no one, and was held in high esteem by most: *I liked Scott; he worked very hard. He cared for the help; he had a little more compassion than the other two.*

The "other two," in the eyes of the employees, might as well have been one. Rick was two years older than Ron. He had a wife who worked in the club and a teenage daughter who often was present. Consequently he was perceived as the more settled and more responsible of the two. But in all other respects the two oldest sons of Dick Schilling were seen by the employees as one. And the end product was neither as uniform nor as admirable as the image projected by their younger brother.

They were highly respected for their dedication and hard work, and they deserved it all. They logged more time on the hill, and worked harder while there, than anyone connected with the club. From early morning until late at night they conducted themselves more like employees than managers—carrying trays, cleaning floors, and doing the same dirty work done by others. They made enormous demands on waitresses, busboys, and kitchen workers. But they demanded at least as much of themselves: *I'd work twelve or thirteen hours and crawl out dead tired; they would still be there doing the same things I had done.*

Rarely did either of the two spend light moments with those who worked at the club. To most, they always seemed too busy to stop and talk, too preoccupied to sit around and listen to the concerns of employees:

*They wanted to get as many people in as possible, get them out fast, and make the most money they could make. They didn't care about anyone. We were just slaves to them, they didn't care about us.*

* * *

*They treated their help like dirt under their feet. You really had to work hard to keep your job. I mean you had to run all the time. You didn't get to take time to slow down at all.*

* * *

*If you walked by Ron and Rick and said "Hi," they just kept on walking, like they never heard you. They wanted the job done. If they saw you do something wrong, they thought nothing of telling you right then and there—in front of anybody—to straighten up and do it right.*

They left very few of the club's employees with ambivalent feelings toward them. They were adored and appreciated by some, despised and barely tolerated by others. They were perceived by still others as arrogant and dictatorial:

*I never felt comfortable in complaining about anything or saying much to them. They gave me the impression that things were going to be run their way; if you didn't like it you might as well quit.*

On the morning of May 28, 1977, things indeed were being run their way. The health of their father had deteriorated a few months earlier, and he had gone to Florida for an extended rest. He had stayed in touch from afar: *I called Southgate every day. I just wanted to know how they were doing, how much they were taking in, and how things were going.* But he had essentially relinquished the operation of the club to his chef, whose responsibilities were in the kitchen, and his oldest sons. He had not designated any one of the three as head manager. But he knew that in the event of an emergency the employees of the club would look to his sons for direction, exactly the way he wanted it, first to Rick and then to Ron.

3

On an ordinary day Beverly Hills did not get busy until about supper time. But it usually came to life much earlier, as managers and employees arrived on the hill to prepare for the influx of diners and drinkers. May 28 started out like an ordinary day. A little activity was already underway at the time of Rick's arrival an hour before noon. The manager of a small band, the Three Way Power, was there to set up equipment for an evening performance. He was unfamiliar with the building and needed help in getting his equipment to the Crystal Room on the second floor. Not many employees were present at this hour, but someone helped. The band manager finished quickly and was out of the building by noon. After his departure, the club was quiet.

On his arrival Rick had every reason to believe that the day ahead would be long and difficult. The number of people anticipated for the two Davidson performances was in the neighborhood of two thousand, and most of that number would have to be served dinner before entering the showroom. Two large dining areas, the Main Dining Room and the Garden Room, had been reserved for this purpose; each of the two was expected to operate at or near capacity for most of the evening. Moreover, every other available room in the building was scheduled for heavy use. A large crowd of four hundred or more was expected to fill the Empire Room for a banquet and dance. The upstairs was reserved for two separate parties, and 120 people were expected to attend each. A barmitzvah party was scheduled for the Viennese Room; slightly less than one hundred guests had promised to attend. With all this and more ahead, the day promised to be hectic for the owners of the club. It started with a guarantee, even if everything could somehow be made to go smoothly, that the patience and stamina of the employees would wear very thin before the day ended.

## 4

Activity at the club gradually intensified as morning faded into afternoon. Toward afternoon, employees arrived on the hill and turned their efforts to preparation of the club for the evening ahead. One of the first areas to draw their attention was near the front of the building—a small party room where later in the day the fire would begin.

The Zebra Room was located in one of the most elegant and charming areas of the entire building. Just outside its main entrance was the beautiful spiral stairway with its iron siderails winding upward to the second story. The open stairwell, which literally was filled with the beauty of a huge chandelier hanging down from the second floor ceiling, was the only thing between the entrance to the room and a small masonry rock wall that contained an attractive decorative fountain and an artificial outdoor scene. Across the corridor was the Hallway of Mirrors that ran all the way back to the main bar.

The Zebra Room itself was almost as appealing as the area in which it was located. Small and L-shaped, the main part was thirty feet long and fifteen feet wide. It had a concrete floor that was hidden under a predominantly red carpet. The ceiling was acoustical tile, one foot squares of gold and white. Two gold-colored chandeliers with brass trim hung down into the room, while two or three other lights receded into the ceiling. On the south end of the room was an artificial fireplace with ceramic, gas-fired logs. The walls on either side were covered with a mirror from ceiling to floor; attractive hardboard paneling covered the other walls. A set of solid wood double doors, stained to match the paneling, was located on the north end of the room to allow for entrance from the Hallway of Mirrors.

Because of its size—the smallest party room in the Club—and its soft elegance, the Zebra Room was used most often for special occasions. By mid-afternoon of May 28, it was being prepared for such an occasion, a wedding reception and dinner for a group of about twenty-five. Banquet tables were set up in the middle of the room in the shape of a T, with a head table backed up to the fireplace on the south wall. Smaller tables were brought in to hold gifts, a champagne fountain, and a cake—all draped appropriately for the occasion. A two-layer wedding cake was delivered to the room, preparations for the party were announced complete, and the employees who had done the work turned their attention to other duties.

Not far away and at about the same time, the Empire Room was prepared to accommodate the Greater Cincinnati Savings and Loan Association's awards banquet. The preparations in this part of the building were neither unique nor difficult for the club's employees. The banquet was in its fifth or sixth year at Beverly Hills and the club's managers knew what the Association expected. More importantly, the Empire Room was particularly suited for the kind of activity scheduled there for the evening. It was large (approximately 60 feet by 120 feet), close to the kitchen, and well equipped for major dinner parties. It had a stage, a set of double doors on each of three sides, and two levels of floor space. The lower level was circular in configuration and filled the center of the room. The stage and the three sets of doors served to break the higher level of floor space into four parts, one for each corner of the room (see Diagram No. 1).

On this occasion tables large enough to accommodate eight people for dinner were scattered evenly throughout the lower level of the room and two sections of the higher level (specifically the two on the south side of the room). A two-tier head table, with chairs for thirty-four guests, was located on the north side of the room on the stage. In each of the northeast and northwest corners of the room, on the higher level of floor space, a temporary bar was set up to serve cocktails to the four hundred or so people expected to attend the evening affair. By late afternoon the big room was ready for the arrival of a group that would consist entirely of savings and loan association employees and their spouses and dates.

Rick and Ron, and to a lesser extent Scott, coordinated the work of the employees throughout the afternoon. But there was one part of the club that occupied very little of their time and attention. The Cabaret Room was in the reliable hands of one of their most trusted employees, a woman who had managed the showroom for a long time. It was her practice to arrive on the hill in late afternoon and to assume nearly total responsibility for the showroom. She would oversee dinner parties slated for that part of the building, assign work stations for the hostesses, waitresses and busboys on duty for the evening, and supervise the seating of patrons for the shows.

On this day she was scheduled to arrive at 4:00 p.m. and was on time as usual. She picked up the reservation sheets at the front desk without paying much attention to the number of people on the lists. She must have known, however, that both performances were sold out, for no reservations had been accepted for days, maybe even weeks. From the front desk she walked down the main corridor and entered the showroom to begin preparations for a very busy evening.

John Davidson had finished his rehearsal and was gone. It was much too early for patrons to arrive in this part of the building, but several employees were already at work. In the service bars, the bartenders were taking inventory of their liquor supply and restocking their shelves from the storage area in the basement. A small group of busboys and waitresses was in the showroom itself setting up for banquets.

Normally the Cabaret Room was not used for dinner parties unless there was no space elsewhere in the club. The evening of May 28, 1977, was not normal in any sense of the word. Two large groups, one of eighty-seven and one of ninety, were scheduled to dine in the room before the first performance and stay beyond dinner for the first show. To accommodate these groups the employees had carried several large banquet tables into the room and placed them near the stage in an area known inside the club as the "pit."

The manager deposited her reservation sheets near the rear doors, checked Davidson's dressing room to see that it was ready, and then unlocked the exit door on the east side of the building. She prepared worksheets that served to assign cocktail waitresses to their work stations for the evening and then proceeded to have the large room set up for a full house. The latter endeavor took some time and effort since the Cabaret Room had almost no permanent fixtures. By design it was adaptable to many situations. Six booths on each side of the stage were stationary. Everything else could be moved in and out of the room.

On this occasion the manager had the room filled with small tables to seat the huge crowd that would dine elsewhere in the club and come only for cocktails and the show. It was after 5:00 p.m. by the time she finished her preparations, got dinner for herself from the kitchen, and returned to the Cabaret Room to await the arrival of patrons. The end result of her preparation, according to information gathered after the fire, is shown on Diagram No. 7 on the following page.

6

A very small group of patrons, the first to arrive on the hill, had come to the club in late afternoon. They had arrived a little before four o'clock for a wedding at the chapel in the garden at the rear of the building. The ceremony had started on time and had been completed a few minutes after the hour. Those in attendance were scheduled to arrive in the Zebra Room for a reception and dinner at about 5:00 p.m. While waiting, they had wandered through the garden and then had entered the sparsely occupied building to enjoy the elegance of the club. Their presence in the building during this time had caused barely a stir, as the employees and managers of the club continued to prepare meticulously for the onslaught just ahead.

In due course the wedding party and their guests made their way to the Zebra Room. When assembled, they numbered twenty-three. The clock had moved only a little past 5:00 p.m. when the waitress took the first order for cocktails. The air inside the room was cool and clear; everything seemed perfectly normal in

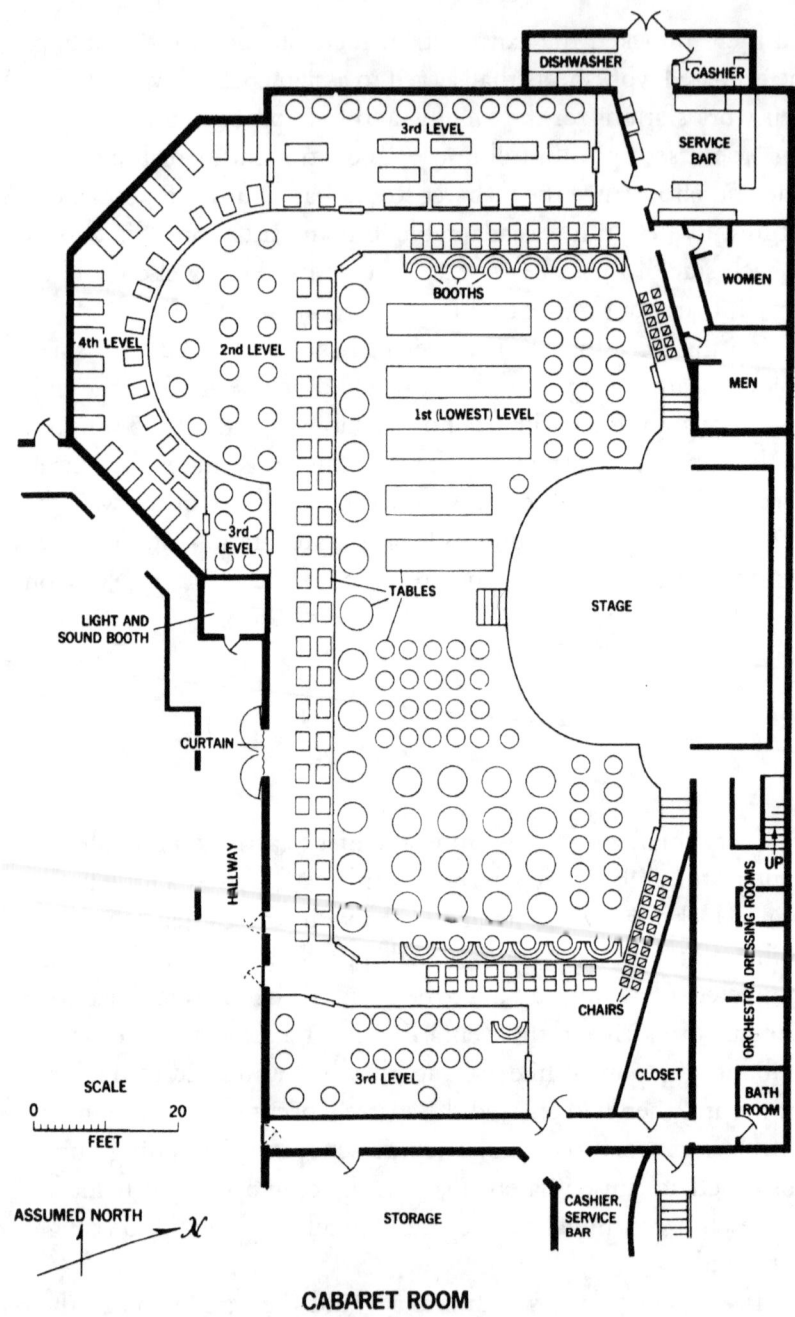

**CABARET ROOM**

**Diagram No. 7**

that small corner of the building. With dinner scheduled to be served no earlier than 6:00 p.m., the wedding group relaxed to wait for the cocktails and the conclusion to a special occasion.

7

Traffic outside the club began to pick up a little after five o'clock, got quite heavy by six, and shortly after that began to stack up in the driveway. Ordinarily the patrons of Beverly Hills did not get the opportunity to park their own vehicles. The club had a contract under which parking service was provided by an outside enterprise. In actuality the enterprise consisted of one man and a group of young boys hired by him to park the vehicles. Unfortunately, on this busiest of days, several of the boys failed to report to work on time. As a consequence cars backed up from the canopy in front of the building all the way down the hill to the main highway. Once this occurred the movement of traffic up the hill was painfully slow. It took about twenty minutes to travel from the driveway entrance to the front door, although the distance was but a few hundred feet. Not everyone endured the unexpected inconvenience with great patience.

The man in charge of the parking operation tried hard to subdue the impatience of his customers: *In this business you try to please the people. I didn't want them to know that my boys were late, so I told them my employees had gone on strike for higher pay.* A harmless misstatement, in his mind sounded better than the truth. In a few days he would come to entertain second thoughts about the wisdom of his indiscretion. Some of the club's patrons would suggest to investigators the possibility of a connection between a strike that did not occur and a tragic fire that did.

Caught in this heavy traffic were a man and a woman who had arrived at Beverly Hills for an unusual purpose. They had come not for a show, a party, or dinner, but rather to fish in a small lake located on the club's property. As the man neared the entrance to the club's driveway he saw that cars were backed up the full length of that driveway and that they were moving at a snail's pace. Nevertheless he moved his automobile in line and proceeded slowly to the top of the hill only to find himself denied access to the property by a parking attendant. The lake was closed for the evening to everyone; the club was simply too busy to fool with visitors. The disappointment of the moment did not linger in the minds of the fisherman and his wife; there would always be another day. But what they observed during the slow journey up the hill remained in their memories.

A cloud of smoke had floated up from the roof of the building and stood out against the evening sky. The woman had seen it first and pointed it out to her husband. It had looked out of place: *The smoke came from the building in a puff, like air had forced it upward, and then it disappeared. It was black, as though someone was burning rubber, and because of its color looked funny.* At this hour the tragedy at Beverly Hills was still a long way off; smoke would not be observed inside the building for almost three hours. The fisherman and his wife may have seen nothing of significance. But they may have seen the first sign of danger.

8

The Empire Room was the first part of the building to receive large numbers of people. The anticipated banquet schedule was the arrival of guests by 6:30, cocktails and dinner by 8:15, the presentation of awards by 9:00, and a dance until 1:00 A.M. The master of ceremonies for the evening and some other program participants had arrived at 5:30 to prepare for the presentation of awards. The guests had started to arrive at about six o'clock but would not fill the large room for almost an hour; the traffic problem outside the entrance was a cause for slight delay. Except for this one minor inconvenience, however, the initial phases of activity in the Empire Room moved ahead smoothly and without incident.

The same is true of activity in another of the club's biggest rooms. The Garden Room was located at the back of the building between the kitchen on the west and the Cabaret Room on the east. It was the newest part of the club, of course, having been in use for only six months. The room was irregular in shape and very large, having over 9,500 square feet of floor space. It was equipped, like other parts of the facility, with folding partitions that could be used to divide the area into four smaller parts. At least some of the partitions were in place on the night of the tragedy.

The most striking feature of the room was a wall made almost entirely of glass that jutted into and overlooked a well-kept garden area at the rear of the building. An unobstructed view of the garden existed from inside, for there were no curtains or drapes on the glass wall. A set of double doors on each side of the room made it possible for guests to walk from the dining area into the garden.

This part of the club—although the largest in the entire building—was not scheduled for a banquet or major party for the evening of the 28th. A substantial number of small groups of people was expected at the club for dinner and a show, consequently some large dining areas were needed for general use. The Garden Room, which would seat several hundred for dinner, had been set aside for that purpose.

It was anticipated that the room would get very heavy use on two occasions, during a period of time before the first performance in the Cabaret Room and then again before the second performance. The first part of the evening went as expected. A few people arrived for cocktails and dinner fairly early—between six and seven o'clock. Heavy use of the room was not expected to occur until a little later. Throughout the early period everything functioned smoothly. Most people came in small groups as expected, relaxed for an enjoyable meal, and planned their schedule around curtain time in the showroom.

During this same period of time the Cabaret Room itself came to life. The first groups of patrons to arrive were those scheduled to be there for dinner. By about six-thirty, most of the two groups were seated at long tables near the stage (in the "pit" area of the room), and soon thereafter the employees began to serve dinner. A condition that would get far more noticeable as the clock moved toward showtime started to develop rather early in the evening: *We were at long tables packed in like sardines. We were joking and laughing, saying we would have to take turns cutting our meat.*

## 9

The second story at Beverly Hills was small in comparison to the first, and divided into two almost equal parts by the corridor that crossed the building from east to west. Each part was equipped with folding partitions that made it possible to subdivide the area into smaller rooms (see Diagram No. 1). For the evening of May 28 the entire floor had been set aside for only two parties. On neither side of the corridor, therefore, was it necessary for the partitions to be put in place.

Activity in this part of the building had picked up fairly early. At about six o'clock a group from the Greater Cincinnati Choral Union started to arrive at the club. The first to arrive had been a dance band of four or five musicians and three singers, and several models. The Choral Union had reserved half the second floor, the part known as Crystal rooms 1, 2, and 3, for the entire evening. Dinner, a fashion show, and a dance, in that order, were expected to last from about seven o'clock until the club closed in the early hours of Sunday morning. The band and models had arrived well ahead of the main group of 120 so that they could prepare for the evening performances.

The other part of the second floor—Crystal rooms 4, 5, and 6—had been reserved for the evening for a dog show banquet. A group of about the same size was expected to be inside the building by about eight o'clock for a buffet dinner and presentation of trophies. By seven o'clock most of the Choral Union party was assembled and ready for dinner. Only a handful of those from the other second floor group had arrived at the club. But one of the group was in a position to observe an unusual sight.

Very near seven o'clock, a young woman who had been a participant in the dog show earlier in the day sat in a car at the top of the driveway near the Beverly Hills entrance. A scene observed by a couple of others about an hour earlier renewed itself and caught her eye: *We were waiting for the parking attendant to take our car. I looked up at the top of the building near the front. Black smoke was coming from the roof. I thought about it for a minute and decided it was nothing.* Perhaps she was right. The clock was still two hours short of 9:01 p.m.

## 10

The circumstances that developed at Beverly Hills on the fateful evening of the 28th were almost totally unkind. At least in the afterthoughts of the event, virtually every circumstance would seem to have contributed in some malevolent way to the day's unfortunate end. Any number of things, with just a particle of luck, could have transformed the catastrophe into a harmless mishap. As though molded by fate, however, they joined instead with other things to turn a life-threatening situation into a monumental tragedy. There was one notable exception.

A few days before the eventful night, a local physician had decided to entertain a small group of professional colleagues. For this occasion he wanted an atmosphere that would be conducive to a quiet evening of fellowship and relaxation, and Beverly Hills seemed to be the perfect spot. So he had made arrangements for a dinner party at the club for the evening of the tragedy.

The physicians and their spouses had originally been scheduled to dine in the Garden Room. But the huge crowd of people expected for the early show in the Cabaret Room had promised to create an overload for the general dining areas including the Garden Room. In anticipation of this the managers of the club had moved the physicians' small party to the Viennese Room. Notice of this move had been so short that the host had been unable to inform his guests of the change prior to their arrival on the hill. So, after he reached the club he found it necessary to station himself in the foyer, meet his colleagues on their arrival, and direct them to the location of the party.

The Viennese Room was located on the main floor of the club to the right of the main bar and fairly close to the front entrance. It was quite large—roughly 100 feet by 40 feet—but was equipped with sliding partitions that made it possible to subdivide the room into smaller areas. This night one of the partitions was put in place to create a small private area on the north end of the room directly across the main corridor from the east entrance to the Empire Room. It was to this small area that the host physician directed his guests. He had completed the task by eight o'clock, and all in the party were assembled for cocktails and dinner.

The remaining two-thirds of the Viennese Room had been set aside for a barmitzvah party for almost one hundred people. The group that would finally assemble for the function would number about eighty-five adults and a small group of young boys, friends of the thirteen-year-old who was being introduced to the religious responsibilities of manhood.

The barmitzvah party had been scheduled to start before eight o'clock. But not everyone was able to get inside the building by that time. Traffic congestion outside still posed a problem for people trying to reach the club; cars were backed up and waiting to reach the main entrance to the building. Those who had managed to arrive on time found in the extreme south end of the Viennese Room an open bar for cocktails and a small band playing dance music. Some ordered cocktails and took to the dance floor to enjoy the band. The young boys in the party set out upon their arrival to explore the corridors and banquet rooms of the club.

## 11

History literally repeated itself at about eight o'clock. A woman who earlier had been in attendance at the dog show in Cincinnati arrived at Beverly Hills to enter the building with her husband and daughter. For some reason her attention was drawn to the area above the front of the club: *A small column of black smoke came from the top of the building.* She noticed it, recorded it in her memory, and entered the building without giving the incident much thought. Within a couple of hours she would come to believe that she had witnessed a matter of great importance. Perhaps she had.

## 12

At nearly the same time, the manager of the Cabaret Room went to the main dressing room in that part of the club. John Davidson asked about the number of reservations for the evening performances, and was told that the house was full. Inside the showroom itself a band took the stage to play a set or two of dance music. A steady stream of patrons was flowing into the big room by this time, always through the rear doors from the corridor that separated the Cabaret Room from the Garden Room.

The employees of the showroom began a struggle in the pit area to clear the banquet tables of dishes. In other parts of the building, guests hurried through the final stages of dinner in an attempt to make the show on time. A line of people formed in the corridor outside the Cabaret Room, waiting to be seated by the hostesses. At this time it was obvious that the show would not open as scheduled at 8:30. An additional fifteen or twenty minutes would be necessary to seat the guests and get the room settled down and ready for the performance.

The conditions of the room—ultimately to become a matter of great controversy—began to disconcert some of the patrons:

> *Our seats were supposed to be down front, but for some reason we didn't get down there. They put us in back. They put five of us real tight against the tables. There wasn't room to sit.*
>
> • • •
>
> *Every time a waitress went past where we were sitting we almost had a tray of drinks in our lap. She had to turn sideways to hold it above her head to get through.*
>
> • • •
>
> *We were seated by a waitress on the top level back against the wall, as far from the stage as we could get. There were ten chairs to every table. People were shoved completely against each other.*

Nonetheless the manager and the hostesses continued to admit people to the room. Additional tables were not added, for there was no space; but more chairs were brought in and placed around or near the tables already there. Some of the guests could barely reach the tables at which they were seated; a few had no table at all.

Soon there was no room on the showroom floor for dancing. So the stage was temporarily converted to that use. The music was inviting and many people danced. The mood of the room was uniformly upbeat. Everybody was having a good time. At some point the band stopped playing dance music and left the stage for a short break before showtime. They moved to the dressing rooms that were to the right of the stage (see Diagram No. 7).

13

The guests had lingered over dinner in the Zebra Room anticipating a second round of cocktails. The wedding reception party in that room was more than three hours old before the guests began to think about bringing it to a close. During this time the fire hidden behind the walls or above the ceiling of the room grew slowly and surreptitiously. No visual signs of danger appeared inside the small room. But noises that were unusual enough to be noticed interrupted the ordinary sounds of the clubs: *They were described by some as sounding like thunder and by others as sounding like furniture being moved. I thought they had a grinding sound. We heard them four or five times, for about two seconds each time.*

More significantly perhaps, physical discomfort not yet encountered in any other part of the building began to bother several members of the party: *People near the door were actually cold and shivering while ten or fifteen feet away we were hot and perspiring.* The waitress was asked to turn up the air conditioner but she reported that it was already running at full capacity. The discomfort in the room worsened as the evening wore on: *I heard one couple say they were going to leave, that it was getting too hot for them, and that they would meet the others at the bride's house or the groom's house.*

The exact time at which the wedding party ended, like the exact time of so many other crucial events during the evening, is difficult to fix. It was probably very close to eight-thirty before the last guest left the room. At this time a familiar sight once again made an appearance over the front of the building, within sight of one of the guests who had just vacated the Zebra Room: *We were standing around in the parking lot talking. My wife and I both noticed smoke coming from the front left corner of the roof. There was one very black puff of smoke followed about four seconds later by another. I looked at my watch and it read 8:27.* The small cloud of smoke that floated above the club was dismissed by its observer as relatively unimportant. But it was peculiar enough at the time to prompt some conversation: *I remarked to my wife that it was probably someone burning trash in an incinerator inside the building or an exhaust from the kitchen.* Perhaps he was right. But the outbreak of fire in the front of the building was now much closer at hand.

14

The showroom band returned to the stage, but no one gave the word to start the show. It was now past eight-thirty. In the north-south corridor a line of people still waited to get in. The occupancy load of nine hundred had been reached and surpassed. Patrons continued to line up outside, and the employees continued to seat them.

The condition developing inside the room—although certainly not unseen before in this part of the club—became a subject of particular concern among employees:

*It was very crowded and we all talked about it Someone said they had overbooked.*

• • •

*I asked the manager how many reservations we had; she said 1,152. That was not counting the people eating dinner there.*

• • •

*I recall asking the manager about the reservations; she said you can bet there are well over a thousand. Everybody's reply was over a thousand that night. They had told us a week or two weeks before that it was completely sold out for the weekend.*

• • •

*The manager went around saying that there were 1,072 reservations. I could maneuver around with difficulty.*

With more thought for personal concern, the size of the crowd also became a subject of conversation among a few of the patrons:

*As we entered we commented on how congested it was. I said to my friends, we could never get out if the place should catch on fire.*

*We had a table near the door. Before the show started, we commented on the crowded conditions and what would happen if a fire broke out. We took comfort in the fact that we were so close to the exit.*

*I said to my wife, "I can't imagine where they will put all these people." We talked about a fire exit and spotted one. I said to her, "We are going out this exit if a fire occurs."*

*I said to one of our principals, "This could be another Coconut Grove the way they are crowding them in; there is an exit over there and one over there. Just be sure and keep that in mind."*

The predominant mood of the group, however, was largely free of such concerns. Cocktails were being served and consumed. Cigarette smoke in the room became thick, and most people would have preferred more space within which to maneuver. But the opening of the show was imminent, and people were generally relaxed and enjoying themselves.

As the clock moved on toward the critical hour of nine the showroom became more and more crowded. Floor space on all four levels of the room got scarce as demand for access to the show was satisfied. Aisles and passageways began to be affected by the continuing effort to seat people for the performance: *There was one table, and the people there didn't want to accommodate us. So the hostess said 'We will seat you in the aisle.' She put a table and four chairs and sat us in the aisle. Directly in front of us she sat another couple directly on top of the stairs.* The obstruction of aisles and passageways that was in progress was being aggravated no doubt by the fact that the room had virtually no permanent fixtures. The chairs used by almost all of the patrons could easily be pushed away from the small tables. And they were being pushed into the aisles on all four levels of the room, mostly because too many were placed around the tables by the club's employees.

Movement of people in all parts of the showroom became quite restricted before the show started. It was difficult for guests to visit the restrooms in the outside corridors: *When I went to the restroom, there was a waitress coming toward me. I had to step between two tables. The two of us could not pass comfortably.* And it was difficult for the employees to do their jobs: *I had to turn sideways to get through with drinks.* In some parts of the room guests were inconvenienced by the growing situation: *He had to get up twice when the waitress came through and move his chair so she could move through the aisle.*

Even the ramps leading from the pit area to the two exits in the corners of the room were affected by the size of the crowd. As one of the employees explained after the fire, chairs were not ordinarily placed on the two ramps until it was obvious "that they had to have them." The showroom manager claimed after the fire that this need never arose but she was unquestionably wrong in her recollection. At some point during the evening, one of the room's hostesses had supervised the placement of two rows of chairs on each ramp. And before showtime guests were seated in the chairs and were served cocktails. The accommodations were barely adequate: *There were no tables, just chairs. The guests held their drinks in their hands. There was a railing; ashtrays were placed on it.* But the guests who occupied the chairs complained very little. They had succeeded in gaining access to the show. That was the important thing at the time.

Although use of the ramps for seating patrons occurred late in the evening, there was nevertheless some impact on traffic flow before showtime:

*We had to go up the ramp in single file because of the chairs.*

• • •

*There was room enough for a waitress to get through because the ones that worked in the pit area had to come through there to get to the service bars.*

• • •

*The right hand side of the stage had five sets of two chairs coming up the ramp. The aisle was blocked by the chairs. I had to turn sideways to get through with drinks.*

The inconvenience and discomfort that resulted was minimal, however. Movement up and down the ramps simply required a little more care and a little more time. Patrons and employees alike had an ample supply of both, at least for the time being.

## 15

Though the Zebra Room was not scheduled for further use during the evening, the waitress who served the wedding group had stayed after the party to straighten up the room. At some point she was joined there by a reservationist who came for a glass of punch. The waitress had removed dishes from the dinner tables, placed them on carrying trays, doused burning candles left by the guests, and vacated the room by about a quarter of nine. The reservationist had followed her out of the room.

A few minutes later the waitress returned to see if the busboys had cleared the room. The carrying trays were still there. And so was something else. The room had not cooled down at all since the departure of the patrons. It seemed particularly hot near the artificial fireplace on the south wall. The waitress left the room once again looking for a busboy, but not before hearing a buzzing sound in the lights.

Soon thereafter a busboy acting on instructions from the waitress entered the room to remove loaded trays. He saw the lights in the ceiling flicker five or six times during a span of about thirty seconds. His curiosity was aroused by the incident but not his concern. He left the room without giving the matter a second thought. Both he and the waitress had missed real signs of trouble.

## 16

Beginning with an introduction of those at the head table, the formal program in the Empire Room had gotten started late. Everyone had finished eating by the time the master of ceremonies relinquished the microphone to the man who was to direct the presentation of awards. The awards were for outstanding performance in a financial education program attended by savings and loan association employees during the prior year. In all, nineteen such awards were scheduled for presentation. The clock had moved beyond half-past-eight before the first presentation was made.

From that point on the awards ceremony plodded along with the clock, taking a little more time than most people expected or wanted. A slight degree of restlessness settled over the crowd, and the attention of a few people turned away from the middle of the room where the awards were being presented to focus momentarily on other matters, mostly trivial and mostly inconsequential. There was one highly unfortunate exception however.

At a table near one of the exits to the room a trio of guests, two employees of a Kentucky savings and loan association and an escort, quietly weighed the pleasures of an evening with John Davidson against an evening of song and dance in the Empire Room. Davidson won out rather easily as the trio decided to leave the banquet and head for the show in the Cabaret Room. In so doing they left behind a friend who had weighed the same considerations but decided to stay with the banquet. Only the friend would be alive on May 29 to describe how casually an individual can sometimes make a fateful choice of life over death.

As the presentation of awards proceeded to the half way point, the clock in the Empire Room moved closer and closer towards the hour of nine. More and more people anticipated the dance that was scheduled to start on the hour. The band that had been hired for the evening was behind the curtain on stage and practically ready to start. Out on the floor a pregnant woman lifted herself out of a chair, departed the company of her husband and friends, and headed for a restroom located at the front of the club. In the middle of the room the master of ceremonies prepared to present the ninth award of the evening; a photographer positioned himself to record the event on film. The exact time is unknown and unascertainable; it was probably still a few minutes before the hour of nine. But the stage for tragedy was set in this part of the building, and absolutely nothing had occurred that could have forewarned the occupants of the terror that was about to erupt just a few feet away.

## 17

The last person to enter the Zebra Room before the outbreak of fire was a cleaning woman. At five minutes before nine, just as the first performance was about to open in the showroom, she entered the room from the Hallway of Mirrors to store a sweeper. She encountered no fire, no smoke, nor other signs of peril. She found the electrical system still operational. At least to casual observation everything about the room appeared normal. The cleaning woman stored the sweeper, turned off the lights, returned to the Hallway of Mirrors, and walked to the area of the main bar.

Not too many people were sitting in the bar at this precise moment. In fact the whole front area was experiencing a slack period. A couple of bartenders were on duty but the barroom piano player was taking a rest. The main dining room was half empty. The first wave of diners had finished and gone to the Cabaret Room; the second was just beginning to arrive at the club. A group of approximately one hundred people was gathered in the foyer patiently awaiting seating arrangements for dinner.

The cleaning woman moved through the barroom and turned to a set of restrooms that separated three parts of the front area: the foyer, the main bar, and the Zebra Room (see Diagram No. 1). In the women's restroom she found a couple of women concerned about the odor of smoke. She felt sure that she knew the source of the problem. Someone had probably put a burning cigarette in a waste paper disposal. It happened all the time in the club. She could easily bring it under control, if only she could find the cigarette.

Sitting in the main bar at this moment was a captain with the Cincinnati Fire Department. He had been in the club for only a few minutes—since about 8:45 p.m.—but had ordered cocktails while waiting to be called for nine o'clock dinner reservations in the Garden Room. Almost simultaneously he received his cocktails and a request from a hostess to go to the Garden Room for his reservations. He and his wife and another couple walked down the Hallway of Mirrors, passed the spiral stairway, and prepared to enter the main corridor. At the other end of that corridor were two fairly long lines of people, one trying to get into the Cabaret Room for the first performance and the other waiting to be seated in the Garden Room. As he headed in that direction he left the area outside the entrance to the Zebra Room. Everything seemed perfectly normal.

18

The showroom band played an overture. The show was finally underway. It was a few minutes before nine o'clock, 8:55 p.m. by the best estimate. John Davidson and his production manager were in a dressing room backstage. In an adjoining room a television set was tuned in to receive a popular show at 9:00 p.m.; a young woman who had a friend in the band was relaxed in front of the set. A two-man comedy team, Teter and McDonald, came on stage and started a performance that was scheduled to last twenty-seven minutes.

There was still some activity offstage in the floor area. The rear doors of the showroom, although ordinarily closed at the beginning of a performance, were open. A line of people stood just outside the doors waiting to get in. Many of those inside thought the room was already full:

*It was jam packed. Elbow to elbow. The waitresses were even having trouble getting around the tables to serve people sitting in the pit in front of the stage.*

• • •

*I would say it was packed. I didn't ask anybody to move when I went to the restroom, but I had to weave my way.*

• • •

*There were so many people in there! The tables were so close together that the waitresses could hardly get through to deliver food. And they were sitting in the aisles.*

*I couldn't see any vacant space at all in the room. It was just totally filled, every ounce of it. I was surprised they could find space for us.*

The hostesses apparently thought otherwise. They continued the process of seating people for the performance.

The job of finding seats for the guests got tougher: *Of course it was very annoying because people were trying to watch the show. They were saying 'sit down' but there was no place to be seated.* Hostesses found it necessary at this time to split groups, seating part in one area and part in another. They placed chairs against walls and in the corners of the room. Not everyone was satisfied with the arrangements: *Our daughter and her friends got disgusted and went back to the doorway and stood.* But most people were willing to accept whatever accommodations were available. As the show moved through its initial stages a small group stood against the southeast wall without hope for seats. A few people were also standing on each side of one of the rear doorways.

On the other side of the room near the double doors leading into the northeast service bar, the most decisive episode of the whole evening was about to unfold.

Ron Schilling was in one of the backstage dressing rooms. His visit to the Cabaret Room at this time was routine. He was not there for any purpose in particular, only to check on the showroom. An eighteen-year-old employee of the club was in the northeast corner of the room near the service bar taking an unauthorized break from his duties as a busboy. His mother had told him that the comedy act in progress was very funny. She had seen it earlier and she was right about its quality. The comedians entertained the large crowd in the true sense. The first part of the performance was delightful and hilarious: *Everybody was laughing and having a good time.* The young employee was no exception.

Ron Schilling left the dressing room backstage and traveled to the northeast service bar. Shortly after his arrival there he saw the busboy disengaged from his duties. He routinely ordered the young man back to work. In so doing, and obviously without appreciating its significance, he set in motion a series of events that would ultimately prove to be the most crucial of the whole tragedy. The busboy, promptly after his brief encounter with the owner, left the Cabaret Room and headed up the north-south corridor toward the front of the building near the Zebra Room. At the entrance to that small room he would find himself uniquely positioned to affect a crisis that was now ready to show its face.

19

From the very beginning of the evening, things had not gone according to plan on the second floor. The small dance band and models with the Choral Union Party had not been served their six o'clock dinner until seven. And the Choral Union party itself, scheduled for a seven o'clock dinner, had not received food even at eight o'clock. Patience had prevailed on this floor for awhile, but indignation finally won out.

Most of the patrons in this group had blamed the waitresses and busboys for the problem. But the problem had unquestionably developed in the kitchen. A large crowd in the Garden Room and in the main dining room had been scheduled to be in the showroom by 8:30 for the first performance; dinner had to be provided to these groups first, and so the parties upstairs had simply been made to wait.

And wait they did. The only thing that had arrived on the second floor by a quarter of nine was atmospheric discomfort. At that moment unpleasant conditions were experienced in widely separated areas of this part of the building. In a dressing room at the top of the stairs, the fashion show models had turned up the air conditioner without getting relief. On the north side of the corridor a group of women had commented about how hot it had become and had removed their wraps. A similar thing had happened on the south side: *Everybody at first assumed that there were too many people in the room. Then it got too hot for that; we assumed that the air conditioner had failed. People were beginning to use their handkerchiefs to wipe their brows and to remove their jackets.* The number of people on the second floor at this time could not have significantly affected the temperature of the area. Something was wrong.

Almost two hours late, food was finally delivered to the second floor. The Choral Union party was served the first course of dinner and a few minutes later the buffet across the corridor was set in place and the people from the dog show prepared to eat. By this time it was very close to 9:00 p.m., and signs of imminent danger were suddenly in abundant supply in this part of the building.

The dance band was sitting near a bar in the Crystal Room planning a performance. The manager thought he smelled something burning, "like varnish," and looked for a waitress. She told him that someone had dropped a cigarette and caused a burn. He was satisfied and returned to his band. The fashion show was an hour late. One of the models left the dressing room at the top of the stairs to check on the progress of dinner. A wisp of smoke drifted into the room as she opened the door and caused some concern. She made inquiry, returned to the room, and reported that a cigarette fire had just been brought under control.

A woman with the Choral Union group was about to eat the last of her salad when a thin stream of gray smoke floated through the door and into the room. She and several others noticed it. One of the coordinators of the fashion show provided a comforting explanation: *It's just a little cigarette in a waste can; it's out. Sit down, be cool, eat your salad. We'll be ready for the show in a minute*. On the other side of the corridor a young girl commented to her parents that the cigarette smoke in the room was terrible, and a woman near the door heard someone outside explain that there had been a cigarette fire downstairs.

A bartender, who was working in a small barroom at the top of the stairs, detected an unusual odor in the air. At the same time he observed powdery strands of smoke hovering around the ceiling above his bar. A waitress standing in the upstairs corridor glanced down the hallway and saw smoke gathered at the top of the open stairway. Light in color, it could have been cigarette smoke, and looked relatively harmless. It would not look that way for long. Conditions around the stairway and in the Crystal rooms were about to change.

## 20

Of course the problem in the front of the club was not a burning cigarette in a waste paper disposal. No one at Beverly Hills knew it yet but the building was on fire. The fire had been in existence for a considerable period of time, hiding somewhere above the ceiling or between the walls of the Zebra Room. It no doubt had spread from the point of ignition to nearby combustibles and had intensified substantially. From the concealed spaces of the Zebra Room black smoke and toxic gases had moved to concealed spaces in other parts of the front of the building. In most of these spaces there was no capacity for additional smoke and gases. The fire would soon be revealed to the occupants of the building.

It would be difficult even to imagine a worse time for a fire to strike a nightclub. The building was full of people who had no reason at all to suspect danger. More than a thousand were in the crowded showroom, largely isolated from the rest of the club, and preoccupied with an entertaining performance on stage. More than a thousand others were dispersed throughout a sprawling structure that had no fire alarm and no sprinkler system. Members of both groups had unknowingly put their lives in the hands of a small group of people who had not been trained in the slightest to deal with an emergency.

Very few of the employees were familiar with the location of fire extinguishers. Even fewer of them knew how to use one properly. Some members of the work force were almost as unfamiliar with the club as the patrons. Only a few had ever entered or left the building except through the front door. None had ever been schooled in emergency evacuation of the building, and no evacuation plan had ever been prepared by the owners of the club. No time is a good time for fire to strike a heavily occupied building. But some times are better than others. The hour of 9:00 p.m., May 28, 1977, was clearly one of the others. It could hardly have been worse.

# *Four*
## Discovery and Notification of the Fire

I

At nine o'clock all parts of the building seemed normal except for the Zebra Room and the second floor. In the Viennese Room the physicians and their spouses were awaiting dessert after a "lovely dinner." On the opposite side of the partition dividing the room, a bartender who had served the barmitzvah party prepared to close shop. Dinner was scheduled for nine and the bar was supposed to close promptly on the hour. Waitresses delivered appetizers to the room, and the dance band took a break. The adults in this group found their places for dinner and seated themselves. The young boys in the party were still exploring the far reaches of the club, at this moment stealing a look through the showroom doors at the comedy team performing on stage.

Perhaps the quietest area of the whole building was the Garden Room. The dining area in this part of the club was occupied by only about two hundred people; when full it seated about six hundred. The employees there had gone through a very busy period and were calmly preparing for an expected second wave of diners. By nine o'clock, activity in the dining room had just begun to increase again slightly. A wedding party of about fifty—following nuptials in the garden area behind the building—had entered the room for the start of dinner. In the main corridor outside the room a short line of people waited for the attention of a hostess. Neither inside nor outside were there any signs of impatience or anxiety. The room was calm and tranquil as the hour of crisis approached. Not a single person in this part of the building had seen anything to arouse curiosity.

Outside the front entrance of the building, the man in charge of parking stood under the canopy chatting with his employees. A few patrons were still arriving at the club for dinner, but activity outside the front door was at the lowest level of the entire evening. The driveway was clear all the way to the main road, and there was no one at the front entrance except the young men who had been busy all evening parking cars. Nothing had occurred yet to alert anyone in this group to the trouble that was about to explode into view at the Zebra Room.

At about this same time the pregnant woman from the Empire Room reached the front area of the building, and the club's beverage manager, the employee who supervised all bars and bartenders, got to the same area from the Viennese Room. The woman walked through the main bar and entered the restroom then occupied by the cleaning lady. The beverage manager walked through the main bar to the foyer and entered a small office that was located just south of the restroom (see Diagram No. 1). Neither of the two experienced anything unusual in passing through the front area of the building. The barroom was not heavily occupied at the time and was relatively quiet. Nothing at all seemed unnatural.

In the main bar at this time, sitting at a small table in the northwest corner of the room, was a man who had brought his handicapped father to the club for dinner. He had been in the building only about fifteen minutes and was waiting for dinner reservations in the Garden Room. From his table in the corner he had an unobstructed view down the Hallway of Mirrors all the way to the north-south corridor (see Diagram No. 1). For some reason, at approximately nine o'clock, he found himself looking down the hallway past the spiral stairway to a point near the entrance to the Zebra Room. He noticed light smoke hanging over the decorative fountain near the stairway. It was about six inches below the ceiling and heavy enough to cause some concern. He watched it for a few moments, wondered where it was coming from, and turned his thoughts to the difficulty his father might have should a sudden evacuation of the building be necessary.

## 2

In the Viennese Room a couple of waitresses who happened to be sisters were ready to serve dinner to the barmitzvah party. They needed serving trays and thought that some could be obtained from the Zebra Room. So they left the Viennese Room, crossed the north-south corridor, and entered the east end of the Hallway of Mirrors. Outside the Zebra Room they had an unobstructed view down that hallway to the north half of the main bar. It was exactly the same view had by the man sitting in the barroom with his handicapped father, but from the opposite end. One of the two waitresses stopped in the Hallway of Mirrors and took advantage of that view.

Above the people sitting at the circular bar she saw an accumulation of gray smoke that was heavy enough to be noticed. The barroom was dimly lit at the time. The bartenders were mixing and serving cocktails; the patrons were engaged in casual conversation and having a good time. The smoke was hanging about a foot from the ceiling and seemed to be circulating through the air but not in a particular direction. No one in the area seemed concerned about it. The waitress watched it momentarily, concluded that it was peculiar looking, and called it to the attention of her sister. But then she moved on toward her destination and rather quickly reached the entrance to the Zebra Room.

Awaiting her at the entrance was a greeting that was equally unexpected and overwhelming: *I turned the door knob, opened the door, and black smoke just poured out.* No flames were visible to the waitress through the partially open door, but the heavy smoke that roared into the Hallway of Mirrors carried with it an unmistakable message. No cigarette or trash can blaze could have caused such an accumulation of black smoke. Unquestionably the building was on fire. Of course neither of the waitresses could have known that the fire had existed for a considerable period of time. But both very clearly understood the magnitude of the threat that exploded through the Zebra Room door into their faces.

The one who had opened the door left her sister stationed at the entrance to the Zebra Room, to warn others of the danger inside, and headed down the Hallway of Mirrors to find one of the Schillings. The man sitting in the northwest corner of the main bar with his father saw part of her journey. He had noticed the light smoke hanging down from the ceiling in the Hallway of Mirrors, had just mentioned it to his father, and was still looking down the corridor toward the spiral stairway: *I noticed a young woman running toward me. She had a scared look on her face and was waving her arms.* In the area of the circular bar she slowed down enough to ask one of the bartenders to call the fire department. The man in the corner looked at his handicapped father and began to think a little more seriously about leaving the building. The waitress raced on through the main bar and headed for the kitchen looking for Rick or Ron Schilling. On the way she spread the message to some other employees: *The Zebra Room is on fire.*

3

Almost simultaneously with the discovery of fire at the Zebra Room entrance, another employee suddenly smelled smoke in a different though nearby part of the building. She was the club reservationist and an hour earlier at eight o'clock had received an unusual phone call. A man had called for reservations to the Davidson performance in the Cabaret Room. After being told that both shows were fully booked he asked: "When was the last time Beverly Hills burned down?" The tone of his inquiry, as perceived by the reservationist, was friendly and not threatening. But he nonetheless made an impression on his listener. When she caught the odor of smoke at approximately nine o'clock she got concerned about it very quickly.

She was seated at the time in a spot called the "cubbyhole"—a very small compartment that was located between the main bar and the Zebra Room (see Diagram No. 1). She looked in the wastepaper basket in the small room and found nothing. Her attention was soon attracted to a set of double doors that opened from the cubbyhole into the Zebra Room. Only minutes earlier she had been in the room enjoying a glass of punch left over from the wedding party. To her amazement she saw dark smoke entering the cubbyhole from around the double doors.

When she pushed the doors open she saw no flames inside the room but found herself face to face with sufficient heat to singe her hair. To use her words, the doorway between the two areas was "hot, hot, hot." And the smoke that came from the room was worse, almost unbearable. *Tears just poured down my face.* She closed the doors to the room, left the cubbyhole, and ran to the front desk with the alarm: *My God, there's a fire!*

The front desk was located barely inside the main bar from the foyer. It was being handled at the time by Marjorie Schilling, wife of Rick. At least two other employees, a hostess and a host, were at the desk when the reservationist sounded the alarm. One of the two was in the process of seating a group of guests for dinner; she took the group to the main dining room and returned quickly to the desk. The other ran swiftly to the cubbyhole, looked inside the Zebra Room, and rushed back to the desk to confirm that the building was indeed on fire. Marjorie Schilling sent the hostess off toward the kitchen to tell the owners about the fire and then placed a call to the Southgate police department and immediately thereafter to the fire department.

From the front desk the reservationist moved quickly to the circular bar and told the head bartender about the problem in the cubbyhole. He rushed away from the bar toward the small compartment and saw for himself what had caused her excitement: *The smoke was so bad it hurt my eyes and throat. I mean it was awfully heavy.* He took a few seconds to obtain a fire extinguisher and then returned to the site of the smoke. The reservationist, Marjorie

Schilling, and the host were still in the area but the smoke had gotten worse during his absence. He saw no flames in the cubbyhole and immediately gave up the idea of trying to control the blaze: *As far as I was concerned it looked like it was too much for anybody to fight with a fire extinguisher.* In his mind it was time to start thinking about getting the patrons out of the building. He headed back to the circular bar to get some help from the other bartenders.

## 4

The fire station in Southgate was very quiet at nine o'clock. Only one man was on duty there. Other members of the volunteer department were in contact with the station through tone-alert radio receivers. At one minute after the hour—9:01 p.m. as logged at the Campbell County Dispatch Center—the silence of the firehouse was shattered by an alarm that announced the possibility of fire at Beverly Hills.

For a long time, of course, the big club had been a sensitive spot for the fire department. Only an old school building in the jurisdiction had a higher priority. The concern of the department for the Schilling property was not just a firefighter's fear of a nightclub fire. There was, in addition, the unexplained fire of 1970, the public controversy that had erupted over the safety of the building, and the grand jury inquiry. The fire department had found itself in the midst of unwanted controversy and had emerged from it with an appreciation of the need to give the big nightclub some special attention.

The initial response to the alarm was swift and effective. The fire chief lived only two blocks from the station. He grabbed his car keys when the alarm sounded and headed for the station. In a matter of seconds he and several firemen were in the stationhouse changing street clothes for fire gear. Other members of his department were already on the way to the fire, having headed straight for the club from their homes at the sound of the alarm. Within a minute or so of that alarm, firefighters were leaving the station in trucks for Beverly Hills. It was only a couple of miles to the club from the station, and the traffic on the streets was light.

At the moment of their departure the firemen of Southgate had no reason to believe that Beverly Hills was a firetrap. They had inspected the building periodically through the years. It was safe. The fire chief himself had been in the Cabaret Room: *I could not find one thing wrong with it. Everything was in order. A separate, recent inspection of the whole structure had been equally comforting: We found the building to be in ship shape, no major violations, if any at all.*

The firemen had no reason at 9:01 PM to doubt their ability to control a fire on the hill outside Southgate. They knew that fire departments from two other localities were scheduled to join their response to the first alarm. And only two weeks had passed since all three departments had rehearsed for a fire at the club and had actually engaged in a drill for such an eventuality. For good reason the firefighters of Southgate felt prepared to respond to the alarm and left the stationhouse with confidence.

5

The waitress who discovered the fire at the Zebra Room entrance could find none of the Schillings on her arrival in the kitchen. But she promptly encountered one of their key employees:

*There's fire in the Zebra Room!*
*Are you kidding?*
*No, I'm serious, there's fire in the Zebra Room.*

The employee headed for the front of the building on the run, and the waitress started looking for another of her sisters who worked in the club. She found her in another part of the kitchen quickly, told her of the need to leave the building, and headed back toward the Zebra Room. Word that the Zebra Room was on fire began immediately to spread to the employees of all parts of the club except one.

At this time the Cabaret Room and its occupants were substantially isolated from the rest of the building. There was no food being brought in from the kitchen. The cocktails being served were provided by the service bars operated exclusively for the showroom. The employees, therefore, had no reason to leave the room for other parts of the building. Moreover, there existed at the time an obvious need to shield the occupants of the room from outside disturbances. The first part of the show was in progress. Performers were on stage.

Only a stroke of luck prevented the isolation of the showroom at this crucial moment from being even worse. The busboy who had been ordered back to work by Ron Schilling was in the main corridor moving toward the front of the building. As he neared the end of that corridor he saw a waitress standing in front of the entrance to the Zebra Room. As he approached she told him of the problem: *The room is on fire*. At first he doubted her word: *I figured maybe a tablecloth was on fire or something was smoking*. But that soon changed. The doors to the small room were closed but smoke suddenly started squeezing into the corridor through the cracks. Very quickly the entrance to the Zebra Room assumed a slightly more threatening appearance.

Without waiting even long enough to look inside the room the busboy moved quickly down the Hallway of Mirrors toward the main bar. Barely beyond the east doorway of that room he stopped. A number of people were sitting at the circular bar drinking cocktails and talking. Concern for their own personal safety was not evident. The young man stood inside the doorway for little more than a second, told the people there that the building was on fire, and retraced his steps through the Hallway of Mirrors. At the end of that hallway he turned toward the Cabaret Room. He was at that moment the most unique occupant of the club—the only person in the building with knowledge of the fire *and* sensitivity to the fact that the large crowd in the showroom was relaxed, preoccupied with an outstanding stage show, and substantially isolated.

## 6

Just inside the front entrance, mostly in the foyer but also in the short hallway near the main bar, a small crowd of patrons was waiting to be seated for dinner. At some point, shortly after arriving in the foyer, a man in that crowd made his way to the front desk to check on reservations. He got there just in time to see the reservationist enter the cubbyhole off to the right, open the door to the Zebra Room, and return to the desk to report that there was fire in the building.

As the employees reacted to the news and spread the word of the fire to the rest of the building, the man returned to his party and calmly reported what he had seen and heard: *Apparently there is a fire in the club, a tablecloth or something*. He created barely a stir among the members of his group. They stayed in the foyer, waiting nonchalantly for their reservations and expecting the fire to be easily controlled; not a single person in the group sensed any urgent need to rush for the front door. For a brief time hardly any patrons located in the front of the club reacted to the emergency. Upon hearing of the fire almost everyone assumed that it was small and that the employees would quickly bring it under control. A sizeable group, probably somewhere between fifty and one hundred, was sitting in the main bar enjoying cocktails and light conversation. Very few of them had even noticed the waitress who had discovered the problem at the Zebra Room entrance come through the barroom asking that the fire department be called. And hardly any had moved toward the safety of the front driveway when the busboy from the Cabaret Room came to the edge of the room to urge those at the circular bar to leave.

The pregnant woman who entered the restroom off the Main Bar encountered a cleaning lady looking in a waste paper container for a burning cigarette. An odor of smoke filled the small room. The two women engaged in a brief conversation about the odor while the employee searched for its source. After a short time the search ended without success, and the cleaning woman left the restroom for the main bar. Almost immediately the other woman's attention was drawn to a vent in the ceiling. Smoke was seeping down through the vent into the restroom. At first it was thin and light, but before long it started to get heavier and darker.

In the small office that adjoined this restroom the beverage manager was seated at a desk preparing a bill for the barmitzvah party's open bar in the Viennese Room. He smelled something burning and looked around the room. A light fixture in the ceiling attracted his attention. It seemed to be the source of smoke that was leaking slowly down from above. His first thought was that the light had somehow sustained a short circuit. But then he observed smoke entering the room from another location in the ceiling. It was heavy enough at this point in time to cause more than a little concern.

7

In the northwest corner of the main bar the man with the handicapped father was still at his small table. He was concerned but not yet alarmed; it had been less than two minutes since the waitress came through asking for the fire department to be called. But then for some reason his eyes turned toward the ceiling of the barroom: I looked up over my head. The room had electrical fixtures flush with the ceiling and about two inches in diameter. I saw smoke coming down out of them. It trickled down out of the light fixtures into the bar area. I looked around; it started coming out of all of them. Others in the barroom at the time soon saw exactly the same sight:

> *I was sitting with my wife when someone came to the bar and said there is a fire. At that very time I looked up and saw smoke coming from two ventilators directly above my head.*
> 
> ● ● ●
> 
> *We were at the bar when someone said there is a fire. I looked up after that and I could see smoke coming out of the ceiling. It was coming from around the vents and the lights.*
> 
> ● ● ●
> 
> *The smoke was coming from the ceiling. It looked weird; it was black smoke just seeping out of a hole where a pipe went into the ceiling for a light.*

# Discovery and Notification of the Fire

*⁂*

*I was at the bar looking up at the ceiling and some of the beautiful pictures. All of a sudden I saw billows of smoke and I was facing it.*

The seriousness of the situation was now beyond doubt for those in the barroom. The man at the table in the corner suggested to his father that perhaps they should start for the front door. People sitting at the circular bar did not wait for instructions; they too started for the outside of the building. The employees attempted initially—but only for a very brief time—to calm the guests by assuring them that the fire was small and under control. Once smoke started leaking down from the ceiling, however, conditions in the area deteriorated quickly. A decision to empty this part of the building was made, and the patrons were admonished by the employees to leave calmly and orderly but as soon as possible. A spontaneous evacuation by some of the guests was already underway.

Before the pregnant woman could make her way out of the restroom, the cleaning lady had returned to give her the bad news: *The building is on fire and people are leaving. You should leave quickly.* An excruciating dilemma was created for the woman by this news. She had no doubt that the building was on fire; she had seen smoke and could now see that people were leaving. Her husband was back in the Empire Room expecting her to return there. Should she try to make her way back to that room or should she evacuate the building? If only she knew what he would do. Would he try to find her or would he leave the building and expect her to do the same? Perhaps she should stay near the restroom and wait? Within a matter of minutes a lot of others would find themselves facing similar agonizing choices.

The beverage manager left the office in which he was working and entered the front area of the club, the foyer and main bar, to see what was wrong. Once he reached this area and discovered that the building was on fire he found himself in a dilemma nearly equal to that which confronted the pregnant woman. Should he attempt to locate the fire and try to control it? Should he broadcast a warning and try to assist people in evacuation of the building? Or should he exercise caution for his own safety and walk out the front door? Every single employee of the club, in the early moments following discovery of the fire, found himself in this quandary. He also found himself prepared to act only by intuition; he had no assigned responsibilities, no prearranged course of action, and no emergency plans to implement. He had only his instincts to guide him at this moment of crisis. The beverage manager left the front of the club and headed for the basement to find a fire extinguisher. His initial reaction was to fight the fire.

The pregnant woman left the restroom and moved quickly to the short hallway that separated the main bar and the foyer (see Diagram No. 1). Unlike most other people in this part of the building she was already under enormous stress. She had been in the club for over three hours and knew that the building was packed with people. As she stood in the hallway outside the restroom she thought of only one fact. Her husband was among a group of four hundred patrons in the Empire Room and at that moment he seemed to be an awfully long way from the front door. Getting to that door in the event of an extreme emergency would not be easy, or so it seemed to her.

The hallway between the barroom and foyer was narrow, only about twelve feet wide. It was clearly inadequate to accommodate a crowd of nearly a thousand that would soon start for the front door from three different directions. Between this hallway and the outside were some additional impediments to a rapid evacuation of the building. A set of double doors that was only six feet wide opened from the foyer into a small vestibule. Within the vestibule was a set of steps that had to be descended to reach the front entrance. A second set of double doors as narrow as the first opened onto a concrete landing that was several feet above ground level. From that landing it was necessary to make a right or left turn and then descend a second flight of steps to reach the driveway outside the club. If measured against the requirements of life safety laws, the front entrance was sufficient by design to facilitate an emergency evacuation of no more than 250 people. With nearly four times that many ready to start for the front door, a bottleneck in the front of the building was almost a certainty from the earliest moments of the fire. The pregnant woman seemed to sense that as she looked back across the barroom and weighed her own personal options.

A powerful urge to return to her husband in the Empire Room gripped her as she stood in the hallway between the foyer and main bar. Somehow she managed to suppress that urge, turned toward the front door, and moved hurriedly through the foyer ahead of the first large group to leave the barroom. She was among the first four or five people to get out of the building after the discovery of fire. And already signs of serious trouble had become all too perceptible outside the building. The piercing sounds of distant sirens disturbed the quiet of the evening and signaled the approach of emergency vehicles. A police cruiser was already parked at the top of the driveway with its top lights flashing, a second was speeding up the hill toward the club, and a third had stopped at the driveway entrance to control traffic.

Very quickly a few more people reached the landing outside the front entrance. Most had seen smoke inside the building but none had seen fire. Hardly any reached the outside with an adequate comprehension of the peril that existed at that moment for the people located more than just a few feet inside the front door. And they acted accordingly:

*We got out and stood right on the steps. Of course nobody thought it was that bad. We thought it might have been just a smoke fire right there in front.*

• • •

*We had been only thirty to forty feet inside the front door. We just walked out and stood there where you go up the steps to the entrance.*

• • •

*When we got outside there were people standing on the porch, thinking it was a small fire and saying "we want to go back in." You had to fight to get down the steps to get away.*

At the beginning of the evacuation perhaps only the woman whose husband was still inside the building sensed the gravity of the developments outside the front entrance. She moved closer to the landing and tried to get people to move away by telling them that others would shortly be driven from the club by fire. In her mind she had very little if any success: *The people did not take me seriously.*

8

The discovery of fire sent several employees other than the waitress who first saw it rushing through the building in search of the Schillings. All three would ultimately be found in or near the kitchen, but not in the same location. The first to get the bad news was Rick. He was located at the time in one of the two corridors that crossed the building from east to west between the Garden Room and Empire Room. A waitress from the front part of the building burst through a doorway separating the two corridors and gave him the word: *Ricky, Ricky, there's a fire!* A waiter from the Garden Room was standing nearby and observed Rick's reaction: *His eyes got real big and he started running like hell down the back hall.* The waiter did the same thing and was on Rick's heels when he turned up the north-south corridor toward the Zebra Room.

Only moments earlier a bartender had entered the north-south corridor from the east side of the Empire Room for the purpose of getting a couple of bottles of champagne for a guest. He met a waitress running down the corridor away from the Zebra Room. As she headed north she told him to keep people away from that room. He rushed immediately to the Zebra Room and found at the entrance the young woman who had been left there by her sister to guard the doors. At his request she opened one of the doors: *Black smoke just rolled out. It was bad.* The door was closed quickly, and the bartender ran back toward the entrance to the Empire Room. He met Rick Schilling coming up the corridor and heard him yell: *Where's the fire! Where's the fire!*

By this time numerous people on the second floor had sensed by sight or smell the signs of fire. Assurances had been given on both sides of the corridor that the problem was nothing more than a "cigarette fire" downstairs. Not everyone who had seen or smelled smoke was completely satisfied with the assurances. One was a woman who was in attendance at the Choral Union party in the Crystal Room on the north side of the upstairs corridor. After hearing of the "cigarette fire" downstairs she departed the Crystal Room, encountered a smokey haze in the hallway outside the room, and moved quickly to the iron railing at the top of the spiral stairway. Rick Schilling, with whom she was acquainted, had just arrived at the entrance to the Zebra Room and was standing below her in the presence of a waitress.

The young woman at the entrance did not have to answer Rick's question about the location of the fire. The doors to the Zebra Room were closed but the smoke was leaking through the cracks into the corridor. The oldest son of Dick Schilling opened one of the doors to see what was inside; he closed it almost immediately. The heat at the entrance was not extreme and flames were not visible from outside the doorway. But Rick did not doubt the gravity of the situation. The smoke in the room was very heavy and very black. The probability that it would stay confined to that room for very long seemed small. There was only one thing to do, and there might not be much time to get it done.

The woman at the railing on the second floor detected a substantial degree of alarm in Rick's voice when he closed the door to the Zebra Room and said: *Call the fire department and get everybody out!* After delivering this order he ran down the Hallway of Mirrors toward the main bar. The young waitress followed in his steps and left the entrance to the Zebra Room unattended. Without a moment of hesitation the woman at the top of the spiral stairway went to the room occupied by the Choral Union group, stood outside the door, and gave a warning that spread rapidly throughout the room: *It's more than a cigarette fire. It's a fire. Get out but don't panic.*

More than half the people on the second floor had now been alerted to the fire. The lives of all were immediately in extreme jeopardy. They had learned of the existence of the fire in the building very early, almost as soon as it had been discovered by the club's employees. But the Zebra Room was directly underneath the spiral stairway. And there was nothing between the fire and the people upstairs except open space and a stairwell that provided an unobstructed passageway for smoke and deadly gases. In a very short time it would be difficult even to think about descending the spiral stairway.

## 9

While the occupants of the second floor were in the process of learning that the building was on fire the awards ceremony in progress in the Empire Room reached its midpoint. The earliest signs of trouble in the club had caused barely a stir among the large crowd in this part of the building. The waitress who left the Zebra Room entrance to find one of the Schillings had crossed the back of the Empire Room on her way to the kitchen. Shortly after that a busboy armed with a fire extinguisher ran through or past the room on his way toward the site of the fire. Very few of the occupants even noticed these events. Of those who did, none saw any reason for alarm. The room was cool, the air was clear, and everyone was relaxed. The master of ceremonies stood in the middle of the floor with a couple of other men, prepared to make another presentation.

Outside the south entrance to the room in the main bar a barroom waitress was engaged in a private conversation with some other employees. She had observed another waitress open the Zebra Room door and had seen smoke rush into the corridor. The topic of conversation: What should be done about the large crowd of people in the Empire Room? There was an expression of concern about the possibility of panic; there was some hope that the fire could be quickly controlled. Rick Schilling had not appeared yet in the barroom to deliver an order for evacuation. A decision was made by the employees to put the Empire Room on alert without ordering or encouraging an evacuation. The barroom waitress was asked to deliver the message.

The master of ceremonies was turned toward the main bar when the waitress entered the room. He knew from prior experience that the employees of the club were under orders not to interrupt programs in the party rooms. He could tell by the look on her face that something was wrong. She walked briskly to the middle of the room, approached one of the men involved in the awards presentation, and gave him the bad news in a voice audible only to him: *There is a small fire in the building. Please don't panic. We don't know yet if evacuation will be necessary, but be ready. When somebody tells you to get out, you get out!* She turned and left the room the same way she entered; the awards ceremony continued.

The bar in the Empire Room was staffed at this time by a single bartender. A second had just left the room to get a couple of bottles of champagne for one of the guests. A cocktail waitress left her station, walked to the bar, and told the bartender that there was a fire in the building. *She looked pretty upset—shaking and nervous. I knew it wasn't a small fire.* The bartender instructed the cashier to get the money together and to leave the building as soon as possible. Then his attention was drawn to the middle of the room where the awards were being presented. A waitress was entering the room from the main bar for the second time in a matter of seconds to interrupt the presentations.

When she entered the room this time, the master of ceremonies saw black smoke through the open door. He had no doubt about the reason for her sudden reappearance. He stopped the awards ceremony to let her make the announcement. She spoke in a soft tone: *There is a small fire in the building and everyone should leave. Don't panic. Keep calm but leave the room.* The reaction to the announcement was immediate. People sitting close enough to hear her got up to leave. The bartender who had sent the cashier out moved to the doors leading to the main bar to direct the evacuation. The master of ceremonies turned and asked that the waitress's warning be repeated over the microphone. The bartender who had left the room only minutes earlier for champagne returned and joined the evacuation effort. His reappearance coincided with Rick's arrival at the entrance to the Zebra Room.

The Empire Room was still free of smoke. None of the patrons except for the master of ceremonies had seen evidence of fire. Very few felt any imminent threat. Most thought that the fire was small and located somewhere else in the building. They did not delay in leaving the room, but there was not a sense of urgency in the air. Most people thought they would be returning within a few minutes to complete the awards ceremony and begin the dance that was scheduled for nine o'clock. Their thoughts were as far removed from reality as they could be. The fire was already out of control. In no time at all it would be threatening to block the only path to safety known to the large group in the Empire Room.

## 10

According to the waitress who followed him down the Hallway of Mirrors, Rick stopped long enough in the front barroom to deliver the same order he had issued at the Zebra Room entrance: *Call the fire station and get everybody out promptly and quietly.* A lot of people had already left the main bar by the time of his arrival, but not everyone. A waitress on duty in the bar area was still at work removing dirty cocktail glasses from tables out in the room. She had heard about the fire and had even seen smoke coming from the Hallway of Mirrors. But she had yet paid no serious attention to it: *I knew it was being taken care of.* She got substantially more concerned about the matter upon seeing one of the owners run through the barroom after ordering an evacuation.

Rick ran to the front desk and located his wife. She reported that the fire department had already been called and was on the way. People were moving through the building toward the front door but no one except Rick seemed to be in a rush: *They were walking very slowly, taking their time.* Rick told his wife to be sure that everybody was notified to get out of the building, and then he repeated the order to a bartender standing nearby. Having done that he turned his attention back to the situation in the Zebra Room. Like everyone else he was not totally aware of the seriousness of that situation. *I didn't think it was as big a problem as it was. I never did see fire, just smoke. I thought it was a tablecloth or something like that on fire.*

He knew, however, that the fire department would have to find the blaze quickly to have any hope of controlling it. And he knew that the best way to get to the Zebra Room from outside the building was through a locked door at the back of the Viennese Room. Someone would have to meet the firemen and show them the way to that door. Rick left the front desk with this in mind and headed for the front door. Firefighters had not arrived yet on the hill, but they would not be very long in getting there. Outside the building the sound of sirens could be heard off in the distance.

On his way out Rick ran straight into the problem that had developed at the front entrance with the very first departures from the building. It was now beginning to have an adverse impact on the progress of the evacuation. At the vestibule he found two "old guys" stationed on each side of the doorway letting people out single file and helping them down the steps inside the small room. He addressed them rather abruptly: *Get out of the way and let the people out of here!* Outside the front door he found that very few people seemed mindful of the need to clear the exit; several had stopped on the steps below the landing and more than a hundred others were standing indifferently in the adjacent driveway under the canopy.

Rick maneuvered down the steps and located the man in charge of parking: *Get everybody away from the building. Fire trucks are going to be here any minute and I don't want people standing in the way when they arrive.* Then after leaving a message for the first truck to come to the Viennese Room door with a fire hose, Rick headed around the southeast corner of the building toward the exit. His destination can best be shown by reference to Diagram 8 (see following page) which shows all of the means of egress that existed from the building on the night of the fire. The one toward which Rick was moving is marked as Exit C. He thought it offered the best access to the fire in the Zebra Room.

While Rick made his way to the outside, a bartender who was working in a small barroom at the top of the spiral stairway descended toward the Hallway of Mirrors and stopped about halfway down the stairs. From there he could see that the smoke on the second floor had come from the double doors leading into the Zebra Room. With no one near the entrance to provide an explanation the bartender looked toward the main bar and noticed that the bartenders working the circular bar had abandoned their stations. He left the spiral stairway quickly and moved down the Hallway of Mirrors toward the front of the club.

On his arrival in the barroom he could see that people were leaving the building, and once he got to the foyer he discovered that employees from the front of the club were actively involved in directing an evacuation. One of the bartenders from the circular

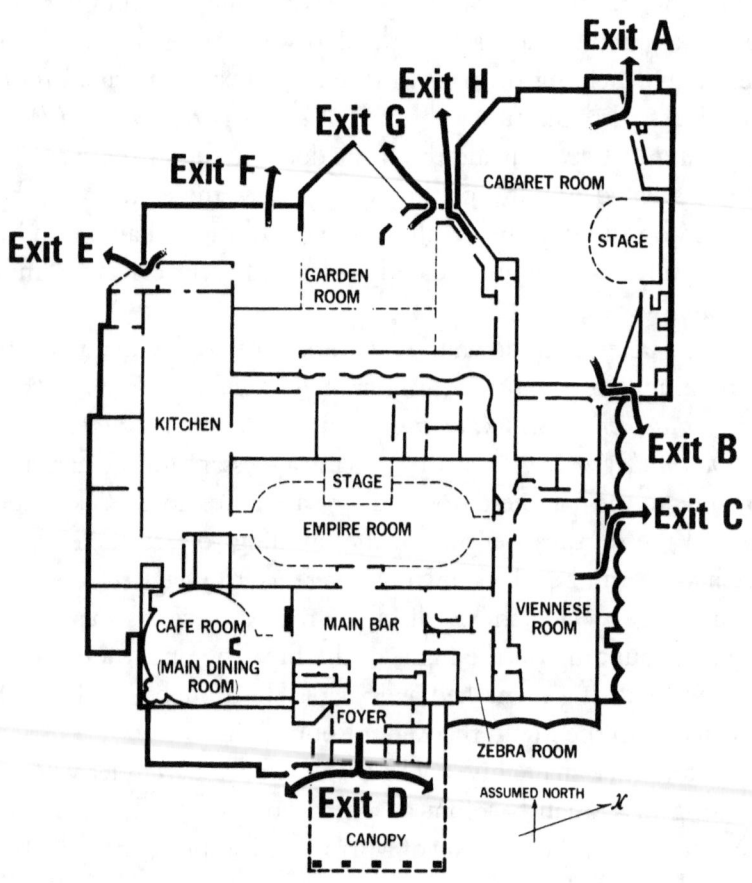

**EXIT CODE**

**Diagram No. 8**

bar was holding a door open for patrons and urging them to get out quickly. Other employees were struggling to hasten the evacuation but were having only limited success. Outside the building on the landing, the steps, and the adjacent driveway, the people were either pausing or stopping. As a result congestion was developing inside the front door, extending from there into the foyer, and steadily inching on back toward the main bar, all at a time when the need to get out of the building was intensifying rapidly. More significantly, no one had yet made it through the main bar from the second floor, the Viennese Room, or the Empire Room. More than 750 people in those three areas of the building were just learning of the need to head for the front driveway.

11

A busboy who was on duty with the barmitzvah party in the Viennese Room found himself in one of the corridors a little after nine o'clock on a return trip from the kitchen. Another employee who was moving hurriedly in the opposite direction paused just long enough to report that the Zebra Room was on fire. The busboy did not hesitate in reacting to the news. His party was located but a few feet across the hallway from the fire. He knew that the fire would quickly put the people in the south end of the Viennese Room in peril. Already thinking about an order for evacuation, he headed for the barmitzvah party.

He passed the Zebra Room entrance on the way: *The doors were closed but there was a slight crack at the top. Smoke was squeezing out.* Not too many occupants of the second floor were coming down the spiral stairway. He stepped into the Viennese Room and found the barmitzvah party undisturbed, still completely unaware of the events underway just outside the door. A few people were standing but most of the group was seated for dinner. The bartender was present but the bar was closed. The band was off to one side but not playing.

The busboy walked to the middle of the room and said in a very calm and collected way that there was a fire and that everyone should leave immediately. The bartender glanced through the doorway and saw a heavy movement of people in the corridor. A mother scanned the room nervously in an unsuccessful attempt to locate her thirteen-year-old son. He and his friends were on the other end of the building watching the show in the Cabaret Room. The seriousness on the face of the busboy was unmistakable to the occupants of the Viennese Room. They responded to the announcement with promptness.

Like others in the building, however, most of the group failed initially to sense the extremity of the situation. A few people walked casually across the room to pick up personal belongings from a chair. Others took the time to pick up cocktails from their tables before starting for the outside. The evacuation was regarded by some as a necessary exercise in extreme precaution. No one had seen or smelled smoke. The air in the room was perfectly clear and comfortable, and had been all evening. *We had no idea, as we started out, that there was a serious fire in the building.*

A few members of the barmitzvah party left the Viennese Room promptly after the announcement. There was light smoke in the corridor outside the room at the time but the Hallway of Mirrors was clear of people and still relatively free of trouble. Most of the smoke leaving the Zebra Room was floating up the spiral stairway to the second floor and was still fairly light. The doors to the Zebra Room were closed; the entrance did not look terribly unfriendly. So the first evacuees from the south end of the Viennese Room moved without difficulty down the Hallway of Mirrors toward the main bar.

12

A few minutes before nine o'clock two busboys on duty with the Choral Union party had left the second floor of the club and gone to the kitchen. They were standing in the kitchen when an employee from the front of the building came through on the run looking for Ron Schilling. Unable to find Ron immediately she grabbed one of the busboys by the jacket and told him of the fire: *It's in the Zebra Room and it's very bad.* The two busboys dropped everything and took off for the site of the fire. They ran through the service hallway behind the Empire Room and approached the Zebra Room from the north-south corridor.

There was no one standing at the entrance to the room when they arrived. The doors were closed; smoke was seeping out through the cracks. Conditions inside the small room had definitely worsened since Rick's departure. One of the two busboys reached for the door knob: *It was so hot that I was afraid to open the door, not knowing what might be on the inside.* The other, thinking they had to ascertain just how bad the fire really was, kicked the door open with his foot. They could not get inside the room; the heat at the doorway was fierce. The boys heard the sound of breaking glass—probably the mirrors that covered the far wall—but saw no flames.

Smoke rushed out the door and up the open stairwell. Another employee was standing on the stairway in the path of the smoke; he yelled for the door to be shut. One of the busboys raced off toward the kitchen to find a fire extinguisher. The other pulled on the door and stepped quickly back from the entrance. He left it cracked. Smoke continued to squeeze into the corridor from the site of the fire, only more heavily than before. The busboy looked down the Hallway of Mirrors toward the front of the club and saw lots of smoke in the area of the circular bar. He ran up the spiral stairway, practically chased in that direction by the smoke leaving the Zebra Room. From the top of the stairs looking back the situation seemed even worse. The smoke appeared to have the stairway almost blocked.

Almost immediately thereafter the evacuation from the second floor got underway. The woman who had heard Rick's evacuation order while standing at the top of the spiral stairway was still there, concerned about what she had seen and heard at the Zebra Room entrance but certainly not alarmed: *I knew it wasn't that far to the front door.* After warning the members of the Choral Union party she had stayed in a doorway to the upstairs room long enough to beckon to her husband who was seated at a table away from the door. She watched him get up from the table and then she hurried back to the head of the spiral stairway.

By this time the smoke floating up the open stairwell from the first floor was very noticeable. The party on the south side of the upstairs corridor, the dog show group, had not learned of the fire. And some of those in the Choral Union party were a little slow in reacting to the warning they had been given. The woman at the top of the stairs was certain that her husband had reacted promptly and that he was right behind her. In fact he had reacted quite differently and was nowhere near the top of the spiral stairway. Nonetheless she joined a few others from the large crowd on the second floor and descended toward the Hallway of Mirrors.

At this point she suddenly realized that the conditions in the stairwell were worse than they looked and worse than she thought. Breathing on the way down was not a thoughtless exercise. By the time she reached the bottom she was talking to herself: *I said, 'Hold your breath, you know it isn't that far to the outside. Breathe only when absolutely necessary.'* In the corridor at the bottom of the stairway she and the others from the second floor joined the exodus from the Viennese Room. Traffic in the Hallway of Mirrors was flowing freely, so she moved down that corridor toward the main bar without difficulty. She still thought her husband was right behind her.

The main body of the barmitzvah party was now leaving the Viennese Room and was quickly disabused of initial thoughts about the nature of the fire: *As we entered the corridor we noticed thick smoke coming out of a nearby room.* The only path to safety known to the group—through the barroom and out the front door—was still open, but the fire had certainly taken on a more menacing appearance. *Smoke was just pouring out of the room; it looked like it was coming out of a chimney.* Conditions in the vicinity of the Zebra Room were now rapidly deteriorating.

So was the composure of the parents separated from their thirteen-year-old sons. Once in the corridor outside the room they found themselves in a dreadful predicament. They had no idea where their sons might be and did not know the building well enough to undertake a search. They could not even be sure that the boys were aware that the building was on fire. And they could only guess as to how thirteen-year-old boys might react to an order for evacuation. Worst of all, they could see that evacuation was no longer a simple precaution. It had clearly become a matter of personal survival.

Still, at least some of them lay back, almost certain that their sons would attempt to find them. All the while the situation in the area continued to worsen. Blacker and heavier smoke poured into the Hallway of Mirrors from the Zebra Room. Changes in the conditions necessary to sustain life in this area were now measurable in terms of seconds not minutes. It was clear that the options available to the parents were gone. It was no longer possible to stay. They would have to go and take their chances that the boys would do the same.

The bartender who had served the barmitzvah party was the last person to leave the south end of the Viennese Room. No one was standing near the Zebra Room entrance as he left his work station and moved toward the Hallway of Mirrors. Smoke was starting to accumulate near the ceiling outside the Zebra Room and seemed to be swirling. The open stairwell looked worse than anything else, and its condition was rapidly becoming more hostile. A few people were still descending the stairs and joining the last of those evacuating the Viennese Room but not without difficulty: *A woman fell down the stairs and landed right in front of me. I figured she was going to be trampled upon and was going to stop the people behind her. So I picked her up and carried her the rest of the way out.* At this point in time it seemed highly doubtful to those leaving the Viennese Room that the evacuation from the second floor could last very long.

13

The main dining room had been very busy early in the evening. But it was only about half full when the fire was discovered at the Zebra Room entrance. An initial wave of people had finished dinner and gone to the Cabaret Room. A second had just been seated.

A hostess from the front desk had entered the room at about nine o'clock with a small group of guests. After seating them for dinner she had cornered a waiter and told him in a quiet voice about the fire. In so doing she had manifested relatively little concern about the matter and certainly no alarm. And then after reporting the fire she had left the dining room and gone back toward the front desk.

The waiter to whom she had given the news was working a station in the front part of the room right off the main bar. Within a short time of his conversation with the hostess, he found himself looking toward the front of the building: *As I looked toward the bar from my station I could see smoke coming through the recessed lighting. I could see it filtering right down through the light fixtures in the ceiling at the bar.* He said nothing at all to the people seated at his station. As other employees had done earlier he ran toward the kitchen to find one of the Schillings.

The smoke accumulating in the main bar did not escape the attention of people in the front part of the dining room for long. One of the guests stopped a waitress and asked if the barroom looked funny. Another saw haze hanging over the bar and stood up just in time to see that people around the bar were somewhat agitated. A waitress stepped forward to explain: *It's a small fire. We will have it under control, please remain seated.* Her efforts to pacify the crowd were largely unsuccessful. Someone rose from a chair and said that the building was on fire, and that the fire was bad. People from the front part of the room started through the barroom for the front door.

Those in the back of the room did not react as quickly to the fire because a large fireplace in the middle of the room obstructed their view of the main bar. A waitress working in the area saw smoke but paid little attention to it. The people at her station noticed it and reacted frantically; one woman jumped up from her table and screamed. A busboy who was standing nearby heard the waitress attempt to calm things down: *Everybody be seated, there is nothing to be worried about. Everything is all right.* At that particular time almost nothing at all was right, and the busboy knew it. He rushed around the corner of the fireplace with the truth: *Everything is not all right. The place is on fire. Get everybody out.* No one wasted additional time in getting up.

The waiter returned to the dining room from the kitchen. During his brief absence the situation had changed radically. Black smoke had nearly filled the main bar. And as he arrived at his station the smoke seemed to be moving in waves across the building toward the dining room. All of the people were gone from the front part of the room. Those in the back were on their feet and moving toward the main bar; they knew of no other way out. Between them and the outside of the building, however, was a set of conditions that was rapidly taking on a terrifying appearance: *It looked like you could walk up and grab the smoke, like it had weight. I have never seen anything so black in my life. It was so dense.*

14

Dick Schilling had a brother-in-law working at the club on the night of the fire. He worked outside the rear doors of the showroom (those opposite the stage) checking patrons against the reservation list and keeping a semblance of order in that part of the main corridor. He was at that station when the busboy who had gone to the front of the building after a brief encounter with Ron Schilling returned to the Cabaret Room with knowledge of the fire. Upon his arrival outside the showroom doors the busboy immediately told a couple of other young employees what he had seen at the Zebra Room entrance. Then he approached Dick Schilling's brother-in-law to inquire as to the whereabouts of the owners.

None of the three brothers was in the vicinity of the showroom at this time. Ron had just left for the kitchen. Neither of the other two had been around the Cabaret Room for at least a couple of hours. The showroom manager was busy seating the last part of the crowd trying to make the first performance. The busboy tried to locate her but had no success. His concern for the safety of the large crowd in the showroom was growing. He decided to share that concern with Dick Schilling's brother-in-law: *I whispered to him that there was a fire in the Zebra Room. He sort of stood there with a bewildered look on his face. And I said, 'What are we going to do? We need to clear the room, or something.'* He stood there trying to think and then turned around.

He moved through the main corridor to the back of the building to see that the exit doors were open. During his absence the busboy moved a podium out of the middle of the hallway. A substantial group of people was in that hallway waiting to get into the Cabaret Room or the Garden Room. He told none of them about the fire but may have suggested to some that they should leave. Dick Schilling's brother-in-law returned to the showroom doors from the north end of the corridor, entered the Cabaret Room and headed across the floor toward the northeast service bar. His destination was a set of exit doors at the back of that small barroom. The busboy stepped inside one of the showroom doors, stood there watching the performance on stage, and agonized over what he should do with the peculiar knowledge he had.

He had been the only person from this part of the club to have been at the site of the fire. Only he had seen black smoke squeeze through the cracks around the Zebra Room doors. He thought the situation was critical. But he had no way of being certain. The fire had not yet escaped from the Zebra Room, and the showroom was a long way from that small party room. Surely the fire department was on the way to the club by this time. Perhaps the fire could be extinguished. All of these things and more were on his mind as he stood near one of the doorways at the rear of the showroom and struggled with the most crucial question of his young life. Should he take the stage and tell more than a thousand people in a crowded room that the building is on fire? The possibility of panic was considerable and on his mind.

He had told Dick Schilling's brother-in-law that he was not about to scream fire. From the back of the room he watched the stage and waited for someone to take action. The comedians continued to perform. They reached the midpoint of their act and moved into a routine about Indians and covered wagons. A minute or two of precious time ticked off the clock. He grew more apprehensive about the situation in the front of the building. *I thought that I should clear the room. I thought that was the most important thing to do at the moment. I saw no sense in looking for the Schillings.*

*It would be a waste of time.* But he was eighteen years old and reluctant to take such action on his own: *So l stood there waiting for something to happen.* But there was no time to wait. There was no time for careful deliberation and no one with whom to deliberate. And for the moment at least there was no one but the busboy to act.

### 15

Ron Schilling was in the kitchen on his way to the Empire Room to check on the savings and loan association banquet. As he reached the south end of that room and neared the door that led into the west side of the Empire Room he was collared by an employee from the front of the club and told of the fire. The excitement on her face and in her voice sent him crashing through the doors to the Empire Room heading for that site. The people in the Empire Room had just been alerted to evacuate and were getting to their feet at that moment to leave.

Just slightly later, Scott Schilling walked out of the kitchen into the main dining room. One of the waitresses from that room met him at the door with the news of fire in the Zebra Room. He ran from the dining room and started through the main bar. People were already leaving from the front part of the dining room, and the barroom was moderately congested with people trying to leave the building. Scott looked down the Hallway of Mirrors toward the Zebra Room and saw smoke coming down that corridor. On his way through the bar he remembered a cabinet located at the top of the stairs leading to the basement. It contained fire extinguishers and was only a few feet away, between the main bar and the gift shop.

He went quickly to the cabinet but found it empty. He knew there were fire extinguishers in the basement and he thought he could get to the Zebra Room quicker by going that way than by trying to make his way through the crowd in the main bar. By the time he got to where the extinguishers were located he had joined up with the club's beverage manager. They each grabbed a cannister and ran up a set of stairs that opened into the kitchen. Once in the kitchen they separated and headed toward the Zebra Room in different directions. The beverage manager made his way to the north end of the kitchen and turned east down the corridor that separated the Empire and Garden rooms. Scott chose a more direct route to the fire. He entered the Empire Room, crossed to the north-south corridor, and ran down that hallway to the fire.

Ron got to the Zebra Room ahead of Scott. No one was in the room or near the entrance when he arrived. The Viennese Room had already emptied. One of the doors to the Zebra Room was standing about six inches open and black smoke was pouring out near the top. A bartender arrived at the entrance on Ron's heels; he brought fire extinguishers with him from the front of the club. From the outside of the room the smoke seemed to be coming from the inside ceiling. The two men stood outside the doorway and discharged the extinguishers in that direction. They had no noticeable effect on the flow of smoke into the corridor.

When Scott arrived he found his brother and the bartender standing in the doorway. The fire seemed still to be confined to the small room, but it clearly was not going to stay that way long unless they could get to it. The youngest son of Dick Schilling got behind Ron and the bartender and joined the battle. The room was full of black smoke with little visibility. There was a glow off to the left of the entrance on the east wall: *I couldn't tell if it was a flame or the reflection from a light fixture.* The three men stooped low to the floor, just outside the entrance, and discharged their fire extinguishers into the small room.

The conditions necessary to sustain human life were rapidly disintegrating in the area. The temperature in the room was soaring; the burning of combustibles in concealed spaces above and beside the room were saturating it with hot gases. The beverage manager approached the area from the north-south corridor; he had taken a longer route to the fire than Scott. Scott, Ron, and the bartender were in the doorway when he arrived but he saw none of them. *I couldn't even get to the first doors, there was so much smoke. I left the extinguisher there without doing anything and ran back toward the Cabaret Room.*

16

The Southgate fire department left the station confident of their ability to handle a fire at Beverly Hills. That confidence disintegrated, however, even before they could reach the scene of the fire. Within a couple of minutes of the official alarm, a fireman got within sight of the building. He had received word of the fire while on the road in his own truck and had gone directly to the club. He knew immediately that the alarm had gone in late. From the highway he could see that the front of the building was already "breathing"—leaking smoke from every opening: *It was just rolling out of every crack and crevice.* The magnitude of the battle in store for the department was clear.

This first man arrived in sight of the club only seconds ahead of a rescue van, which carried the fire chief and three firemen, and the first piece of fire equipment. The situation looked no better to the chief: *As we came up the highway to where we could see the building, smoke was coming out of the eaves of the roof the entire length of the building.* By the time the van got to the top of the hill, people were streaming out of the club like cattle. And right outside the front door, on a small landing about six to eight steps above ground level, they were stopping, as though lost or in a state of shock. The firemen had no doubt that the conditions inside the building were already growing difficult. And it was only 9:04 p.m. according to the official estimate of the department, only three minutes after the alarm had sounded.

17

At approximately nine o'clock a large group of people, perhaps as many as seventy, stood in the north-south corridor waiting to be seated for the show in the Cabaret Room or dinner in the Garden Room. Among the group was the captain of the Cincinnati Fire Department who had walked from the main bar past the Zebra

Room only minutes earlier and had noticed absolutely nothing. Inside the Garden Room a waitress was greeting a party of four that had just been brought in from the corridor and seated at her station. She filled water glasses on the table, took the party's cocktail order, and headed for the kitchen.

As she entered the east-west corridor between the Empire and Garden rooms an employee ran past her with a fire extinguisher in his hand. She paid little attention and went on to the kitchen, where she found a group of employees talking about a fire in the building. A woman had come from the front of the club only moments earlier and told Ron Schilling that the Zebra Room was full of smoke. As she looked toward the front of the building, she could see patrons streaming into the far end of the kitchen near the service stairway to the second floor; she was told that an evacuation of the building had been ordered. She turned around and started back to the Garden Room.

During her absence an employee who had been on duty in the front of the club entered the Garden Room from the north-south corridor in a state of extreme agitation. The guests sitting in that part of the room could hardly fail to notice her condition: *She was just about a basket case, able to walk, but crying and very distressed.* She approached one of the waitresses and broke the news that set in motion the evacuation of this part of the building: *The Zebra Room is on fire. It is filled with smoke. I am supposed to get everybody out of here.* The word spread rapidly among the occupants of the room. By the time the waitress who had gone to the kitchen got back to her station, the employees were going from table to table telling people to leave; the guests were in the process of getting up.

A couple of waitresses left the Garden Room and headed in a hurry toward the front of the building. The Cincinnati fireman and his party were still standing with the group in the north-south corridor; his wife was almost knocked down as the waitresses went past. A third waitress walked out of the Garden Room and stopped within view of the people standing in the corridor. The fireman had a good look at all three employees: *They were on the verge of panic, but trying hard to subdue it.* Something was wrong and he knew it. Within seconds a hostess from the Garden Room moved a rope that divided the two groups of people in the corridor, told them that there was a small fire in the club, and asked that they leave through the rear of the building. No one in the crowd had seen any signs of fire; but they moved quickly toward the exit at the north end of the hallway.

On their way out they walked past the entrances to the Cabaret Room. At least momentarily one of the doors to that room stood open and allowed a woman to look in from the corridor. The room appeared to be packed with people. The lights had been turned down low; two comedians were performing on stage. For some reason the woman seemed to sense more keenly than most the danger lurking in the corridor behind her. What she saw in the Cabaret Room at that moment left her muttering to herself: *Why in God's name aren't they getting the people out of the Cabaret Room. They are just sitting there. The guys on stage are telling jokes.*

18

Time was running out for the people in the Cabaret Room. The evacuation order in effect in every other part of the building had still not reached the showroom crowd. Dick Schilling's brother-in-law had returned to the rear of the room after opening the exit doors in the northeast service bar. The busboy standing at the rear doors thought he had waited as long as he could for someone else to act: *At that moment I just decided to clear the room myself.* He left the back of the room, walked briskly across the middle of the floor, and stepped onto the stage. The young woman watching television backstage recorded the time in her mind as eight minutes after nine o'clock. John Davidson's manager was looking on from offstage. He glanced at his watch. It showed 9:08.

A substantial part of the audience thought the busboy was part of the comedy routine. The musicians on stage knew otherwise: *When he came on we all looked at each other. We knew it wasn't part of the act.* And so did the comedians. They also knew that something was critically wrong: *He was very serious, certainly wasn't smiling.*

*He meant business. That's about the best way I can put it.* One of the comedians handed him the microphone immediately and he turned nervously to face the audience. Beads of perspiration clung to his brow as he strained to keep calm. The room was large and the lights were dimmed; most people failed to see the nervousness on his face. But they were prepared to listen to what he had to say. Total silence fell over the audience. The band had already stopped playing. There wasn't a sound in the room when he began to speak.

He chose his words carefully and delivered them with composure: *Turn around and look toward the back of the room. You will see a green exit sign. Notice it. Look to the corners of the room off to my left and right. There are other exit signs there. Notice them also. I want the left side of the room to go to this exit (pointing to left of stage) and the right side of the room to go to this exit (pointing to right of stage). There is a small fire on the other side of the building. There is no reason to panic or rush but you should leave.* His objective had been to issue a solemn warning about the fire without causing undue alarm and disastrous panic. His voice broke slightly a couple of times during the delivery but he finished without difficulty and handed the microphone back to one of the comedians.

There was no instant movement of people in mass toward the exits. He had succeeded in avoiding panic, at least for the moment. More significantly, he had managed to convey the right message to some of the people and had started them on their way to safety:

> *I took my wife's hand and we followed his instructions immediately after he stopped talking.*
>
> • • •
>
> *I took him seriously because his face had perspiration running down it He was trying his best to keep calm. I felt that he was really trying to restrain himself. We looked at each other and got up.*
>
> • • •
>
> *His voice was nervous. He was very serious. It was obvious to me that he meant what he was saying. I said to my group, "It is time to go." We got up and left.*
>
> • • •
>
> *I thought he was part of the act until he said "fire." I knew they would not joke about something like that. So we got up.*

But not everyone in the room got up to leave when he finished. More than just a few people failed to take the warning seriously and failed to treat the matter as one of urgency:

*We were relaxed and enjoying the show. When the busboy came on the stage, it just didn't register with people. That's all I can say.*

*I told my girlfriend that I thought it was just a precaution and that we might as well just sit and wait for a lot of the crowd to get out.*

*Everybody thought it was part of the act. I should have known by the guy's face that he wasn't kidding. But I for one— and members of my party as well—said "this is funny." I guess he stood there for another 45 seconds trying to convey to the people that it was no joke, that there really was a fire.*

The busboy left the stage and started back through the middle of the room toward the rear doors. A lot of people were on their feet moving toward the exits; a lot of others were not. The busboy was surprised: *I saw people sitting in their seats and staring at me like I was a nut.* As he neared the rear of the room he jumped up on a couch and shouted again for people to leave. The comedians immediately addressed the audience, repeated the warning that there was a fire in the building, and removed all doubt that the busboy was part of the comedy routine. The possibility of panic was also on their minds.

They told the huge crowd that the fire was apparently small, that everyone would be returning to the showroom in a few minutes, and that the performance would continue. More people got out of their seats and moved toward the exits. But very, very few did so with any great degree of haste. Some did not move at all. They sat at their tables, continuing to drink their cocktails, and waited, some for the congestion at the doors to clear and others for the show to resume. Those leaving as well as those staying were calm and unafraid. After all, the fire was "small" and on the "other side of the building."

## *Five*

### ESCAPE FROM THE FRONT

I

As soon as smoke had started filtering into the main bar from the light fixtures in the ceiling, the man who was at the club with his handicapped father had decided to leave. Their table in the northwest corner of the barroom had been located as far from the front entrance as any in the bar area. But like everyone else in this part of the building, they had still been quite close to the front door. Because of the condition of his father, however, it would take them a long time to reach the safety of the front driveway. Under the best of circumstances—no doors, no steps, and no congestion— movement for his father from one place to another was a slow and difficult exercise. The man had anticipated this and they had started for the outside at the first signs of danger. They had been among the first to leave.

They were far from the first to get out. The advantage of their early departure had quickly disappeared. Even before they got out of the barroom itself a widespread reaction to the discovery of fire had begun. They had gotten barely away from their table before employees of the main bar had turned up the lights and started directing people to evacuate the building, and by the time they had reached the hallway connecting the main bar and the foyer, smoke had begun to accumulate near the ceiling throughout the front area of the club, and large numbers of people had begun to stream into the barroom from all directions. The evacuation of his father that had looked so easy a minute or so earlier would now be difficult. The two sets of doors and the two sets of steps at the front entrance were still ahead, and the congestion he had hoped to avoid was upon them.

More people had arrived at the front door from the Viennese Room, the second floor, and the main dining room. From the concrete landing to the double doors on the south side of the foyer, the exit was clogged; and from that set of doors all the way back to the main bar more and more patrons lined up in the foyer and the short hallway and waited nervously for an opportunity to squeeze through the vestibule. The problem outside the building continued to hamper the evacuation. Some employees struggled to speed the movement of patrons down the steps and out of the way, but they were not able to relieve the pressure that was building up inside the front door.

All the while the conditions in the front part of the building were changing rapidly. By the time the man and his handicapped father had inched past the gift shop and entered the foyer, smoke was hanging down from the ceiling like a cloud and was getting blacker all the time. Although still above head level, it was beginning to affect those moving toward the outside: *At first it burned your eyes and then started to affect your breathing.* The safety of the driveway was within sight of everyone inside the main bar, but the long line at the front door barely seemed to move. Nonetheless, for awhile, a remarkable degree of composure prevailed in the foyer and beyond. But as more and more patrons arrived in the barroom and discovered that their path to safety was blocked, the situation changed. The people behind yelled at those ahead to hurry and also pushed a little to keep the line moving toward the front door: *It started to get a little rough in the hallway.* Before the evacuation toward the driveway had reached its midpoint, the large crowd in the front of the club was under a threat at least as great as the deadly smoke hanging from the ceiling. The potential for panic inside the overtaxed exit was enormous.

## 2

Inside the Empire Room no smoke was visible. As soon as the request for evacuation had been made by the master of ceremonies for the awards banquet, a small group of patrons had gotten up from their tables on the extreme east side of the room, entered the north-south corridor, and headed for the front door. All of the others, more than four hundred, had gotten to their feet upon hearing the evacuation order and headed for the main bar. As they got underway very few had sensed the imminent threat to life: *Everybody took it lightly. The fellows had drinks in their hands. Someone said, 'Do you think they will get it cleaned up so we can go back and finish?'* Consequently very few if any were prepared for the conditions just outside the big room.

When they reached the doors to the main bar and looked up the short flight of steps just ahead, there was no longer any room for doubt about the seriousness of the threat. The smoke in the barroom was hanging about two feet from the ceiling. It was as black as charcoal by this time and thoroughly wicked in appearance: *To look up and see the black smoke we had to walk into was just a little hairy. It was very frightening. But we had no choice.* The sight ahead made the idea of staying in the Empire Room unthinkable; and like nearly everyone else in the building the people in the room thought of the front door as the only way out. So in their minds there was no real choice; the temporary safety of the Empire Room had to be sacrificed for the unfriendly condition of the main bar.

The initial shock of seeing heavy smoke in the main bar intensified immediately for the first group to leave the Empire Room. They climbed the two or three steps necessary to reach the barroom anticipating an unobstructed path to safety and expecting to reach the outside in a matter of seconds. Instead they found a crowd of excited people bottlenecked on the far side of the room and barely moving toward the front door. From where they entered the main bar they observed a scene that resembled an exodus from a crowded theater or stadium except for one overwhelming difference—a dark cloud hanging above the crowd and growing more ominous with every passing moment.

Once inside the main bar the people from the Empire Room encountered the elongated circular bar. It made direct flight to the front door impossible; a turn to the left or the right was necessary to circumvent the obstruction. Those who turned left found themselves caught in the crowd trying to get away from the Viennese Room and the second floor, and those who turned right ran into the smaller group trying to leave from the main dining room. Conditions were a little worse on the east side of the circular bar because of its proximity to the Zebra Room, but the people coming from the Hallway of Mirrors were slightly more orderly than those entering the barroom from the main dining room.

The main dining room was still relatively free of smoke, but a few of the people from that part of the building showed some early signs of panic. Among the group was a substantial number of elderly patrons. As they entered the barroom from the dining area, the Hallway of Mirrors was directly in sight: *The smoke looked like it was coming in waves across the front bar towards the dining room.* A couple of women screamed when they saw the smoke and started pushing those ahead of them. Others in the crowd tried to exert a calming influence and had considerable success: *Everybody was saying keep calm, don't push, don't push.* For the most part a high degree of order and self-composure prevailed throughout the room. A woman from the Empire Room fell while trying to navigate around the circular bar; the crowd stopped, picked her up, and inched on toward the front door.

### 3

Ron Schilling, his brother Scott, and a bartender were standing in the doorway of the Zebra Room. They had been there no more than a couple of minutes. The fire was confined to the small party room, and the battle to bring it under control was still underway. The three men fought against an antagonist that was largely invisible. There was a glow on the east wall, but nothing else that looked like the flames of a fire. The three young men discharged their fire extinguishers aimlessly into the thick black smoke of the room hoping somehow to reach a target. At the time they had no way of knowing that their struggle was futile from the outset, and they had no way of anticipating that it would end so suddenly and so explosively.

The fire analysis experts later called it "flashover." Everything in the Zebra Room that would burn—wood tables and chairs, hardboard paneling, carpeting, hot gases, etc.— ignited simultaneously. All at once and without warning there was a loud noise ("like air suddenly rushing out of a inflated tube") and a tremendous release of energy. Scott and the bartender were literally blown out of the entrance into the Hallway of Mirrors. Ron was propelled across the corridor and knocked into the mirrors on the opposite wall.

In the north-south corridor, just a few feet away, a waitress from the Garden Room and two busboys from the Viennese Room stood and watched the events at the Zebra Room entrance. They saw Ron Schilling pick himself up after the explosion and struggle back toward the entrance to close the doors. A much heavier stream of black smoke was now pouring into the corridor from the burning room. The heat inside the Zebra Room thwarted the effort and the doors stood open. Ron left the area and ran down the Hallway of Mirrors toward the main bar: *I thought the fire was going to spread that way.* The bartender ran into the north-south corridor and started toward the Cabaret Room. Scott looked up the stairwell toward the second floor; black smoke had rendered the stairway almost impassable. He followed the bartender into the north-south corridor. An employee who was standing near the Empire Room doors saw him run out of the smoke and heard him yell: *Get the hell out of here. The whole place is going up.*

One of the busboys from the Viennese Room stayed in the area for a few seconds longer than the other employees. He moved to the Zebra Room entrance for a final attempt at closing the door on the fire. With a serving tray from the Viennese Room he crouched low to the floor and tried unsuccessfully to pull the doors shut. The heat in the room was simply too great. It singed his hair and drove him quickly out of the Hallway of Mirrors and into the north-south corridor. The fire had not yet escaped from the Zebra Room, but there was smoke everywhere.

## 4

A second floor waitress had been in the upstairs restrooms for a couple of minutes trying to find the source of what others had said was a "cigarette burn." Still concerned about the smoke she had seen in the second floor corridor she left the restrooms and walked to the top of the spiral stairway. There she found what she had been looking for and much more. From the first floor the smoke rushed up the open stairwell and hit her in the face: *It just filled the upstairs in seconds. I have never seen anything happen so fast. I mean in a matter of seconds the whole upstairs was saturated and we were all gagging and choking.*

At that moment several of the fashion show models were in a dressing room at the top of the stairs trying frantically to get dressed. Only seconds earlier a companion had come to the door to warn that the building was on fire. The models reacted to the warning without delay, left the dressing room on the run, and headed for the front door. The sight they confronted at the top of the spiral stairway was terrifying: *There was so much smoke you could hardly see. The only way I knew to leave was out the front so I started down the stairs. I had to feel my way down, the smoke was so thick. I had my hand on the rail and knew I was at the bottom only when my ankle buckled.*

The smoke from the Zebra Room filled the area around the stairway in a matter of seconds and then moved rapidly down the hallway that separated the second floor dining areas. The people on the north side of the corridor in Crystal Rooms 1, 2, and 3 (see Diagram No. 2) had just learned of the fire and the need to leave. But before they could react to the warning the deadly smoke had moved into their midst:

> We looked up and saw this great big ball of black smoke rolling about midair past the door. It just looked like you could reach up with both arms and grab it. A man stuck his head in the door and said "we've got to get out of here."

*You could see the smoke come under the door. I yelled to my sister to get up and out because the hallway was full of smoke. She just sat. I went to her table, got her by the arm and slung her out the side door, and told her to get out of there. Everybody then started getting up and moving.*

*It just seemed to me like somebody took smoke and just threw it into the room. It entered like a cloud. Everyone got up to get out; they knew there had to be fire somewhere.*

The people on the other side of the second floor corridor in Crystal Room 4, 5, and 6 got even less notice of the threat that had slipped silently up the open stairwell. Some had overheard conversations in the hallway about a downstairs "cigarette burn," but no one came to the dining room ahead of the smoke to sound a warning:

*At some point our daughter said "the cigarette smoke is terrible." I looked around and said that is not cigarette smoke. My husband looked and said "we must get out of here."*

*I looked up and our room was getting really smoky. And you could see the smoke pouring into the room through the air ducts. One of our people rushed into the room and said we must leave.*

*I don't recall anybody coming in and telling us to leave. We saw smoke and everybody had the same idea at the same time—get up and get out.*

On neither side of the corridor was there time to think about the magnitude of the peril nor to plan an avenue of escape. There was time only to get up and leave. More than two hundred people got to their feet practically in unison and started for the head of the spiral stairway.

By the time the first part of the crowd reached the stairs their anxiety and concern had changed to undiluted fear. The huge chandelier that hung from the second floor ceiling was barely visible through the smoke and the people courageous enough to move toward the Hallway of Mirrors without hesitation were literally disappearing into the cloud that had accumulated in the stairwell. Escape to the first floor by use of the spiral stairway was still possible, but no one in the group gathered at the top of the stairs could have failed to see that the only known path to safety from the second floor would soon be blocked. There was yet no fire on the stairs and none in the hallway below, but the conditions of the stairwell were becoming deadly. Worse, only a very small part of the second floor crowd had made it to the Hallway of Mirrors.

At the extreme west end of the upstairs corridor on the opposite side of the floor from the spiral stairway there was an elevator (see Diagram No. 2). Earlier in the day the manager of the dance band scheduled to perform in the Crystal Room for the Choral Union party had used that elevator to move equipment to the second floor for the performance. Near the elevator was a narrow wooden stairway that descended from the upstairs corridor to the kitchen on the first floor. The stairway was used by employees to serve the dining rooms on the second floor and was totally concealed from the view of patrons. At nine o'clock on the night of the fire, only employees of the club and the manager of the small dance band knew of the existence of the service stairway on the west side of the building. When the fire in the Zebra Room made its presence known in the upstairs dining rooms only they, the employees and the one guest, knew that the spiral stairway was not the sole path to safety from the Crystal Room.

The band manager was as far from the spiral stairway as anyone on the second floor when heavy smoke from the Zebra Room started through the upstairs corridor. He was standing with the members of his band near the bar at the rear of the Crystal Room on the north side of the floor. The sudden appearance of black smoke in the area was as shocking to him as to those located much nearer the spiral stairway, but his reaction to it was entirely different. Unlike the members of the Choral Union party and the members of the group across the corridor he did not jump to his feet at the first sight of smoke and head directly into the path of the fire. The narrow stairway near the elevator flashed through his mind almost at once.

His first thought was to stop the people rushing toward the spiral stairway: *Wait! Don't go that way. There's a way out the back!* But his effort to get their attention was to no avail. On both sides of the corridor the occupants of the second floor moved en masse toward the only escape from the smoke known to them. Only a handful stayed behind to join the band manager as he prepared to leave the Crystal Room for the service stairway on the west side of the building.

Escape from the Crystal Room did not provide the band manager and his companions immediate relief. The conditions in the corridor outside the room were just as perilous, and the members of the small group quickly found themselves running through a cloud of smoke. Nonetheless they reached the opening to the stairway without difficulty and ran furiously down the steps to the first floor. What they encountered in the kitchen was different from what they had expected to find on the first floor. In the Crystal Room at that moment people were fighting desperately for survival. In the kitchen there wasn't a hint of danger. The employees in this part of the club were standing calmly at their stations— cooking, cleaning, unconcerned, and apparently oblivious. The intruders from the second floor were incredulous: *I can remember very vividly one man standing there just smiling.*

The leader of the small group from the Crystal Room stopped long enough to tell the employees that the building was on fire and to ask for directions to the outside. The kitchen employees knew about the smoke in the Zebra Room but the magnitude of the problem had obviously not registered with most: *For about forty-five seconds they just looked at me, like they didn't believe me.* Having just left the Crystal Room the band manager was in no frame of mind to reason with skeptics: *Look, you goddamned fools, the building is on fire! How in the hell do you get out of here?*

The first door they directed him to was locked, and so was the second. In his mind there was no time for a third. On his own he located an open door at the north end of the kitchen and led his small group from the second floor out of the burning building. As he walked through the exit he turned and looked back across the kitchen. At the far end, other patrons had entered the room looking for a way out of the building. Perhaps others among the large group on the second floor had discovered the existence of the service stairway near the elevator.

5

The man and his handicapped father had finally worked their way through the foyer to the front door. At times the anxious crowd seemed barely to move toward the safety of the driveway. It had taken only two or three minutes to reach the exit, but it had seemed like forever. They had departed from the northwest corner of the main bar as soon as smoke started filtering into the room from the light fixtures in the ceiling. As they descended the flight of steps in the vestibule the man looked back through the interior of the building toward the barroom. The sight was almost beyond belief because of the suddenness with which it had come into existence: *I could no longer see the main bar area because of the smoke. I am sure the lights were still on; the smoke was just too black.* Fortunately only one door separated the man and his father from the outside of the building. As they moved through the crowded vestibule an enormous sense of relief settled in; they were practically out.

At about this time the first part of the Southgate fire department arrived outside the club. A fireman who had heard the alarm while on the road in his own truck was the first to get to the top of the hill; a rescue van with the fire chief and three other men arrived right behind him. The efforts of the Beverly Hills employees to deal with the congestion outside the front entrance had been only partially successful: *When we arrived people were just milling around in front like they were lost. Once they got outside the building they didn't move away; they just stood there kind of like they were in shock.* An employee approached the firefighters as they hurried to don their gear and gave them instructions left by Rick Schilling: The fire is on the east side of the building. You can reach it through an exit right around the corner. The rescue van had no equipment with which to extinguish a blaze; but the first fire engine to leave the station was within sight of the club and would arrive within a matter of seconds.

The fire chief jumped from the van as soon as it stopped and headed for the main entrance: *People were streaming out of the place like cattle; but on the landing outside the front door, as they reached fresh air, they were stopping.* The chief and one of the club's employees climbed to the landing from the driveway and started pushing and shoving people out of the way; in short order they managed to get a steady flow of evacuees down the steps on each side of the landing. Below the landing other firemen were moving people down the driveway away from the front entrance.

The chief had seen heavy smoke escaping from the building near the roofline; he entered the front door to find the source. Movement through the crowded vestibule was difficult but he managed to reach the edge of the foyer. He found no fire, but he saw "an awful lot of smoke." And he saw people packed tightly together, practically head to head, as far back through the club as he could see, "which wasn't too damn far." Although he stood at the top of the steps for only a second or two he could see the conditions inside the building changing rapidly; in a short time the foyer would be saturated with smoke and totally uninhabitable. He turned, retraced his steps through the vestibule, and left the building. The flow through the front door was as free as the circumstances would permit. Neither the chief nor anyone else could do much to help. The people in the foyer, the short hallway, and the main bar would have to struggle on their own to get out.

6

*If the waiter hadn't gotten there when he did we were dead, that's all there is to it.* The employee who got to the second floor just in time was the Crystal Room headwaiter. He had learned of the Zebra Room fire from a waitress after returning to the upstairs dining room from the kitchen and was headed toward the spiral stairway when the patrons on the second floor first moved toward safety. The upstairs corridor was very narrow, and near the spiral stairway it was filled within seconds after people saw the heavy smoke.

The headwaiter's path was blocked almost immediately: *I had started for the Zebra Room at the bottom of the main steps but I couldn't even get to the end of the hallway before the smoke poured in on us.* So he entered the dining room on the south side of the second floor and moved toward the spiral stairway. But on seeing the smoke in that room he quickly abandoned the idea of getting to the stairway. He had just used the service stairway on the west side of the building and knew it was clear: *I yelled at the top of my lungs for everyone to go out the back way.*

With no hope of reaching the spiral stairway because of the crowded corridor, part of the second floor crowd had no choice but to rely on the word of the headwaiter. So they turned with no idea of what was ahead and started across the building in the direction of the service stairway near the elevator. A bartender who had gone to the kitchen and returned to the second floor with supplies saw them coming: *They were in a real hurry. A few women were highly excited. There was no panic, but they were flat moving out when they came down that corridor.* He directed them down the stairway and told them there was an exit at the far end of the kitchen.

At the other end of the upstairs corridor the second floor employees were trying to get people out of the dining rooms and struggling to halt the rush toward the spiral stairway. *I remember seeing the waitresses standing there with napkins up to their faces saying, 'Come this way, you can get out this way.'* The dense smoke in the open stairwell had rendered the use of the main stairway extremely treacherous. But the patrons were determined to use it nonetheless: *They would get halfway down the steps and jump. One man jumped all the way from the second floor.* Two young women fell on the steps, and others trampled on over them trying to get to the first floor. A couple of busboys helped the women to their feet and stood momentarily in the path of the crowd trying to turn it toward the service stairway near the elevator.

Suddenly the lights in that part of the club went off leaving those still there in total darkness in unfamiliar surroundings: *I couldn't* have seen my finger if I had put it one quarter of an inch in front of my eyes.* Already, before the darkness fell over them, the patrons had lost much of their capacity to orient to their surroundings. When the lights went off they lost the rest, and quickly found themselves in the worst imaginable predicament. They couldn't possibly stay where they were but under the circumstances they had no way to leave. All hope of finding the stairway near the elevator disappeared in the darkness; in both the corridor and the dining rooms the evacuation came to a sudden halt.

The conditions that now existed in this part of the building were horrible for those trapped in the dark: *I had the feeling the smoke was up over my head and behind me. I could feel the heat, and could hear glasses and dishes popping in the room we just left.* Any effort by one person to render aid or comfort to another was largely futile: *The girl in front of me was coughing real bad. I tried to reach to pat her on the back; as I reached out she moved away from me a little more.* With no familiarity with the building and no way to acquire even a minimal sense of direction, the patrons were totally helpless. With no realistic choice, they halted their efforts to escape, dropped to the floor, and waited in stunned silence for the lights. Only the soft voice of one of the club's waitresses broke that silence: *Turn the lights on, turn the lights on.* She knew, as most of the others must also have known, that there was little hope of reaching the outside in the dark.

For approximately thirty seconds, the second floor was in darkness and then for some unknown reason the lights came back on. The smoke was heavier than before, but there was sufficient light for the patrons to find their way to and through the corridor. Those near the service stairway headed hurriedly down the steps toward the kitchen allowing the flow of people to resume. The employees moved quickly to take advantage of what seemed to be a fleeting opportunity to avoid certain catastrophe. As many patrons as possible were pushed toward the west side of the second floor and away from the spiral stairway. An attempt was made to check the upstairs rooms for stragglers. One of the waitresses stood in a doorway to one of the dining rooms and yelled into the smoke: *Is everybody out, is everybody out?* And then, as suddenly as before, darkness returned to the second floor. This time, except for a single momentary flicker, the condition was permanent.

The evacuation toward the kitchen slowed down as it had done before and in a very short time completely stalled. Feelings of hopelessness and despair returned to the upstairs corridor. The smoke and darkness had virtually beaten the patrons into submission. They were wedged in the narrow hallway or lost in the dining rooms with almost no hope of moving to safety: *Everybody stopped yelling, got quiet. The smoke got to my eyes and my throat. My chest started to burn. I just gave up, backed up against the wall and felt myself going to the floor.*

Few people have ever looked death so directly in the eye and lived to reflect on the experience: *We really thought we were going to die. We couldn't breathe. I was gasping for breath and my eyes were burning so bad I couldn't even open them. One of the waiters grabbed me and kept holding me because I was so sick.* For some in the group there was nothing left but prayer: *Lord here I am, let your will be done. Oh, Lord have mercy. My companions were all around me, on the floor, but I couldn't see them, or anything. I was standing there waiting to die.*

Without a doubt the struggle for survival on the second floor would have ended at this point had it not been for the decisive and determined actions of one employee. The headwaiter, after initiating the movement of people toward the service stairway, had gone to the set of doors closest to the spiral stairway, the one on the east wall of Crystal Room 1 (see Diagram No. 2). It was his intention to check for patrons in the upstairs dressing rooms. He had opened those doors only to discover that the situation around the main stairway was far worse than he had expected. The heat was tremendous and there was dense smoke from the ceiling to the floor. He had retreated from those doors and was heading toward the stairway on the other end of the floor when the lights went out and the evacuation stalled.

Immediately he thought of a door that led from the upstairs corridor to the roof of the building: *I had been out of that room to the roof many times before. I knew it would be like a big porch. It would be safe.* He also knew that the door was always kept locked but thought that with some help he might be able to break it open; at least there was some hope. So he enlisted the aid of a couple of hefty patrons and had them crash against the locked door with all the power they could collectively muster. The sound of bodies banging against the door echoed from one end of the corridor to the other. But the effort was futile. The door was an impenetrable barrier to the outside: *They kept beating on the door and kicking it with their feet. They finally said "It's no use. We are all going to die. We can't get out of here."*

The options for the occupants of the second floor were still the same—escape down the narrow stairway to the kitchen or certain death. The headwaiter got against one of the corridor walls and maneuvered through the bewildered patrons to the opening to the service stairway. Through the smoke and darkness he told the group that he was an employee and could lead them to safety. He headed down the steps feeling his way along in the dark and leading those behind somewhat like a locomotive pulling a train. Descent down the stairs to the kitchen under the horrible circumstances that existed at the time was not particularly easy even for him and the other employees. For those unfamiliar with the escape route the journey from the second floor to the kitchen was the longest and most difficult of their lives: *We were all trying to get down the steps, but when you are in total darkness you really aren't aware of what is happening around you. We had a hard time getting down the steps.* Smoke had filled the upstairs all the way to the elevator and had even moved into the service stairwell. After it began, the flow of people through the corridor and down the stairs toward the kitchen was steady. Unfortunately there was precious little time left for those still on the floor.

7

The tension in the main bar by this time was as thick as the heavy black smoke that hung down from the ceiling. The congestion on the south side of the room, at the bottleneck, had grown worse. A flood of people had entered the room from three directions, the main dining room, the Empire Room, and the Hallway of Mirrors, while only a trickle had been able to exit through the narrow hallway leading to the foyer and beyond. By the time the flow of patrons down the Hallway of Mirrors ended, the barroom was nearly full of people. And there was still a group of more than three hundred in the Empire Room pushing toward the front door believing it to be the only means of escape. The conditions in the main bar and on toward the front of the building had also grown worse. Smoke was accumulating at an accelerated pace: *By the time I got out of the room the smoke was down to about five-and-a-half-feet from the floor. It was below shoulder level and you had to bend over to breathe. That was difficult, everybody was packed in so tight.* As the smoke dropped lower and lower into the room, the patrons shielded their faces as best they could and inched on slowly toward the exit. As the conditions worsened, shouts from the back of the room for those ahead to hurry got louder and more frequent. The employees in the area continued their crucial efforts to avoid panic: *Take your time, hold your heads down, and put your hands over your mouths. We're almost out, we're almost out.*

It became more and more difficult to crouch underneath the smoke. Finally it became impossible, and the people in the front of the building were enveloped in smoke. The artificial lights in the ceiling were barely visible. Breathing was very difficult. From the circular bar all the way to the front door, the patrons began to fear for their lives: *The people around me started coughing more and more. I can remember a waitress behind me; all I could see was the bottom of the uniform. I put my napkin up to my face and tried to cough into it. My eyes were burning from the smoke. I was scared. I didn't think we were going to get out.* In the foyer, just a few feet from the front door, a woman fighting for a breath of clean air lost control and started screaming: *We are going to die, we are going to die!* Only the sounds of sirens outside the front exit could be heard over the chain reaction that echoed through the front of the club after her scream.

In the barroom, with smoke hanging half way to the floor, a small group from the main dining room stood helplessly at the back of the large crowd waiting to squeeze through the narrow hallway to the foyer: *We couldn't go forward, and we couldn't stand the smoke.* Moments earlier a waitress had stopped them from entering the kitchen through a door located at the northwest corner of the dining room. With that door as their destination they reversed directions and left the barroom determined to find another way out. In the main dining room they discovered that things had changed during their brief absence. Smoke had filled the room, and all of the diners were gone except for the last part of a group then being herded toward the kitchen by a waiter. Near the door in the corner of the dining room, the small party from the barroom joined the back of the group headed toward the kitchen and entered an area that was just being awakened fully to the crisis. Most of the kitchen employees were still at their stations, a few even working, but a steady flow of people was descending the stairs from the second floor in a state of panic, and an evacuation through the kitchen toward the back of the building was in high gear. Smoke had not entered the kitchen but that was soon to change. The developments in the Zebra Room were hastening the deterioration of conditions in the whole building.

8

As Scott Schilling left the Zebra Room he yelled to some employees that the whole building was going up. He was right. At that time there was absolutely no hope of controlling the fire. The Zebra Room was like a furnace. It had a fuel supply and an available vent, the open doors leading into the Hallway of Mirrors. Shortly after flashover, the smoke, flames, and hot gases rushed through the doorway, crossed the narrow corridor, and hit the wall on the far side. At that wall the fire split into parts. One headed down the Hallway of Mirrors toward the main bar, another went up the spiral stairway to the second floor, and a third entered the north-south corridor. The fire was being propelled along the ceiling of the corridors by the energy released in the Zebra Room. The paneled walls were burning, and the carpeting and padding on the floors were being ignited by the heat from above. The fire was truly raging and spreading with incredible speed.

After leaving the Zebra Room entrance Ron Schilling stopped at the double doors between the Empire Room and the main bar to give instructions to the employees: *Stop the evacuation through the front and divert the people still in the Empire Room to the kitchen!* Then he made his way to the staircase on the other side of the barroom (between the gift shop and the main bar on Diagram No. 1) and headed for the basement. His destination was the Crystal rooms on the second floor, which he could reach from the basement via the service stairway near the elevator. At that moment, the fire in the Hallway of Mirrors had enormously intensified the life-threatening conditions already existing on the second floor.

Shortly after Ron's departure for the basement, the employees of the Empire Room slammed shut the doors leading to the main bar and stopped the exodus toward the front door. The last two people to enter the barroom, a husband and wife, immediately found themselves engulfed in thick black smoke and unable to breathe. For the first time fire itself was visible in the front of the building. From the Zebra Room it had consumed the wall paneling in the Hallway of Mirrors and had moved toward the bar area. Luckily most, if not all, of the people in the barroom at this time had come from the Empire Room, and many of them had been in the club often enough to find their way to the front door through heavy smoke. At the first sight of fire, a few patrons screamed but most acted sensibly. Several of the men still in the barroom shouted instructions and encouragement to the others: *Get down on the floor, keep moving, and stay calm. We will make it.*

The heat in the barroom, even on the floor, had soared, but the last couple out of the Empire Room followed the instructions to the letter. They dropped to the floor, tried to shield their faces from the smoke with clothing, and crawled around the circular bar on the way to the front door. Their hopes of survival at the time were small: *Before we hit the first curve of the bar my husband said he didn't think we were going to make it. I told him if he got out not to come back. I didn't know what his stamina was but I didn't think I could get out.* On the other side of the circular bar they bumped into a woman who was hysterical; she was sitting on the floor up against the bar crying like a child. After screaming at her—*if you keep doing that you are going to kill everybody*—they pushed her toward the front door ahead of them. As they moved away from the circular bar and toward the foyer the walls on the east side of the room in and around the cubbyhole were burning and the fire had moved to the middle of the floor behind them. The circular bar itself was on fire.

Fortunately, the pace of the evacuation through the front of the building had quickened substantially. By the time the last people to leave the Empire Room reached the hallway on the south side of the barroom, the congestion in the foyer had evaporated, and the safety of the driveway was within sight: *I was down on my knees going out, because the smoke and heat were so intense. But I could see a brightness out of my left eye.* With their path to the exit relatively unobstructed they moved quickly through the foyer and vestibule to the landing above the driveway. The journey from the Empire Room, although it seemed to have lasted forever, had taken no more than two or three minutes for the fifty to a hundred patrons who made it.

Hundreds of people stood outside the building watching the front door as the last people came through. Darkness had not yet fallen over Southgate, although it was a few minutes after nine o'clock when the last person staggered down the steps to the driveway. Heavy smoke had darkened the evening sky over the club and was now pouring out the top of the front door. The situation on the outside looked as ominous as it had looked on the inside. Over a hundred artificial lights burned in the roof of the canopy, but few if any could be seen through the black smoke that had accumulated above the entrance. Despite all this, when the evacuation to the driveway ended, a certain sense of relief spread through the large crowd standing in the parking lot in front of the building. Although stunned by their harrowing escape from the club, most of those in the crowd assumed that everyone had made it safely out of the building. Only a few had good reason to believe otherwise.

A small group of parents who knew nothing of the whereabouts of their thirteen-year-old sons stood outside the front entrance and

*Main Dining Room before the fire*

Used by permission of the Kentucky State Police

*Spiral Stairway before the fire*

*Spiral Stairway after the fire, view from below*

Photo: National Fire Protection Association

Spiral Stairway after the fire, view from above

Photo: National Fire Protection Association

*Photo: National Fire Protection Association*

*Cabaret Room*

*Copyright 1977, The Courier-Journal. Reprinted by permission*

Kentucky State Police stand watch over the remains of the Beverly Hills Supper Club while rescue workers rest in back of the club's burned out shell

*Firemen carry a statue past the twisted remains of the Beverly Hills Supper Club*

Copyright 1977, The Louisville Times. Reprinted by permission

*Little remains of the building that was once called "the showplace of the nation"*

*Copyright 1982, The Courier-Journal. Reprinted by permission*

watched in shock as black smoke rolled through the doorway and blocked the exit. The woman who had left the second floor thinking her husband was right behind her was at the bottom of the outside steps in a state of hysteria. A fireman tried to give her assurance that her husband was out. She had watched the evacuation carefully and knew better: *He was right behind me; he did not come out!* After blocking her attempt to reenter the building the fireman moved her gently away from the entrance. For both the parents and this woman, the end of the evacuation through the front door was the beginning of a period of indescribable anguish. In a very short time the news that hundreds of people were trapped inside the burning building would reach the front of the club.

One other person was extremely distressed as the evacuation stopped. At that moment the pregnant woman who left the building without her husband stood motionless in the driveway near the canopy. She had remained near the entrance studying every face that squeezed through the front door. Her husband had not made it. She noticed that most of the last group out had come from the Empire Room, barely ahead of the heavy smoke, and that some had obviously experienced great difficulty in reaching safety: *A person at my table, the one most affected, had black streaks up her nose and just kept coughing and coughing, and saying that she couldn't even see to get through the bar.* She moved through the crowd asking members of the savings and loan party if they had seen her husband. None had. She lost her composure and broke down. And she lost her hope: *I imagined him to be trapped in the fire, I remember thinking that he probably was dead.*

9

At some point before Ron Schilling halted the flight through the main bar a bartender working the Empire Room started an evacuation of patrons through the kitchen. Consequently, for a very brief period the large banquet room had emptied in two different directions—toward the double doors on the south side and toward the double doors on the west side (see Diagram No. 1). During this time the conditions of the room were entirely normal in appearance and the evacuation toward the kitchen was orderly and in some ways even casual: *People were talking and joking on the way out.*

The conditions in the front of the building at this time were getting worse very rapidly, but the occupants of the Empire Room did not know this. So when the employees implemented the instructions of Ron Schilling and closed the doors to the main bar, the rest of the banquet crowd turned toward the back of the building and moved quietly and without haste toward the doors leading to the kitchen: *There was no panic. They moved slowly and calmly. Some were carrying their drinks and chatting.* Very few showed signs of distress. Most of the crowd simply responded in orderly fashion to the announcement that there was a small fire in the building. Perhaps only one man in the crowd of more than four hundred had reason for unusual anxiety.

This man's difficulty began to some extent with the initial call for evacuation. His pregnant wife had gone to the front of the building a few minutes earlier to find a restroom, and he expected her to return. For awhile after the evacuation started he did not move toward the main bar or the kitchen. He stayed near his table and watched the doors to the barroom for his wife. At first he was more irritated than frightened: *I really didn't think there was a serious fire. I figured it was minor, that it was a precautionary measure to leave, so I wasn't in any real great hurry to get out.* At some point, he saw smoke in the main bar, but he continued to wait for the return of his wife.

During this time, the fire in the Zebra Room burst into the corridor and moved down the Hallway of Mirrors toward the barroom. Gradually most of the banquet crowd left him behind. The conditions in the large room remained normal, but his dilemma nonetheless grew. Should he go or should he stay? Would his wife leave the building or would she try to return to his side? Ultimately, after a few minutes of uncertainty, he reached a point of decision. No longer did it make any sense to stay. He got in line and moved with the last part of his group toward the doors that led from the Empire Room into the kitchen.

By this time the scene in the kitchen had changed substantially. No longer was there any doubt about the seriousness of the situation. The employees had left their work stations to help with the evacuation effort. One of them was standing on top of a table directing people toward the back of the building: *Keep moving, you'll make it, keep moving.* At the north end of the room, however, a serious obstacle to quick evacuation had developed. The door to the outside led to a loading dock that had a very narrow set of concrete steps down to the driveway. Instead of jumping two or three feet to ground level, the people leaving the dock were descending the steps in single file. With people entering the kitchen from three different directions, a bottleneck was developing inside the exit and slowing the evacuation. Meanwhile, the first strand of smoke to enter the area floated into the south end of the kitchen. It may have come from the second floor via the service stairway but more likely it came from the main dining room. It quickly gave the large group moving toward the exit at the far end of the kitchen something to worry about.

All but a small part of the savings and loan association crowd had made it out of the Empire Room by this time. At the back of the group was the master of ceremonies for the awards banquet; he had stayed behind to see that everyone got out safely. As he prepared to leave, two busboys came from the kitchen with fire extinguishers, ran across the room at full speed, and entered the main bar; the sound of fire extinguishers being discharged in the barroom followed in a matter of seconds. At almost that same moment a member of the savings and loan association group came running across the room from the doors that led to the north-south corridor. He leaped over an iron railing and, with a wild look on his face, addressed the master of ceremonies: *We've got to get out of here, we've got to get out now! The fire is right there!*

Surprisingly the Empire Room was still free of smoke. The master of ceremonies pacified the other man—*Calm down, we are as good as out*—and turned with him toward the kitchen. As he did so a small group of patrons entered the other side of the room from the north-south corridor. Some of the party of physicians in the north end of the Viennese Room had learned of the fire much too late to exit through the front of the building, and had been directed by a busboy to enter the Empire Room and cross to the kitchen. As they proceeded in that direction the master of ceremonies moved ahead of them and followed the last part of his group out of the room.

The situation in the kitchen had grown worse. *There was a lot of light smoke in the room, like something had been burning in a skillet; it was not real black but was awfully irritating to the eyes.* A woman who was apparently a nurse stood in the room, as the master of ceremonies entered, trying to tell people how to protect themselves from the smoke: *Get a napkin or something, wet it down with water, and hold it over your face. It will help you breathe.* The exit on the north wall was clearly visible through the smoke and everyone in the room was moving in that direction.

Not more than half way there, however, the last group out of the Empire Room bumped up against the crowd waiting to squeeze through the narrow door to the loading dock. Outside that door a group of patrons and employees were working to get people off the platform at a faster rate. As they succeeded, the evacuation from the building accelerated to some degree. Still the crowd in the kitchen dwindled slowly; the flow of people to the room, at least from the second floor, had not stopped yet. The master of ceremonies from the Empire Room looked at his wife; she had picked up a napkin to cover her face. He could have left the banquet room much earlier. At that point he must have wished that he had. Circumstances were to get a lot worse for him and his wife.

## 10

The Garden Room was in the final stages of evacuation by this time. It had been the easiest part of the building to empty. The employees of the room had learned of the problem in the front of the building quite early. A waiter had gone down the north-south corridor on the heels of Rick Schilling, had seen smoke in the Zebra Room, and had decided promptly on evacuation: *After seeing the smoke I figured we had to start getting people out.* When he returned to the Garden Room he spread the word about the fire to other employees and started moving patrons toward the back of the building. The room was not heavily occupied at the time, and the people there could easily see that there was a direct avenue to safety—no corridors and very little distance to the outside.

On each side of the glass wall at the north end of the room there was an exit that led directly into the garden (see Exits F and G on Diagram No. 8, p. 106). In the first stages of the evacuation a slight problem developed at the exit on the east side of the glass wall (at Exit G). A few patrons recognized the problem quickly and tried unsuccessfully to correct it: *My God, what is wrong with you people; get away from here, this place is going to blow up!* A little later an employee grabbed a microphone that had been used for a wedding ceremony in the garden and asked the crowd to move as far away from the building as possible. His effort succeeded in keeping the exit open, and within a couple of minutes after the evacuation had started all of the patrons of the Garden Room were outside the club. So was the large group of people who had been standing in the north-south corridor between the Garden Room and Cabaret Room waiting for dinner or for the show.

Near the end of the evacuation, after all of the patrons were out of the room, a hostess who had been working in the area all evening walked through the exit on the east side of the glass wall and started toward the garden. She got no more than a couple of steps from the exit before Marjorie Schilling, anxiously looking for her husband and teenage daughter, rushed from the building and grabbed her from behind:

> *Have you seen Rick and Kim?*
> *No, I haven't seen them.*
> *I've got to find them, I'm going back in.*
> *You can't do that, the building is on fire.*
> *I'm going. I've got to find Rick and Kim.*
> *If you do, I'm going with you.*

The two women entered the building and headed up the north-south corridor toward the front of the club. They ran at full speed all the way from the rear doors (at Exits G and H on Diagram No.

8) to a point halfway between the Empire Room entrance and the Zebra Room; they stopped in between only to check the Viennese Room for occupants. On the way they encountered not a single person in the corridor.

By this time the fire at the Zebra Room had made its first move toward the north-south corridor. The smoke in the area was so thick and so black that nothing was visible through it. As the two women stood in the hallway, a few busboys with fire extinguishers in their hands ran out of the smoke and screamed at them: "Get the hell out of here!" They turned and retreated toward the back of the building as far as the double doors on the east side of the Empire Room. When they opened those doors and saw that the large room was still free of smoke they left the corridor and headed across the building toward the kitchen. Only one waitress was in the room as they entered and she started immediately screaming at them to get out.

Halfway across the room the hostess changed directions and headed for the main bar; she had left her purse there earlier in the day and wanted to retrieve it. The barroom was totally saturated with smoke by this time, and when the hostess opened the doors at the back of the Empire Room and looked toward the circular bar, the smoke was so black that she could see no more than a few inches beyond the doorway. As quickly as she had decided to retrieve her purse, she abandoned the idea. When heavy smoke rushed through the open doors she pushed them shut and joined Marjorie Schilling in a sprint for the kitchen. Marjorie was still looking for her husband and daughter.

11

Despite the efforts of the employees to push the second floor patrons toward the service stairway on the west side of the building, many of them were struggling to descend the spiral stairway when flashover occurred in the Zebra Room. With nothing to block its path, the fire that exploded into the Hallway of Mirrors turned toward the second floor and started up the carpeted stairway. The group at the top of the stairs suddenly found itself facing more than the grim prospect of wading through heavy black smoke: *By the time I got to the steps they were just blazing. I thought, 'Oh my God, the steps are on fire.' And then I heard a man say, 'My God, the steps are burning.'* Descent to the Hallway of Mirrors had been treacherous and extremely difficult for some time. Now it was impossible.

For a moment the people caught on the steps stood helplessly in the smoke and watched as their only known path to safety vanished. The larger group at the top of the staircase had not seen the fire and were still trying to go down. Those who were further down and closer to the fire began to panic: *The women started screaming, and the men were hollering, 'Let me out of here! Go back the other way, go back!' The fire was shooting up the steps, and the people from behind were still pushing us toward the first floor.* In the pandemonium that followed two women tripped on the steps and fell. *The people near them just trampled over them. They were lying there screaming, 'Help me. Help me.' But there was nobody to help. Everybody was stepping over them or walking on them trying to get out.*

The conditions that existed in the open stairwell at this moment were so bad that survival itself was only barely thinkable. A woman who was standing near the two people who had fallen was in a position to feel the full force of the peril on the steps:

> *It was like somebody had thrown a gob of soot into my mouth. I remember trying to breathe, coughing and gagging, inhaling and exhaling nothing but smoke. I have never encountered anything like it before. I remember saying, "Oh Lord, please don't let this happen to me."*

Fortunately the group at the top of the stairs quickly discovered that the spiral stairway was on fire and that escape through the Hallway of Mirrors was impossible. They turned and headed across the building toward the service stairway near the elevator. The panic that had prevailed momentarily in the stairwell ended, and the people on the steps, including those who had fallen, made it back to the second floor ahead of the fire. Not all of them, however, were in shape to save themselves: *A man grabbed hold of my arm. I was choking. Then a woman grabbed my other arm. She said, 'You've got to help yourself.'* Somehow, through the smoke, the darkness, and the terrifying conditions, the entire group moved away from the fire and toward the only avenue of escape still open to them.

The short, hellish trip across the building for this last group to leave the spiral stairway seemed endless. The service stairway near the elevator was nothing but a hope as they moved through the darkness of the corridor past the upstairs dining rooms. No longer were the smoke and toxic gases just punishing. Their throats and chests burned as though the fire had somehow penetrated their bodies. There was a little air near the floor, but breathing was nearly impossible. Then near the end of the corridor, still not sure there was a way out ahead, the group found itself at the back of a line of people of unknown length that was inching its way through the corridor toward an unknown destination.

For some the new obstacle was a crushing blow to their hopes for survival. But then through the darkness a man's voice sounded out: *I work here. I know the building. I can't see you, but I know the building. I'll take you to the kitchen. Crawl.* On hands and knees they crawled through the remainder of the hallway and turned down the narrow stairway toward the first floor. On a small landing half way down they experienced a precious sign of relief from the insufferable conditions of the second floor: *A breath of air hit us in the face; it felt like a new world. I used my clothes to shield my face from the smoke. But I must have had a pint of it in my lungs.*

At the top of the stairway one of the Crystal Room bartenders crouched in the smoke and started the last patron down the steps toward the kitchen. He took a moment to satisfy himself that the upstairs evacuation was complete and then descended the narrow stairway to the first floor. By the time he got to the bottom he was coughing and gagging and gasping for breath. As he left the stairwell he entered the kitchen which was gradually filling with smoke from the front of the building. It was still very light in comparison to the smoke on the second floor, but the fire was obviously moving across the building from the Zebra Room and pushing a mass of black smoke ahead of it. Time for evacuation of the kitchen was short, and most of the employees seemed to sense that. All but a few worked furiously to get the people out. A small group of three or four, however, stood near the door between the kitchen and the service stairway and labored momentarily over what seemed like a more pressing matter.

Ron Schilling had arrived in the area from the basement. He was still concerned for the occupants of the second floor. The headwaiter and other upstairs employees thought that everyone had made it off the floor, but they weren't certain. Because the heavy smoke had come so suddenly, the rooms could not be checked for patrons. A final search was necessary, if there was still time.

A busboy climbed the steps to the upstairs corridor. He managed to move to the doors leading into the dining room. He yelled into the darkness on both sides of the corridor; nobody answered. The fire had not yet moved away from the main stairway, but the smoke that filled the air was unbearable. A tablecloth that the busboy used to cover his face provided no relief. Breathing was impossible. He turned quickly toward the service stairway and retraced his steps to the kitchen. The other employees concluded that nothing more could be done about the second floor. Ron Schilling checked the empty Empire Room for patrons and then turned his attention to evacuation of the kitchen. The upstairs headwaiter was still unable to forget his concern for the people he had earlier served in the Crystal rooms. He headed for the outside still thinking about the locked door from the upstairs corridor to the roof.

By this time employees from the Garden Room had come to the kitchen to render aid and had started a second escape route from that room to the back of the building. From the kitchen they were moving patrons a short distance down the service corridor behind the Empire Room, diverting them from there to the Garden Room, and sending them to the outside through the exits on each side of the glass wall (see Exits F and G on Diagram No. 8). The pressure on the exit at the north end of the kitchen had subsided, and the escape from the front part of the building had entered its final phase.

All of the first floor banquet and party areas, the Empire Room, the Viennese Room, and the Zebra Room, were now empty. All of the patrons and employees were gone from the foyer, the main bar, and the main dining room. The second floor was empty. Many people were still in the kitchen and others were strung out in the service corridor and the Garden Room. But everyone was moving steadily toward safety. However, in one of the dressing rooms on the extreme east side of the second floor were two people who were not so fortunate.

Earlier in the evening, a couple of young women came to Beverly Hills to coordinate the fashion show and dinner for the Choral Union party in the Crystal Room. Soon after their arrival they entered one of the upstairs dressing rooms, depositing some clothing and personal items there, and moved on to the dining room for an early meal with the fashion show models. During the remainder of the evening they moved back and forth between the dressing rooms and the dining room in preparation for the performance. Then when smoke rushed to the second floor from the Zebra Room, the two women went down the service stairway on the west side of the building. They left in that direction in one of the first groups to depart, and rather easily worked their way through the exit at the north end of the kitchen.

From the loading dock outside the kitchen they moved a few feet away from the building and stopped. A man who had known them for a long time stood nearby as they talked worriedly about money that had been left on the second floor, apparently in one of the upstairs dressing rooms. At the end of that conversation one of the two turned toward the building and started for the kitchen door. The other followed immediately in her footsteps and reentered the building. They were last seen at the kitchen door. Their movements thereafter are partly a matter of conjecture.

Presumably they moved hastily to the south end of the kitchen, climbed the service stairway to the upstairs corridor, and crossed the building toward the spiral stairway. The conditions on the second floor had gotten worse during their brief absence from the building. In all probability the whole floor was dark, and the smoke in the corridor surely must have been insufferable. Nonetheless the two women pushed on. They moved past the dining rooms and the spiral stairway and managed somehow to get all the way to the extreme east side of the second floor.

From that remote corner of the sprawling club they never returned. As the kitchen emptied and the group of people in the east-west corridor moved toward safety, the bodies of the two young women lay on the floor of one of the upstairs dressing rooms. More than a thousand people had been in the front half of the building when fire was discovered. Only these two failed to survive. In all likelihood they were the first fatalities of the tragedy—dead of smoke inhalation.

# Six

## Escape From the Showroom

I

In the showroom audience not too long after the busboy's announcement that the building was on fire, a young woman looked at an elderly couple sitting unconcerned and motionless at a table in the area near the stage. She approached and urged them to get up: *He is not kidding. There is really a fire.* They smiled, as if to acknowledge her kindness, but just sat and watched others move slowly toward exits that were already becoming congested. At a different table, in another part of the room, a woman rose from a chair and started to leave. A friend reacted differently to the warning: *Come on, sit down, it's nothing.* With misgivings the woman reconsidered: *Well, maybe I am making a big issue out of nothing.* She sat back down. In still another part of the room a man turned to his wife: *If that's all it is, let's just sit. We'll wait and let the crowd clear.*

Within a short time after the announcement, lines formed at the double doors on each side of the stage as people converged from the four levels of the room. As they moved toward the outside, many thought about what the busboy had said:

*I remember he said a small fire on the other side of the building, the other side and it was small.*

...

*When he said we have a small fire I thought there was no hurry to get out. I didn't know it was bad.*

...

*He said not to panic, that it was a small fire. My mother-in-law and sister-in-law wouldn't leave. My husband said "This is part of the act, I am not going."*

Not a single sign of panic or disorder occurred in any part of the room. No one pushed, hurried, or tried to take unfair advantage of others. The strong helped the weak, the young helped the old. Very few in the crowd of a thousand felt seriously threatened by the "small fire" on the "other side" of the building. They had been asked to leave, and most were in the process of complying with that request. Few were in a hurry, for nearly everyone was sure that the evacuation was purely precautionary.

Throughout the room compliance with the evacuation order was approached with a certain degree of indifference. The musicians on stage unhooked their instruments from electrical fixtures and casually collected their music. A few sauntered off toward the dressing room backstage: *We really didn't think things were that serious. We took our instruments so they wouldn't get knocked off.* A waiter who was certain that the problem was a grease fire in the kitchen turned to address the customers he had been serving: *Remember what table you have. I don't want to get stuck with your liquor bill.* The patrons located near the stage made jokes with the comedians: *Are we going to have to listen to the same old jokes when we return?* The comedians, still at the microphone attempting to blunt the possibility of panic, responded in kind: *People have walked out on us before, but this is ridiculous.*

## 2

The busboy's announcement from the Cabaret Room stage had served to send a small number of people rushing up the north-south corridor toward the front of the building. An employee who operated the showroom sound equipment from a small booth at the end of the corridor had headed for the Zebra Room. He intended to join the fight to bring the blaze under control. The small group of boys standing at the rear doors watching the comedians had headed for the Viennese Room to join their parents. They had no way of knowing that their parents had already left the building.

Flashover had occurred in the Zebra Room just after the busboy spoke. A few of the club's employees had stayed in the area around the fire momentarily but only for the purpose of seeing that the patrons had all departed. A waitress from the Garden Room was in the group when the young boys arrived to join their parents:

> *Go back! You can't get through this way! Our parents are here, in the Viennese Room! There's nobody here. Get out of the building!*

Without waiting for the boys to respond she herded them north toward the back doors. Near the entrance to the Cabaret Room she delivered them to another employee and joined the evacuation effort in the Garden Room. The young boys were promptly taken out of the building through the north end of the corridor.

The peril to the people in the Cabaret Room had reached colossal proportions by this time. A huge body of smoke and gases had amassed in the south end of the main corridor and was growing with every passing second. It contained sufficient quantities of toxic gases to cause nearly instant unconsciousness and it was headed north toward the rear of the building. There was nothing in its path to block or slow its movement. The north-south corridor provided an unobstructed passageway from the origin of the fire to the showroom. An immediate evacuation of the room was needed to avert disaster. No longer was there any margin at all for error.

The comedians were still on stage engaging some of the patrons in lighthearted conversation. Many of the musicians were also there. A few were trying to contribute to the comedians' efforts to keep the audience calm. But most simply failed to comprehend the seriousness of the threat:

> *I immediately left my piano. As I walked away I looked and the rest of the band was still sitting there. Nobody looked like they were going to get up. The conductor came on stage; he tried to get the band members to pass in their music books.*

> *The audience was a little slow in responding to the announcement; the band was even slower in knowing what to do. As the comedians worked to keep the audience calm, by assuring them that the show would continue after everyone was out and the fire was controlled, we took our time about getting off the stand and off the stage. I took my instrument with me and headed for the dressing room backstage to get my case.*

> *After the announcement we took our instruments with us. We really did not think that things were that serious. When we got backstage we stood around putting our horns away. I noticed a wisp of smoke along the ceiling. I don't know why, we still didn't take it too seriously.*

The dressing rooms toward which the musicians moved were to the right of the stage. Adjoining them was a narrow hallway that led almost directly to the exit on the east side of the building (see Diagram No. 7, p. 66). As the musicians eased across the stage in that direction they had little reason to fear for their safety. The conditions of the showroom were as normal as they had been all evening, and the exit toward which they moved was close and easily accessible. At least it seemed so at that time.

The response of the patrons in the earliest part of the evacuation was not significantly different from that of the musicians. A few people jumped from their seats instantly and moved to the outside as quickly as possible, but most of the large crowd acted with much less haste. They maintained composure and took their time in getting to their feet. Some stood around and finished their drinks while waiting for others to clear out. Outside the building, particularly at Exits A and B (see Diagram No. 8, p. 106), the early evacuees stood barely beyond the exterior doors. They had been told by the comedians that the show would resume as soon as the fire could be controlled. Many believed that return to the Cabaret Room was simply a matter of time. They moved grudgingly away from the exits to make room for others to escape. For a short time a few did not move at all.

Inside the building the general characteristics of the evacuation from the showroom were taking shape. The large crowd had broken into three parts as the initial move toward safety began. One part had turned away from the stage and headed toward the doors leading into the north-south corridor. Another had moved toward the exit sign over the double doors in the southeast corner of the room. The largest part had started toward the double door leading to the service bar at the northeast corner of the building. Some of the people in each of the three groups were extremely anxious to get to an exit, but they were badly outnumbered by those who were unafraid of the fire. Consequently there was no real sense of urgency in the first movement toward any of the exits.

There was yet an even more remarkable characteristic of the early phases of the evacuation. At this crucial moment there were many patrons in all parts of the large room that had not taken the first step toward safety:

> *Patrons in our area were slow to heed the warning. When we exited many were still just sitting at their tables.*
> 
> • • •
> 
> *I left quickly but others seemed to think it was a joke. They sat there, quite a few of them. They were kidding back and forth with the comedians.*
> 
> • • •
> 
> *A lot of people just didn't want to give up their seats. I really think they didn't believe it was as serious as it was, and they didn't want to lose their seats, because they didn't move.*

By this time the fire in the front of the building had spread beyond the Zebra Room. It was raging out of control in the Hallway of Mirrors and was burning toward the north-south corridor. In the showroom there wasn't the slightest sign of imminent danger. Nor was there a single person in the whole room who had seen the smoke or fire in the building. Only the busboy's warning was operating to push the large crowd toward safety. Under the circumstances that was simply not enough. A tragedy of catastrophic dimensions in this part of the building was now a certainty.

3

The waitress who had ushered the young boys away from the Viennese Room after flashover at the Zebra Room stayed in the Garden Room for a minute or so to help with the evacuation there. She suddenly remembered a small band that was scheduled to play for a dance in the Empire Room at nine o'clock. Immediately she rushed from the Garden Room and entered the corridor that crossed the building from east to west. She headed for a soundproof compartment behind the stage of the Empire Room.

From the corridor she reached that area very quickly and found that members of the band were still there, carefully packing away their instruments. Someone had already informed them of the fire and of the need to leave. But the waitress was a little more emphatic: *Get the hell out of here! You don't have time for that!* The musicians better understood the message this time. They scrambled for the door as the waitress moved on toward the stage for a look across the Empire Room.

None of the savings and loan association group was still there. But no smoke had entered the large room from the main bar or the north-south corridor. From the stage the waitress looked toward the double doors on the east side of the room. At that moment the bartender who had been at the Zebra Room entrance with Ron and Scott Schilling opened those doors to see if the crowd in the Empire Room had been warned to leave. He stood there only long enough to yell at the waitress to get out of the building and then headed north toward the back exits. Heavy smoke entered the room before he was able to let the doors close. The waitress wasted no time on the stage. She retraced her steps and returned to the service corridor on the south side of the Garden Room.

In the meantime the busboy who had warned the Cabaret Room crowd had entered the north-south corridor. A few people—obviously those who had reacted to the warning immediately—were already exiting in that direction. Dick Schilling's brother-in-law was standing outside the room directing them toward the exits at the back of the building (see Exits G and H on Diagram No. 8). There was a strong odor of smoke where he stood, but no visible signs of fire, and from the showroom doors to the garden the main corridor was relatively free of people. Understandably, there was no fear on the faces of the first evacuees from the big room and no delay in their departure.

After leaving the Cabaret Room the busboy turned toward the rear of the building and went to the small room in the corridor that housed the electrical controls for the showroom (see Diagram No. 7). Only the stage lights had been on inside the showroom when he asked the guests to evacuate. He intended to get the houselights turned on as soon as possible so that the people could more easily and more quickly make their way to the exits. That accomplished, he turned south toward the Zebra Room to see what had happened with the fire.

He moved past the doors of the Cabaret Room and reached the intersection of the two corridors. Then he glanced south toward the Zebra Room. The sight ahead stopped him in his tracks. *I sort of stood there amazed, at the smoke coming up the hallway; I was stunned.* The smoke was moving toward him about as fast as a person can walk and was hanging about half way to the floor. There was no fire in the corridor that he could see, but the smoke clearly had some kind of sustaining force behind it. For a few seconds he stood near the corridor intersection and watched as the deadly mass moved past the Viennese Room to the double doors on the east side of the Empire Room. And then he saw Scott Schilling and some other employees emerge from the smoke on the run. Without much hesitation he turned toward the back of the building and headed for the exits at the end of the corridor.

4

On his way through the north-south corridor Scott Schilling told everybody in sight to get out of the building. At the intersection of the two corridors, knowing that the smoke was not too far behind, he turned down the narrow hallway between the Cabaret Room and the storage room and headed toward the exit on the east side of the building (see Exit B on Diagram No. 8). The manager of the showroom had already come to that part of the building to open the exit doors and to get people started toward safety. She was standing in the doorway of the Cabaret Room when Scott arrived, holding one of the double doors open, urging people to hurry.

The houselights were on at the time, and she had a clear view across the room. The comedians were at the microphone urging people to move to the exits. Not everyone had reacted to the busboy's warning; a few people were still at their tables apparently unconcerned about the fire. A disproportionate part of the crowd had moved toward the exit on the other side of the stage (see Exit A on Diagram No. 8). The employees located in the service bar on that corner of the building had a good opportunity to observe the mood and demeanor of those moving in that direction.

> *When people were going through the doors toward the exit to the chapel, they were just joking away, "Give me a rum and coke to go." And "wow, we're going to get better seats when we get back in." They took it just serious enough to walk out.*
>
> ...
>
> *I mean they were joking, really. They would laugh and say, "That's alright Mary, just take our drinks to the table, we'll be right back." They were joking, I guess, until the smoke started coming.*
>
> ...
>
> *When they were walking out they were laughing, had their drinks in their hands, smoking cigarettes. One woman commented when she got to the garden area about how nice the garden was, and said, "Maybe they will serve drinks out here until this thing is over."*

On the opposite side of the room the failure of the patrons to comprehend the degree of danger was equally widespread. The movement in that direction, although smaller in size, was no different from the one going toward the left of stage. It was woefully lacking the urgency needed to deliver the people to safety. Up the ramp to the right of stage and through the aisles, the patrons moved slowly and casually toward the exit. Few appeared frightened. On the way out one of them looked at the showroom manager and joked about being in a fire drill. All of the people around him laughed, but not the manager. Only she had seen the smoke in the north-south corridor. The others had been told that the fire in the club was "small" and "on the other side of the building," and for the moment they were taking that warning to be the literal truth.

5

The busboy who had warned the showroom crowd wasted no time in heading for safety after seeing Scott Schilling run out of the smoke. As he moved past the showroom doors he encountered a slightly heavier flow of people leaving the Cabaret Room. However, the north-south corridor was still relatively clear all the way to the exits. Dick Schilling's brother-in-law was still standing outside the showroom doors to keep patrons from turning toward the front of the building. Another employee had joined him there. Together the two of them had the evacuation moving in an orderly fashion toward the garden. Not many patrons had noticed the problem up the corridor, and most of those who had were reacting to it with remarkably good sense:

> *I looked to the left, on leaving the Cabaret Room with my mother, and saw this black smoke booming down the hall. I grabbed her and started as fast as I could, I realized that it was really, really bad.*

The busboy moved to the exits at the back of the building without difficulty or delay. Very few of the people behind him would find the path to safety so open. One of the doors at the end of the corridor, identified on Diagram No. 8 as Exit H, was locked. The people leaving the Cabaret Room via the main corridor, as well as those trying to leave the building from the east side of the Garden Room, were all being funnelled through a single set of double doors at Exit G. The busboy stopped inside the exit long enough to attempt to force open the locked door. In the meantime the exodus from the Cabaret Room picked up some momentum. More people than the double doors at Exit G could accommodate efficiently departed the showroom and headed through the corridor. The busboy gave up on the locked door rather quickly and walked to the outside. In a very short time the escape route behind him was full of people all the way from the back of the building to the showroom doors.

Then at that crucial moment the evacuation from the Cabaret Room to the garden via the north-south corridor suffered a familiar setback:

> *We had a bottleneck because of the people in the garden. I guess they didn't think it was that bad. They were mingling in the garden and we couldn't get out of the door. Some employees started yelling at them and I joined in—"Get out of the way so we can get out of here!" And then I got scared. I was so close to the door. But it was so far away. We weren't moving.*

All the while the peril in the front of the building was rushing toward the back. The main body of smoke had moved past the Empire Room and was rapidly closing in on the corridor intersection. Some lighter smoke that was being pushed ahead of it had already arrived outside the Cabaret Room doors. Breathing was still easy, but the composure of the patrons was beginning to weaken. From the back of the crowd a man yelled angrily at those ahead: *Move faster! There are people back here and smoke around us! Hurry!* He and most of those around him started pushing gently toward the exits at the back of the building. The flow through the corridor improved a little but not enough to make much difference to those still inside the showroom. Dick Schilling's brother-in-law and the employee working with him were behind the crowd trying to direct the evacuation. They had started taking some patrons across the building by using the hallway between the Empire and Garden rooms and sending them to the outside through the Garden Room. However, they were rapidly running out of time. The heavy smoke from the front of the building had reached the corridor intersection.

6

West of that intersection, in the short hallway on the south side of the Garden Room, a couple of waitresses were working frantically to complete the evacuation that had been started through the service corridor to relieve the congestion in the north end of the kitchen. For a short time the exodus in that direction had proceeded smoothly and uneventfully. Employees of the kitchen and Garden Room had stationed themselves along the escape route to direct traffic and render assistance. No congestion had developed along the way to impede the flow of patrons from the kitchen and nothing had happened in the Garden Room to create difficulty at that end.

But then the situation changed suddenly and completely. Without warning the conditions in the area between the Empire Room and the Garden Room began to worsen. From the corridor intersection a huge mass of thick smoke turned west across the building and moved violently into the hallway on the south side of the Garden Room. One of the two waitresses there saw it coming from the main corridor and thought it looked like a tornado. Without a doubt it came very fast. In a matter of seconds the whole hallway was full of black smoke from ceiling to floor, and the evacuation from the kitchen to the Garden Room had come to an abrupt and permanent end. The sudden change in conditions did more than merely close another avenue of escape from the fire. It trapped a small group of patrons in the smoke-filled area between the two large banquet rooms and left them with little more than a faint hope for survival.

Part of the group managed somehow to turn around and head back to the kitchen. For the rest there was no time or opportunity for that. They found themselves instantly in what seemed like a maze of hallways, engulfed in suffocating smoke and darkness, and scared literally out of their wits:

> *The minute I walked through that door the smoke was from the ceiling to the floor, and I couldn't see a few inches in front of me. I tried to feel my way to a door but became disoriented. I thought, "I am not going to make it out of here and might as well quit struggling; if I go down and someone comes along they will crawl on over me."*

The two waitresses who had watched the smoke storm into the short hallway had no chance to give them help. They barely had time to scramble out of the path of the smoke and head for the exits on the back side of the Garden Room.

In no time at all after the smoke from the main corridor poured into this hallway it started through the large opening in the east wall of the Garden Room—the one directly opposite the rear doors of the Cabaret Room (see Diagram No. 1). Not many people were in the large dining room at the time but those that were instantly found themselves under an imminent threat of death. A waitress who was fully cognizant of the problem in the north-south corridor was standing in the east part of the room at that moment trying to issue an effective warning to the patrons: *Hurry, hurry, it is coming! And it is really bad! Get out and get away from the building.*

The people to whom she spoke were moving rapidly across the room in a northeasterly direction toward Exit G. They had come to the Garden Room from the kitchen. Very quickly they discovered for themselves that the waitress's warning was no exaggeration: *I could see the smoke at the time. It was about two feet from the ceiling and was rolling. Ahead of us we could hear people shouting and screaming.* The shouting and screaming heard in the Garden Room came from the north end of the main corridor. The heavy smoke from the front of the building had just roared in on the people trying to get out of the Cabaret Room.

The employee working outside the showroom doors with Dick Schilling's brother-in-law got caught by that cloud of black smoke: *As soon as it hit me I couldn't breathe. It took my breath away and I immediately hit the floor.* Many of the patrons who had made it to the corridor from the showroom did the same thing. Some maintained a semblance of composure. Most did not. A few fought their way through the confusion and reentered the Cabaret Room to escape the blinding smoke. Dick Schilling's brother-in-law was at the back of the crowd when the panic struck. He concluded very quickly that there was nothing more he could do to help. *I stayed until I couldn't stand it any longer.*

The main corridor ahead of him was full of people. So he moved across the building in a westerly direction, entered the Garden Room from the east-west corridor, and headed for the exit on the east side of the glass wall. He found the conditions in the Garden Room somewhat better than those in the north-south corridor. But they too were deteriorating rapidly. From the ceiling the smoke had already dropped below head level. By bending over to stay underneath the worst of it, however, he was able to move across the large room to Exit G without substantial difficulty. And much of the congestion that had existed earlier at that exit was gone by the time he got there. From both the Garden Room and the extreme north end of the main corridor, people were moving to the outside at a rapid rate. The path to safety was suddenly opening up for the large group still located near the showroom doors. Unfortunately the time left for them to reach the outside had nearly run out.

The north-south corridor was sustaining at least two separate fires that were on the move toward the back of the building. There was a *visible fire rolling along underneath the ceiling and a secondary fire traveling along on the carpet face, trailing behind the ceiling fire.*[14] To the north of the fire the corridor was serving as a chimney for the rapid movement of the heavy smoke that was being pushed ahead of the flames. An employee who escaped the Garden Room barely ahead of Dick Schilling's brother-in-law discovered just how quickly the deadly smoke had reached Exit G: *Smoke was pouring out the door. I walked right into it. It came down to about my chest. It was that low already.*

## 7

From the narrow hallway on the south side of the Cabaret Room one of the club's employees entered the storage room and rushed to the back wall of the two restrooms located in that part of the building (see Diagram No. 1). A few minutes earlier, without the slightest suspicion that there was a problem in the club, a trio of waitresses had entered the ladies restroom at that location for a brief respite from the drudgery of the dining room. No one except the waitresses were in the restroom when the employee banged his fists against the back wall to get the attention of those inside: *Is there anybody in there? The building is on fire! You've got to get out!*

The waitresses were startled by the banging sounds behind them but none of the three immediately understood the warning the employee was trying to deliver. For at least a minute thereafter they stood in the restroom, prepared themselves for a return to work, and engaged in casual conversation about the disturbance outside the room. After a while they concluded that their supervisors must have sent someone looking for them: "We are probably in trouble now." Then one of the three left the room to check on the matter.

Her departure took her into a short hallway that connected the ladies restroom with the north-south corridor (see Diagram No. 1). Just outside the restroom door, even before she had taken a full step, she stopped and faced the most terrifying sight of her life. The fire had moved north in the main corridor and was now near the double doors on the east side of the Empire Room: *As I started out the door I saw this big stream of heavy black smoke. And then I saw red and yellow flames.*

Most of the smoke in the main corridor was being pushed toward the back of the building by the fire, but some had managed to slip out of the stream and turn toward the ladies restroom. Normal breathing down that way had already become difficult. But that was the very least of the waitress's concerns as she stood in that short hallway. Her only avenue of escape from the restroom was through the north-south corridor. She and the other two waitresses were all but trapped behind the fire.

But then from the fiery corridor she heard the familiar voice of a cousin who worked at the club as a busboy: *Don't come out yet. Go back in and wait. We'll get you out.* She reentered the restroom as directed and gave her companions a chilling report of the problem confronting them: *There's a big fire in the corridor. We're trapped in here with no way to get out. You can already see the flames.* The busboy in the corridor moved quickly to obtain a fire extinguisher. Two other busboys were with him to help. All three had been in the front of the building trying to extinguish the fire in the main bar. They had abandoned their efforts to control the blaze and were retreating toward the exits at the back of the building with the fire coming rapidly behind them when they saw the waitress standing helplessly in the short hallway off the main corridor.

The three waitresses left the restroom to face the fire. One of the busboys discharged an extinguisher against the burning walls of the corridor. The movement of the fire toward the back of the building was arrested long enough for the young women to dash across the corridor to the double doors leading into the Empire Room. One of the three fainted on the way across and had to be dragged out of the path of the fire by one of the busboys. But all three got through the doorway to the Empire Room without burns. Only the young man with the fire extinguisher had difficulty in the hallway. Before he could get out of the corridor and into the banquet room, the flames from the fire ignited his jacket. One of the waitresses quickly reached into the corridor to help him rip the burning clothing off his back. Then he headed through the smoke on the run toward the back of the building. The others started across the Empire Room toward the kitchen.

The Empire Room had ceased to be a place of refuge. From ceiling to floor it was full of light smoke and more was entering rapidly through the doors leading into the main bar: *We had to hold our breath as we moved through; if we breathed it hurt.* No flames had entered the room but the fire out front at that moment was making its first move toward the center of the building.

With one of the busboys carrying the unconscious waitress, the employees moved quickly toward the kitchen. By the time they got halfway there the wall that separated the Empire Room and the main bar began to disintegrate, particularly the portion east of the double doors. Glass that constituted part of the structure of the wall shattered from the pressure inside the barroom and gave the fire unobstructed access to the Empire Room. The small group moved on across the room as quickly as possible. They got to the other side with almost no time to spare.

After reaching the doors leading into the kitchen one of the waitresses glanced back toward the north-south corridor. Flames were shooting into the large room from the main bar. A few seconds later, after the busboys and waitresses got through to the kitchen, an employee who had been helping evacuate people from that part of the club opened the doors to the Empire Room and took the last look across the building that anyone had: *The fire had spread into the room. It was moving in circles just eating up the carpet and had reached the walls of the stage on the other side of the room.*

The situation in the kitchen, as the final escape across the Empire Room ended, was not too bad in comparison to the situation that existed in the rest of the building. The smoke was rapidly getting worse; it had even started to squeeze through the cracks around the closed doors to the Empire Room. But the previous congestion at the exit in the north end of the kitchen had subsided and the escape to the loading dock outside the building was in high gear. The evacuation from the kitchen to the Garden Room was over but it had fully served its purpose. There was good reason to hope that everyone would make it to the loading dock ahead of the fire. Most of the group nearing the exit at the north end of the room had come from the second floor; they were extremely fortunate to have made it to the kitchen. The waitresses from the restroom across the building were no less fortunate and they knew it: *But for the three busboys we would all be dead.*

## 8

The fire in the front of the building and down the main corridor had clearly become more intense. Somewhere in the structure it had overpowered the air handling system and was sending smoke and toxic gases toward the showroom through the air conditioning ducts. In the north-south corridor, not too far from the Cabaret Room, the fire was really roaring. It was producing an extremely heavy volume of smoke that had no way to vent to the outside, and it was releasing sufficient thermal energy to propel the deadly smoke through the club at ever increasing speeds.

In the lowest level of the Cabaret Room, in the area called the "pit," a couple of waitresses worked calmly to help some older patrons toward the exit outside the northeast corner of the room. Suddenly one of the two looked at the other and screamed: *My God! There really is a fire!* At that moment a terrified group of patrons who had just left the showroom returned from the north-south corridor obviously looking for another way out of the building. No one looking toward the back of the room could have failed to see the fear on their faces. But that fear was only a small part of the horrifying scene that existed at the showroom doors. Above the heads of the scared patrons, actually chasing them into the showroom, was the worst looking smoke anyone had yet seen in the building: *It just rolled into the room. It was the blackest smoke I'd ever seen. If you could just take oil and get it to roll in midair then that was the way the smoke was.*

The three doors at the back of the showroom, the ones used earlier in the evening to fill the room with people, were standing wide open. Black smoke poured through from the corridor. In every part of the large room occupants discovered to their instant horror that the fire was not on the other side of the building:

> *The smoke came in very fast. I couldn't believe it. It was like it was rushing toward everybody at once.*
>
> •••
>
> *Then all of a sudden, just out of nowhere, the smoke just piled into the room. Before my eyes it was just there.*
>
> •••

*When I looked back it was just barreling through the back doors. I don't know where it came from.*

Hundreds of patrons were still trying to reach the doors to the right and left of stage (those leading to Exits A and B) when the smoke roared in. To every single one of them it had a totally terrifying appearance.

For a few seconds the occupants reacted to the sudden change of circumstances with extreme agitation but no panic. The employees struggled to maintain order in the evacuation: *I kept yelling to them to be calm and walk out safely.* And for a brief time the patrons responded favorably. Those returning from the north-south corridor paused momentarily near the back of the showroom for a rational choice of exit. Most headed for the doors leading to Exit B since a smaller part of the crowd had moved in that direction. The people on the ramps left and right of stage took chairs that impeded their movement toward the exits and tossed them out of the way. In the long lines that extended back from the doors in the two corners of the room the people near the back yelled for those ahead to hurry. They pushed toward the outside to quicken the pace of their escape, but very gently. There was no instant disorder in the room.

But it was increasingly difficult to maintain composure. The deadly smoke from the main corridor left almost no capacity in anyone to be rational for very long. As it quickly moved away from the back doors and started through the room, it pushed from the minds of the occupants all but a single thought: *I've got to get out of here. I'm going to die if I don't get to that door.*

For some "that door" was a very long way off, and the difficulty of getting there was unmistakable. In both of the crucial corners of the room the aisles were packed full of nervous people. Long lines still extended back from the doorways well into the large room. More significantly, beyond the doorways but still inside the exits, there was a substantial number of patrons who did not know that the black cloud had just roared into the showroom from the north-south corridor. Consequently they continued to move toward the outside as though the threat to life behind them was negligible.

For example, in the hallway between the Cabaret Room and storage room, beyond the showroom doors but inside the exit door, a man stopped to let a band member and his girlfriend move laboriously to the outside with a musical instrument and a television set. Behind him, but out of sight in the showroom, a man at the rear of one of the long lines turned to his wife and told her they were in deep trouble. In the service bar on the other side of the room at the northeast corner of the building several patrons slowed down on their way to safety to joke with some employees. One of the employees acknowledged their humor with a smile. Behind them on the other side of the doors leading to the service bar, a man with fear on his face looked at his young daughter and made a crucial decision: *Go. Don't wait for us. Just get out of here if you can!*

9

The off-duty captain from the Cincinnati Fire Department moved his family away from the building and started looking for a knowledgeable employee. He was in the garden area at the time, outside the exits at the end of the north-south corridor. He had seen only light smoke in the building before evacuating and thought the fire might be controllable. Soon he found a busboy who told him that the fire was in a small party room in the front of the building and agreed to take him there. Together they reentered the building at Exit G and moved through the east side of the Garden Room toward the origin of the fire. They reached the hallway on the south side of the Garden Room and turned toward the corridor intersection. Immediately the fireman discovered that the situation in the club was far worse than he thought. There was darkness in the area because of heavy smoke and a tremendous amount of heat at head level: *Right then I realized there was a fire of pretty good proportions ahead.*

At about this time Dick Schilling's brother-in-law was approached in the garden area by an employee and told that someone was trapped in the electrical controls booth up the main corridor toward the Cabaret Room (see Diagram No. 7). The exits at the end of that corridor were now only partly visible from the garden and terribly menacing in appearance. Black smoke was pouring through to the outside and the people reaching safety were gasping for a breath of air. Nevertheless Dick Schilling's brother-in-law re-entered the club at those exits, with another employee at his heels, and started through the corridor toward the Cabaret Room.

Inside the building the two men encountered a hallway full of dense smoke and terrified patrons struggling to reach an exit. Against the flow of traffic to the outside the two men crouched low to the floor and moved up the corridor to the controls booth. In that small compartment they found nothing but heavy smoke. South of there, however, they discovered a few patrons still staggering out of the Cabaret Room trying to find a way to the outside. The employee tried to direct them toward the exit at the end of the corridor and Dick Schilling's brother-in-law gave them some necessary advice: *Get down on the floor. There is a little air here and you can breathe.* Then the two men turned toward the garden and started crawling on hands and knees to stay underneath the smoke.

The fireman and the busboy reached the corridor intersection and made a turn toward the Zebra Room. Almost immediately the busboy began to scream. The fire was just a few feet up the corridor and bearing down on the two men rapidly: *The kid started to panic, I don't know what he was saying. I grabbed him by the back and said 'Let's get out.'* The heat above their heads was tremendous and the dense smoke had dropped to within eighteen inches of the floor. By the time they turned around and started crawling toward the back of the building the fire at the ceiling had roared in over their heads. Even the fireman had to struggle to maintain composure: *This is the closest I ever came to panic. I have never in all my life seen a fire travel like that.* Somehow the two men crawled back to the Garden Room ahead of the flames, stood up in the tremendous heat that had arrived there, and ran for the doors on the east side of the glass wall.

Soon the situation in the Garden Room got a lot worse. With incredible suddenness smoke and deadly gases swept across the room in a westerly direction and caught the last group of evacuees from the kitchen trying to find their way to the exit on the west side of the glass wall (Exit F on Diagram No. 8). Fortunately not all of the employees who had been directing the evacuation through the Garden Room had abandoned the building to the fire. Under the worst possible conditions they were still in the room searching through the smoke for stragglers. A few were actually leading patrons through the smoke by the hand:

> *I could see nothing in the room at all; I felt that at any moment we were going to run into something. And my wife was stating that she couldn't go any further, but this woman had a good grip on her and was literally dragging her out. The smoke was so hot I felt as though I was standing in fire. It seemed like we were in there for an eternity. The lady just literally led us to the outside.*

The smoke through which they were moving was now as black as smoke from a burning tire. But one by one the evacuees from the kitchen found their way out of the maze of hallways behind the Empire Room and entered the Garden Room. Among the last to make it through was a woman who had been in the north end of the Viennese Room before the fire with the party of physicians. She had fallen behind the rest of her party during the evacuation, got separated from her husband somewhere in the east-west corridors, and ended up lost in the heavy smoke that roared into the hallway on the south side of the Garden Room. For a seemingly endless period of time she had crawled around on the floor trying to find a door that would lead her out of the maze. Near the floor she had found some oxygen but the smoke and gases in the area were so bad that her throat had burned like it was on fire when she tried to breathe. With hope for survival all but gone she escaped the corridor and staggered toward a faint light she saw in the distance. An employee or perhaps a patron trying to help the employees was still there to render aid: *Someone grabbed my fingers, worked his way up to my wrist, and started pulling me out.* At the exit door she looked back over her shoulder for her husband. Had he been there she couldn't have seen him through the smoke. But he wasn't there. Like all the others who had come from the kitchen he had made it to the garden area behind the building. The evacuation of the Garden Room was over. Everyone had made it safely to the outside.

In the same time span, perhaps a few seconds later, the exodus from the north-south corridor also ended, but not so successfully. Fire arrived outside the Cabaret Room not long after the Cincinnati fireman made it to safety. That fire blocked one of the three avenues of escape from the showroom instantly, and then it literally chased the people still in the corridor out the back of the building. All of them managed to get to the garden area alive, but the last two or three to get out paid a heavy price:

> When I got to the outside a man bumped into the back of me. I turned around and he was all burned. His hair was gone and his eyebrows were gone. His hands were burned and he was holding them down by his side. There was skin hanging from them like noodles. His wife seemed to be burned as bad as he. She was somewhat in shock and was starting to collapse. She had blisters all over her arms.

A man who had arrived in the garden barely ahead of the last people was looking toward the building when the end finally came: *No one was coming out the exit any more, just solid black smoke which seemed to be gushing rather than rolling out, like something was pushing it.* And then the fire from the front of the building arrived. Flames shot through the exits at the end of the corridor with tremendous force: *It was like you see in a war movie with a flame thrower, as though someone was inside the building shooting flames to the outside.* The people near the exits moved away from the building as quickly as possible. None of them yet knew of the magnitude of the problem in the Cabaret Room, but they were nonetheless overwhelmed for the moment by the suddenness with which a pleasant evening had changed into an awful nightmare: *It was like a big flash; I never saw anything so quick in all my life. It was like a big tornado; all of a sudden, 'whoosh,' just like that. I just can't believe it went so fast.*

## 10

The black smoke from the main corridor moved across the Cabaret Room rapidly and with the same devastating impact it had had in other parts of the building:

> *I was surprised how fast the smoke circulated through the room. Within in seconds it seemed like the whole room was completely covered with smoke. And it hurt to breathe. It was not like I think smoke ought to be. I was burning way down deep in my chest, a really hard deep burning sensation.*

Before it reached the far side of the room, however, something worse than smoke roared into the room toward the scared patrons.

On its arrival outside the Cabaret Room the fire in the corridor instantly spread through the showroom doors and shot flames fifteen to twenty feet into the room. From the double doors to the right and left of the stage the back of the room looked like a ball of fire. To the patrons the fire was even more terrifying than the deadly smoke that had preceded it:

> *I call it a vicious fire, not creeping or one that you could see coming. It came into that room with such force that it seemed the whole room just exploded, like somebody had saturated it with gasoline. It was a nasty fire, that's the only way I can describe it. It was out to get you.*

A semblance of order had prevailed in the showroom before the flames arrived. To a remarkable degree the crowd had managed under terribly threatening conditions to subdue the natural urges that lead to panic. But all that changed, in an instant when the fire exploded through the rear doors;

> *There were a lot of elderly people in our group. We had helped them as much as we could. But when we saw the fire coming we went over the rail. At that time it was a matter of fighting for your own life. We had been trying to save the people in our tour but it got down to dog eat dog. Save your own life.*

It seemed overwhelmingly certain to the large number still in the room when the fire appeared that there was no hope for the survival of all. Some people would surely have to die. At least it seemed that way. From that moment the occupants of the room were at the mercy of their overpowering and irrepressible instinct for self-survival. Screams for help announced the arrival in the showroom of still another antagonist of the patrons. This one was far more deadly than the fire at the back of the room or the toxic gases floating through the air. Uncontrollable panic struck the crowd and all order to the evacuation collapsed: *People were fighting one another like animals. They saw the smoke and fire. That's when they went berserk.* The waitresses and other employees tried to restore order but there must have been thirty to forty panic stricken patrons for every employee.

A man located in one of the higher levels of the room picked up some chairs that were in his path and threw them to the pit area below. It made no difference to him that there were people in the landing area. Soon after that lots of chairs and small tables were flying through the air as patrons tried to squeeze closer to the doors leading to the exits. And on both sides of the room, as the congestion at those doors worsened, terrified patrons and employees did whatever they could to improve their own chances for escape:

*People started jumping off the top tier over the metal railing and landing on the tables. Others were hollering and screaming and running up on the stage. Some of the people there were telling them that there was no exit backstage. But they weren't listening. They just went on.*

* * *

*I knew I couldn't make it to the door if I got at the end of the line. So I climbed over a rail and jumped from booth to booth until I reached the door. I don't know how but I managed to squeeze into the crowd and got out of the door. As I came through the first door people were starting to fall down. I helped a couple of them to their feet but I was scared. I still don't know how much farther it was to the outside. So I decided to look out for myself.*

* * *

*I screamed at her to get up on the tables. We did that and ran across the tables on the second level toward the service bar and jumped down into the crowd. And we were fighting these people to get through, and the smoke had just about covered our heads when we got to the door.*

The congestion at the doors leading to the two open exits mushroomed very quickly. Within seconds after fire entered through the rear doors hundreds of people were bunched together in the southeast and northeast corners of the room as close to the outside as they could get. At the double doors on each side of the stage they gathered eight abreast and tried to squeeze through doorways that were barely wide enough for two. A high level of disorder prevailed on both sides of the room, but it was far more dangerous to life in the northeast corner. A greatly disproportionate number of the total patrons in the room had moved in that direction after the initial warning about the fire.

A cocktail waitress and bartender stood in the service bar at that location trying as best they could to avert a sudden catastrophe. They screamed at the people inside the showroom: *Calm down or you won't make it through!* They pleaded with them to file through the doorway in two lines. But inside the showroom nobody was listening. The whole crowd was now engulfed in smoke that was getting thicker all the time. The fire raged at their backs. Ahead of them was a doorway that seemed to be beyond reach. Needless to say most felt helplessly trapped. So they reacted to the circumstances in perfectly normal fashion.

Those at the back of the crowd pushed and shoved as hard as possible against those ahead. And more and more people tried to shortcut their way to safety to the disadvantage of others. The panic that the employees, the comedians, and the others had tried so desperately to avoid had gained control of the situation. At least it had taken control of the part of the evacuation moving toward Exit A:

*It was just a big mob of people pushing toward the outside. You had no choice but to push along with them. And you had to fight just to stay in line. Otherwise you would have been ground up against the wall somewhere.*

## 11

At the west end of the hallway on the south side of the Cabaret Room where it intersected with the north-south corridor, there was a door that was camouflaged by design to look like part of the main corridor wall (see Diagram No. 7 for its location). Earlier it was inconsequential to the evacuation of the building. Most of the patrons knew nothing of its existence because of the camouflage. And very few of the employees used it, perhaps only the showroom manager, Scott Schilling, and a handful of others. But when the fire from the front of the building reached the corridor intersection, and then stormed into the Cabaret Room, the camouflaged door began to play a highly critical role in the evacuation of the showroom because for a period of time it served to shield the hallway south of the Cabaret Room from the problems in the main corridor. In so doing it kept the escape route to Exit B relatively free of smoke and completely free of fire. Unfortunately hardly any other physical feature of the building in the vicinity of this exit worked to the advantage of those who chose to leave the showroom in this direction. Several worked to their distinct disadvantage.

The exit sign that hung over the double doors in the southeast corner of the showroom fooled nearly every occupant of the room except the employees. Almost without exception the patrons thought that the double doors led directly to the outside. The configuration of the route that had to be travelled to complete the escape was a serious impediment to a rapid evacuation. Two ninety degree turns, one left and one right, were needed to get from the showroom doors to the outside of the building, although the distance was less than twenty feet (see Diagram No. 7). Only in the absence of complications brought on by a raging fire could most people have been expected to make those turns without difficulty. At the end of their flight toward safety, those who moved toward Exit B encountered still another obstacle to a rapid evacuation.

On leaving the building they found themselves standing on a landing that was suspended eight feet or more above ground level. The landing was very small, approximately five feet square, and had a metal railing on each of two sides. It was connected to the ground by a set of wooden steps that were narrow and quite steep. Below the steps there was a path that had been worn in the grass alongside the east exterior of the club. There was no sidewalk or driveway on this side of the club, only a steep embankment that dropped rapidly away from the building. With these features, the exit on this side of the building was sufficient under the standards of the Life Safety Code for the prompt escape under emergency circumstances of only 112 people. At least three and perhaps four times that many started for the exit after the initial announcement in the showroom that the club had to be emptied. Not very many had completed the journey by the time fire poured into the back of the room.

12

With fire at the back of the showroom the pace of the evacuation toward Exit B intensified quickly and substantially. The faces of those reaching the landing outside the exit began to reflect the seriousness of the situation behind them. The conditions of the showroom had become life-threatening almost instantly: *There's no way to describe the heat. It was a horrible engulfing heat. You could not breathe at all. And it was extremely dark because of the smoke.*

Significant amounts of black smoke began to reach the narrow hallway from the north-south corridor, the storage room, and even the Cabaret Room. Breathing became a problem all along the escape route. At the same time the protective shield at the west end of the hallway—the camouflaged door—was being consumed by the fire in the main corridor. Some of the people moving toward the exit seemed to sense the threat that was closing in on them: *It felt like we were walking directly into the fire. It got hotter and hotter the more we walked. I thought, 'God, we're walking right into the path of the fire.'* But there was hardly anything they could do about it, except to push harder and more desperately toward the outside.

The people in the showroom and some of those in the outer hallway thought that the pushing and shoving was constructive.

Perhaps it was for awhile. At least it served to give the evacuation a needed element of desperation, and it served initially to quicken the escape all along the way. As it worsened, however, it gave those inside the exit door something else to worry about:

> *I was trying to just stay on my feet, get to the exit, and calm the people around me. They were screaming, "Oh God, oh God." I wondered if I could hold my breath long enough to get to the exit. And I was worried about being trampled.*

On the landing and stairs outside the exit, the pushing and shoving had a far more disastrous effect:

> *The woman in front of me stumbled and her head was behind one step and her feet behind another. She was bent like this and I couldn't move. I looked down at her and she looked up at me and I started screaming, "Get this woman. Get this woman." She was holding up everyone in back of us. Then I got pushed from behind and I slid over her all the way to the bottom of the steps.*

Momentarily the exodus toward the east side of the club slowed as a number of patrons tried to stop long enough to dislodge the trapped woman from the steps. But their efforts proved to be totally futile. Those inside the building were determined above all else to get out, and anyone hesitating for even a moment on the landing outside the exit soon found himself flying head first toward the ground below.

Scott Schilling was standing at the bottom of the steps trying to help with the evacuation. He had gone to the front driveway after leaving the building and had returned to this exit. He was not aware of the desperate situation in the Cabaret Room and the number of people still there, but the obvious need of those inside to escape the building as rapidly as possible was apparent. Less than five minutes earlier he had been driven away from the Zebra Room by the flashover there. Already light smoke was floating through the door at Exit B above the heads of the fleeing patrons. It was black, like that which Scott had left in the north-south corridor earlier, and sufficiently heavy to leave no doubt that the people inside were in extreme jeopardy.

As quickly as possible Scott and some patrons who were trying to help at the exit moved to rescue the trapped woman. They moved her aside to keep people from trampling over her and somehow dislodged her from the steps without halting the evacuation. To lessen the difficulty of getting from the landing to the ground, a couple of men then broke the railing off the steps, allowing some of the patrons to jump to the grass below from high on the steps.

At about this time a fireman arrived on the east side of the building from the front driveway. For the moment, however, there was little he or anyone else could do at the exit except to help people down the narrow steps. It was obvious that any attempt to enter the building would obstruct the evacuation. So the fireman instructed the people standing in the grass below the landing to move farther away from the exit, and then he joined the effort at the steps. Many of those to whom he directed the order still had relatives or friends inside the building. Most complied with his instruction by simply moving a short distance to another location within clear view of the exit door.

Scott Schilling headed for the front of the building. Soon after his departure the volume of smoke leaving Exit B increased substantially. A further deterioration of conditions in the hallway on the south side of the Cabaret Room had obviously occurred. The fireman abruptly left the exit and ran as fast as he could to his truck in the front driveway. Once there he addressed a fire department dispatcher: *Get as many oxygen tanks as you can, from any place in the county. We're going to need them and more.*

13

The heavy black smoke that entered the showroom reached the crowd gathered at the double doors to the left of the stage in an incredibly short time. It made normal breathing impossible in that part of the room and enshrouded the three hundred or so people there in near darkness. The fire at the back of the room could be seen through the dense smoke. But hardly anything else was clearly visible: *All I could see were images of people; I couldn't see anybody's face.*

To reach the outside from that part of the Cabaret Room it was necessary to make a single ninety degree turn to the left, move about twenty-five feet through the northeast service bar to Exit A, and then step through a set of double doors to level ground at the back of the building (see Diagram No. 7). With only one turn along the way and no steps outside the exit door the evacuation in this direction should have been easier and more effective than the one toward Exit B. But as events developed it turned out to be neither as easy nor as effective.

For a brief period after fire entered the showroom, the service bar near the exit remained free of smoke. Two bartenders who had worked that station all evening were there at the time to direct the evacuation. One of the two stood just inside the bar to direct evacuees toward safety. The other stood near the exit door. At some point he picked up an elderly woman who had been knocked to the floor, dragged her out of the path of the stampede through the barroom, and pushed her on to the outside. The one nearer the showroom struggled vainly at the double doors to restore some semblance of order to the evacuation. But under the circumstances there was really very little that either of the two could do to help with the escape effort. The increasing panic on this side of the Cabaret Room threatened to bring the evacuation to a complete halt.

With women crying, and men screaming and yelling, a furious battle was being waged just inside the showroom for access to the doorway leading to the service bar. Only two or three people could squeeze through the doorway at once, and by this time no one was making it through easily:

*We were fighting these people to get through. The smoke had just about covered our heads when we got to the door. I grabbed hold of a man's belt, with the smoke and fire at my back, and he pulled me through.*

• • •

*I got through but my mother-in-law got stuck. People had her pinned up against the doorway. When I got through and noticed she wasn't there I heard her yelling. I reached around the door and got her arm and pulled her through.*

* * *

*My wife and I got separated; she got pushed ahead of me. The next thing I knew I was within reaching distance of the center post of the doorway, I grabbed that post and with all my might blew through the door. But I got caught on the center post and people were smashing against it so hard I couldn't get my arm out. I kept yanking and yanking. Finally I made it.*

Almost everyone joined the violent engagement at the showroom doors. They did so without personal animosity or hostility toward one another, but there was no restraint in their behavior. They treated the engagement for what it was, or at least for what it seemed to be, a ferocious struggle for survival that could be won by only a few.

Then suddenly black smoke in the showroom started floating into the service bar above the heads of those caught in the doorway. At the same time additional smoke began to pour into the small room from air vents in the ceiling. It came in torrents from both sources and filled the bar in a matter of seconds. The bartender standing at the exit door yelled at the top of his voice to the one standing near the showroom: *Let's get the hell out of here!* But he had no time to wait for his friend to react to the warning. He left the building, fearing for his life, and joined the large group of patrons in the garden to watch the exit door for the sight of a familiar face.

For a few seconds the stampede of people through the service bar to safety continued unabated, but then it slowed abruptly to a trickle. Some of those outside the exit believed that everyone had escaped. A young woman who had just barely made it to safety knew better. She turned toward a companion with tears on her face: *I don't think everybody made it out.* The bartender standing nearby had even less doubt than she. But perhaps he had simply missed seeing his friend get out.

14

A sizeable number of people, perhaps as many as a hundred, was inside Exit B when the evacuation in that direction started its final collapse. None in the group was any less terrified than those trying to reach Exit A, but very few of them had permitted their fears to dominate and totally determine their behavior. Consequently the greatest threat to life on this side of the showroom was not panic. Instead it was the worsening conditions in the hallway on the south side of the Cabaret Room. With the fire in the north-south corridor so close to this narrow passageway, the heat in the area between the showroom doors and the exit had become so intense that a few people even contemplated returning to the showroom and the terrible conditions they had just escaped. The smoke in this hallway was even more punishing on the patrons than the heat.

There was a little air near the floor that could have provided relief but under the circumstances it was totally inaccessible. The evacuees were simply unable or afraid to drop to their knees even to breathe. Most had been in the smoke for a relatively long time. Very few could have had an oxygen reserve left:

*We got in the corridor and made a left turn. The smoke was very, very bad. It got in my throat and my lungs. We were all coughing. My girlfriend had her face in my back so she wouldn't breathe the fumes I had taken in a lot of smoke. How much more I could have absorbed I just don't know.*

• • •

*The hallway was filled with this tremendous black smoke; it was something. You could hardly breathe. And I had held my breath as long as I could.*

• • •

*To be perfectly honest, in that hallway I panicked as much as anybody ever did. At that point I couldn't breathe and I was out of breath. I tried. All I could take in was smoke.*

Fortunately the landing outside the exit was not too far from the showroom doors, and the movement of the crowd was now furious. Virtually body to body the patrons were running from the building and stumbling or falling down the steps to the grass below. In a very, very short time the whole group could have made it to safety, but the conditions inside the exit got even worse.

The smoke got so black and thick, particularly in the hallway outside the Cabaret Room, that visibility dropped to zero. Not too many people were still in the showroom when this occurred and those that were had a good line on the exit sign ahead of them. Most moved through the darkness to the showroom doors without added hardship. But in the hallway beyond those doors they experienced disappointment and fear that were almost indescribable:

> *I thought when we got to the door we would be outside. I really wasn't too scared going up the ramp or even when we lost visibility and I couldn't see. But when we got into this hallway I was never so scared in my life.*
>
> . . .
>
> *We turned left and I knew I was going to die. I felt as though we were in a dead end, because the doors didn't open to the outside. They opened into this hallway. I couldn't believe I was going to die, but I knew I was.*

In a short time the unbroken chain of people that extended from the showroom doors to the landing outside the exit disintegrated. The patrons then lost their ability to follow one another to the outside. On leaving the showroom some turned to the right and headed away from the exit. Others turned correctly to the left at the showroom doors but moved beyond the exit door to backstage dressing rooms from which there was no means of escape (see Diagram No. 7). Soon fifty people or more were lost in the smoke within a few feet of the exit. For all but a few there was very little hope.

The fire in the main corridor suddenly broke through the door that had been protecting the escape route on the south side of the Cabaret Room. Suddenly flames poured through the narrow hallway toward Exit B and streaked to the outside like "a gust of strong wind." Below the landing a young couple who had just escaped stood in the grass watching the exit door as two friends burst through to the outside. Flames were right at their heads. They seemed to be on fire. In a second or so, as the couple watched their friends tumble safely down the steps out of the fire, the evacuation through Exit B ended. Five or six more people managed to get through the smoke to the outside before heavy flames engulfed the upper part of the exit. Then the exit door slammed shut from the outside as the crowd on the east side of the building looked on in shock.

Only a police officer and a young man were near the exit at the time. The young man moved up the steps toward the landing to reopen the door, but the police officer quickly intervened: "Wait, don't open it. The oxygen will fuel the fire!" Then he grabbed a plank that had been part of the banister along the steps and moved toward the landing himself. In the grass below the exit, just a few feet away, a woman whose husband had pushed her to safety at the very last moment saw the officer near the door and instantly became hysterical. She screamed louder than the people trapped inside the burning building: *You've got to open that door, you've got to open the door! I've got a husband in there, and some other people! They're right there! You've got to open that door!* She was the only one in a party of six to make it all the way to the exit from the "pit." A couple of patrons tried to calm her down and provide some comfort, but she only backed away and screamed louder than before.

Toward the front driveway, but still within sight of the exit door, a cocktail waitress stood in the company of her sister and another employee who thought her father was still in the showroom trying to escape through Exit B. As the policeman moved toward the door with the plank in his hand the employee watching for her father started to scream. The cocktail waitress and her sister were totally horrified by what they saw at the exit door:

> *I don't know why the flow of people had stopped. But the policeman walked across the landing and was closing the door. The people inside were screaming, and I am sure that it was an arm I saw, on fire at the top, trying to poke out. I thought the policeman was trying to shut the door so that the oxygen would be caught and that he would open it again. But he didn't. He barred the door.*

The waitress left her sister and the other employee standing in the grass near the driveway and rushed toward the exit. On the way there she encountered a woman lying on the ground crying for her husband: *She was screaming that her husband had kicked her out, that he was still inside the door, but that they wouldn't let him out.* After a brief and unsuccessful effort to help the crying woman the waitress turned toward the building and looked again at the exit. This time she saw John Davidson on the landing above the steps trying to get the door open. The policeman's body was pushing against it. Ultimately the door was successfully reopened but nobody thereafter escaped to the landing without help. The police officer had succeeded in bringing the escape to a tragic and premature end—at least it was so reported in the aftermath of the fire by media coverage that sensationalized the last few seconds of the evacuation through Exit B.

But the events that ended the escape through Exit B did not in fact occur the way they looked or the way they were sensationally reported in news accounts of the fire. John Davidson was indeed near the exit toward the end of the evacuation. A drummer from the band had rushed to his dressing room immediately after word of the fire reached the showroom and warned him of the need to leave. He had reacted to the warning without hesitation and had moved through Exit B without difficulty and ahead of the crowd. No more than thirty or forty people had made it to safety by the time he reached the grassy hillside below the building. For a time after his escape he stood near the landing and held the exit door open so that people trying to leave the building could more quickly descend the narrow steps. But when flames shot through to the outside he released the door and moved back away from the steps and landing.

The door at Exit B was equipped with a self-closing device. Almost immediately after the appearance of fire it slammed shut on its own because there was no one on the inside to push it open. Davidson made no effort thereafter to reopen the door. Instead he stood near the exit and watched the activities of a police officer and a young man. The police officer climbed to the top of the steps with a plank in his hand and crouched very low to the landing. He was there not to bar the door as it appeared to some of those standing toward the front driveway but to open it:

> *I proceeded up the steps and attempted to hook the point of the wood to the door so as to open it from approximately six feet away, hopefully to avoid engulfing myself, and the young man in flames. After a few seconds I hooked the door and opened it a few inches. I yelled for the young man to go ahead. He opened the door and wired it to the railing alongside the landing.*

For some reason no fire poured to the outside after the door was reopened. But the smoke was heavier than before. In a couple of seconds a man blackened with smoke staggered through the exit doorway and collapsed in the arms of the policeman. The officer carried him to the grass below and returned to the landing just in time to help a second patron who managed somehow to survive the hallway fire and get to the exit after the door was reopened. But then no one else came to the outside. The officer quickly dropped to his knees at the exit door, got the young man to hold one of his feet, and crawled into the building as far as his body would extend. Even near the floor the smoke was now so bad that the officer could neither see nor breathe. And the heat was all but unbearable. He stretched his arms and body as far into the hallway as he could reach in every direction but found none of the people he was certain were still inside. The smoke forced him back to the landing just as a couple of firemen arrived from the front driveway.

The two firemen entered the building without hesitation and headed through the smoke toward voices still screaming for help from inside the open door. The officer moved off the landing out of the way. The conditions in the hallway on the south side of the Cabaret Room proved to be too much even for the experienced firefighters. They moved no more than ten feet toward the showroom doors, turned around immediately without reaching any of the patrons in the hallway, and did the only thing sensible under the circumstances. They retreated to the landing outside the building gasping for breath and knowing that none of those still inside the exit had any chance for survival without help.

## 15

The northwest service bar was now immersed in total darkness. A few of those at the showroom doors on that side of the Cabaret Room had nonetheless been able to fight their way through to the bar. In that small room they faced an enormous difficulty that had not existed earlier. No longer was there an employee there to turn them toward the outside, and in the black smoke that had filled the room there was no way to see the need for a left turn toward the exit door. So they did the natural thing on leaving the showroom. They maintained a straight course and missed the turn that would have sent them toward the garden. In a matter of seconds a group of more than twenty was lost in that part of the service bar from which there was no means of egress. Some were trapped behind a long wooden counter that crossed the room almost from wall to wall (see Diagram No. 7). Others were simply lost in the smoke. All were trying to feel their way to a door that was in another part of the room. And then—with more than a hundred people still inside the showroom doors screaming for help—the evacuation toward Exit A came to an end.

While trying to fight her way out of the Cabaret Room a woman was knocked to the floor in the doorway between the showroom and the service bar. She got a limb stuck behind one of the doors, perhaps while trying to get to her feet, and could not free herself to move on. The anterior section of her body finally came to rest in the doorway while lying across the path to safety. In the darkness a couple of other patrons promptly fell in the same spot. Then a cocktail waiter stumbled over somebody or something just inside the showroom and added to the bodies in the doorway. The people behind him fell like dominoes.

Instantly the waiter found himself with his feet in the Cabaret Room, his head in the service bar, and his whole body near the bottom of a pile of screaming people stacked in the doorway. He was conscious and clearheaded and knew the way to the exit. But he couldn't move as much as a centimeter toward the garden at the back of the building. Neither could any of the others. The doorway between the showroom and the service bar was now completely blocked. The people in the Cabaret Room were hopelessly trapped. They moved as close to the blocked doorway as they could get and dropped to the floor to wait. The fire was at their backs. The smoke had taken away their breath. They had nothing left but a faint hope for survival through rescue.

From outside the building the doorway at Exit A now looked like a chimney. Except for a couple of feet at ground level it was serving as a vent for the black smoke that had filled the service bar. Only the bartender who had escaped moments earlier and a busboy from the Garden Room were near the exit doors. Both were crouched underneath the smoke trying to answer the cries of distress from inside the building: *This way, come this way! The door is over here. Stay on the floor and crawl!* Neither of the two could see very far into the building, certainly not as far as the showroom doors. They assumed that the people hidden by the smoke had the capacity to crawl to safety on their own. Soon they learned differently.

Among the desperate cries for help from the other end of the service bar was the familiar voice of a fellow employee. The Cabaret Room had only one cocktail waiter. Through the smoke and above the screams that filled the service bar, the bartender heard and recognized the shrill voice of that waiter. And from the exit door he tried to communicate with him:

"Donnie, Donnie, this way. I can't get to you!"
"I can't get free! My legs are stuck!"
"You've got to pull loose! We can't help you!"
"I can't! I can't!"

The bartender moved reluctantly into the service bar and started toward the showroom doors. But the heat and smoke inside the building were simply too much to endure. They quickly drove him back to the outside.

At the other end of the service bar the cocktail waiter was indeed helpless. He was at the bottom of a mass of tangled bodies that was several feet high. Some of those on top of him were unconscious. Most of the others were hysterical. The waiter was unable to move a single muscle without a struggle and had absolutely no hope of moving toward the exit. But he had not yet surrendered to the fire. Near the floor there was some oxygen. It was difficult and painful but he could breathe. The bodies above him provided a shield against the searing heat leaving the Cabaret Room. He had suffered no burns. He was no more than twenty-five feet from the safety of the garden. He knew that the bartender and some others were at the exit door to help. Unlike most of those around him he didn't scream for help. He had hope for rescue.

# *Seven*

## RESCUE AND RECOVERY

I

After escaping the building, one of the physicians from the Viennese Room moved his wife and the wives of some other physicians to the rear of the garden area and started for the front driveway. Hundreds of excited people blanketed the grounds at the back of the club as he departed. None in his immediate vicinity seemed seriously injured or in need of help, so he moved quickly through the crowd in the garden, ran the full length of the narrow driveway on the west side of the building, and headed for a rescue van that was parked on the east side of the front canopy. On reaching that van he found a radio with an emergency frequency, and put it to immediate use. He called one of the major hospitals near the club, identified himself, and sent a message that would soon ring a lot truer than he expected: *I'm calling from the Beverly Hills Supper Club. There's a real bad fire here. I have yet encountered no one in need of medical treatment but the casualty potential is tremendous.*

From the rescue van the physician ran across the driveway toward a large crowd standing in the grass on the east side of the building intently watching Exit B. Several uniformed men were standing on the steps below the exit, apparently waiting to enter the building, while a fireman with a heavy hose tried to aid them by spraying water in the direction of the exit door. Only one person was lying on the ground below the exit and she needed nothing from the physician other than assurances that she would soon be all right. He gave her those assurances after a cursory examination, left her in the good hands of some relatives, and decided that his services might be needed more desperately elsewhere.

He watched the work of the fire department at Exit B for a few seconds and headed for the garden area at the back of the building. He took the long way around, returning to the front driveway and retracing his steps along the west side of the club, but he moved toward his destination with haste. The situation at the back of the building was in a state of rapid change. Already it was vastly different from when he left only a few minutes earlier.

2

A minute or two after the last person exited from the Garden Room (through Exit E on Diagram No. 8), the evacuation through the kitchen stopped. Everyone in that area was out. The last patrons to reach the loading dock outside this exit had come to the kitchen in the final phase of the second floor evacuation. They left the building barely ahead of a small group of employees who had directed the last part of the exodus from the kitchen. The smoke in this part of the club, although mild in comparison to what had entered the Garden and Cabaret rooms, had gotten very bad toward the end of the escape. A bartender who had come from the Empire Room to help was one of the last people to reach the safety of the loading dock. He thought that there was little or no time to spare when he got out: *It seemed like everything went black at the door, and the smoke started to pour out. We got off the loading dock immediately and moved into the parking lot.*

Ron Schilling was also among the last group to leave the building from the kitchen. After exiting at that location, he stayed in the driveway below the loading dock for a few seconds just to be sure that everyone made it to safety and then headed through the parking lot toward the front of the building. At this time he had no inkling at all about the problem that had developed in the Cabaret Room: *I thought everybody was out of the place.* Still the events in the front of the building had inflicted a devastating blow to his state of mind. And soon after he reached the front of the building he found his brother Rick in a comparable state of distress.

Rick had come to the front driveway after unlocking the exit door on the east side of the building (Exit C on Diagram No. 8) so that firefighters could get to the vicinity of the Zebra Room. While standing inside that exit door he had seen for himself that the fire had broken away from that small room and had spread through the main corridor toward the back of the building. Nonetheless he had rushed to the front driveway believing, or at least hoping, that it was not too late to control the fire and save the building.

Fire departments from three cities in the area had responded to the first alarm and had equipment at the scene at that time. At least four trucks that could pump water and more than twenty-five firefighters were already on the hill. The trucks were hooked up to two hydrants near the club and one down the driveway, and the firemen were busy at two tasks, laying water lines according to previously laid plans and responding to reports received on arrival that people were trapped in the front of the building and on the roof. Very quickly the demands at the scene had outstripped the capacity of the three departments. Already they had put in a call for additional help.

From the beginning Rick thought it absolutely essential to get a water line through the exit door he had unlocked at the back of the Viennese Room, and he pressed that viewpoint vigorously on his arrival at the front of the building. For obvious reasons, though, not every fireman he confronted was in a position to respond immediately to his demand. Most were attending to preassigned responsibilities. As promptly as possible, however, an order was issued and firemen started around the east side of the building with a line. Rather quickly it became obvious to Rick that the effort of the firefighters to get to the fire in time would fail. Understandably he lost his patience with the futile effort and finally his composure: *He was screaming and hollering at us to get in there with water.* By the time his brother Ron arrived out front and located him he had partially regained his composure and had begun to turn his thoughts to concerns of a more personal nature, the safety and whereabouts of his wife and daughter.

The third brother was also at the front of the club at this moment but not with Ron and Rick. Scott was on the roof of the building with an employee and a fireman. A little earlier he had encountered near the front entrance the second floor headwaiter who delivered some disquieting news: *I'm concerned about the people in the Crystal rooms; I'm not sure everybody got out.* From what he had seen at the spiral stairway following flashover the youngest Schilling had plenty of reason to share that concern. So the two men promptly sought out a fireman, grabbed a ladder from one of the fire trucks, scaled the front wall of the building (exterior to the Check Room), and moved across the first floor roof to the door the headwaiter had earlier tried to open from inside the upstairs corridor (see Diagram No. 2). Once again that door proved to be a barrier. It was locked and could not be opened from the outside without a key.

After obtaining an axe from one of the trucks on the ground, the three men managed to break through to the corridor. Thick black smoke poured through the door as soon as it was opened and headed for the night sky. None of the three standing there doubted how bad it must be inside. The second floor of the building was clearly incapable of sustaining life for very long. The fireman had an air tank and gas mask on the roof but the two were not compatible. So he forged through the smoke without a tank and moved into the building a few feet toward the upstairs dining rooms. From that position he yelled through the smoke and darkness for survivors and waited for answers that never came. In a few seconds he returned to the roof and joined the others in a hasty retreat to the safety of the driveway.

Meanwhile the three fire departments had managed to get a water line on the roof, two lines through the main entrance toward the fire in the barroom and beyond, and a fourth and fifth through the kitchen door on the west side of the building. Several additional fire trucks had arrived on the hill to take up positions that had been preplanned in case of a large-scale fire. Approximately sixty firefighters were now under the command of the Southgate fire chief and the number was growing rapidly. More than two thousand people were standing around the club watching exits that were all emitting heavy volumes of smoke. Above the building a dark cloud hung in a clear sky that had not yet been completely darkened by night, and from every direction the sound of sirens announced the approach of emergency and rescue vehicles. In no more than twenty minutes the area around the Supper Club had acquired all the characteristics of a major catastrophe.

The worst was yet to come. The fire chief was still trying to pinpoint the exact location of the blaze. He knew only that he had a tremendous fire somewhere in the large building. At this time he received another report of people being trapped. The earlier ones had proved false, but this one involved the showroom at the back of the building. Immediately the chief dispatched a couple of men to the back to check on the report. The operation at the front of the building continued under his direction. In a very short time an urgent call for help came to the front by radio transmission: *We've got a real mess back here. People are trapped in the showroom, perhaps hundreds of them. We need all the help you can spare.*

The water lines at the front of the building were immediately abandoned under orders of the chief. The principal mission of the firefighters was suddenly changed to rescue. All but a handful headed around the building in the direction of the showroom exits. The fire chief promptly put in a radio call for more rescue units, all available ambulances in the county and surrounding area, and more pumpers. Even without visiting the back of the building he knew now that the situation at Beverly Hills had developed into a "signal 69"—an all-out disaster.

3

The smoke in the service bar at the northeast corner of the building appeared extremely intimidating after the evacuation through Exit A ended. Neither the bartender who had already once tried unsuccessfully to reach the cocktail waiter nor any of the other two or three employees who had joined him at the exit were eager to challenge the conditions inside the building. But the cries for help from near the Cabaret Room quickly proved to be irresistible as it soon became clear that the people hidden by the smoke were hopelessly trapped. So one by one the bartender and the employees overcame their concerns for personal safety and plunged through the smoke to test the conditions inside the exit.

No more than halfway throughout the service bar they encountered a few patrons crawling around on the floor trying to find their way to the exit. But they also encountered conditions no less punishing than they expected—staggering heat, thick smoke, and air so toxic that a single breath burned all the way to the bottom of their lungs. At least one of the employees found the punishment inside the exit unbearable and retreated to the outside. The others discovered that they could survive long enough in the service bar to grab a patron and get to the exit without undue personal risk, and that's what they began to do.

Soon they got some badly needed assistance from an experienced though unexpected source. From the garden area at the back of the building the off-duty captain from the Cincinnati Fire Department saw the developments at Exit A and rushed across the grounds to join the rescue effort in its earliest stages. When he arrived none of the trapped patrons was able to get to the outside without help. Smoke was pouring out of the service bar at the time, and the employees involved in the rescue were trying without success to shield their faces with handkerchiefs.

The fireman got near the floor at the exit door where there was some oxygen, and moved in a direct line toward the screams emanating from the rear of the service bar. Never in his long experience had he seen anything even remotely approaching what he found at the showroom doors:

> *There was just a wall of arms and heads, people piled up at the double doors screaming and waving their arms. I called out for a couple of the employees to give me a hand and I started pulling people, reaching for heads and arms, coats, or anything. They were piled four or five feet high all the way across the doorway. It was just a nightmare.*

Near the bottom of the pile was the cocktail waiter. He was in fair shape though feeling almost numb and thinking he had waited interminably for help to come. From his place underneath the smoke he had watched the bartender and others work their way through the service bar toward him and had helped himself tremendously by controlling his emotions under the most torturous circumstances imaginable:

> *I talked to myself while lying there. I thought it was all over but I kept saying, "Get hold of yourself and take it easy." When you've got a crowd of screaming people around you that's hard to do. It seemed like a long time I laid there and I tried not to breathe. I held my breath so that I wouldn't use much air.*

As the fireman and others worked to free the people above him the waiter began to feel more certain about survival. But he wasn't so sure about the prospects for most of those trapped with him. Many had stopped screaming, and it wasn't because of the arrival of help.

Exhaustion came quickly in the heat and smoke of the service bar. A lack of oxygen ultimately conquered almost all of the rescuers. Some were subdued more quickly than others. The off-duty fireman worked at the showroom doors freeing patrons from the mass of tangled bodies there and pushing them to the employees for removal to the outside until he could barely lift his own arms to the level of his face. But like the small group of employees working in the smoke alongside him he pushed himself beyond his own limits. Under the circumstances even that seemed inadequate:

> *I had this woman by the arms trying to pull her free, and down out of the smoke, but I couldn't do it. I tried to pull her horizontally but her legs must have been locked in with other people. I stood up and grabbed more of her arms, and she even grabbed mine. I tried to pull her free but I couldn't. The heat was so intense. I feel ashamed of myself but I had to leave her.*

He retreated through the service bar toward safety, coughing smoke from his lungs and gasping for breath like everyone else. He reached the exit door just as additional employees arrived to help with the rescue. Scott Schilling and the bartender who earlier stood by his side at the Zebra Room entrance arrived from the front of the building. Dick Schilling's brother-in-law and the busboy who made the announcement from the showroom stage were there from the area at the back of the Garden Room. Some others from the kitchen and elsewhere had also come to help.

At about this time the fire apparently vented itself somewhere in the building by burning through the roof because the density of the smoke inside Exit A dropped slightly. It was not quite as dark as before and that helped the rescuers a little. Inside the service bar, however, conditions remained survivable by the barest margin. The fire in the Cabaret Room was expanding, particularly on the south wall and near the rear doors, and it was sending ever increasing levels of heat through the service bar. The air was "hotter than hell" and the smoke no more than eighteen inches off the floor. It was still impossible to stay in the small room for a very long period of time.

Under these circumstances the employees struggled feverishly to untangle the pile of bodies stacked in the showroom doorway. The routine they used was simple:

*The voices called out for help from a pile of people two-and-a-half to three feet high. I couldn't see a thing. I felt around and grabbed the person who held out his hands, pulled him to the outside, and returned for someone else.*

But the difficulties they confronted at the showroom doors were truly overwhelming:

*Whoever grabbed on and held the tightest I'd pull out. Once I got to the door, where I could get a breath, someone else would help out and I'd return. Again I'd feel around until someone grabbed me. I'd take him out, holding my breath, with no time to spare. After a while I couldn't return. I was just totally exhausted.*

*There was a woman we couldn't get out because others were on her legs. We just about pulled her arms out of their sockets but we couldn't move her. Then there was this man on top, a heavy guy reaching his arms up. It was my thought to get him off the top so I could do something with those on the bottom. I had him wrap his arms around my neck and I pushed against the door as hard as I could. I moved him about two feet and by this time he was out of it. He didn't have strength to help me and I didn't have the strength to lift him. He just looked at me and shook his head; there was nothing I could do. And then there was a young girl. She was on top, not screaming or anything, but in fine shape. I started to walk out with her but her leg was wrapped around a table. I don't know how the table got there, but her leg was wrapped around it and she couldn't pull it loose. I can't tell you the ones I left there. I couldn't take it any more. That's when I left. It was terrible, just terrible.*

4

The physician who made the call to the hospital reached the northwest corner of the building and started across the grounds at the back of the club. Things had changed substantially during his journey to the front driveway. Fire was now pouring through the exit doors at the end of the north-south corridor. The Garden Room had taken on both a terrifying and spectacular appearance. It was *a mass of flames and looked like a greenhouse full of orange fire*. No one in the large crowd near that room could have believed that survival inside the building was possible for even a second, and no one could have been sure that the occupants had all made it to safety ahead of the fire.

A large number of people moved aimlessly through the garden area trying to locate relatives and friends from whom they were separated. All were extremely nervous. A few were hysterical. At least two women attempted to reenter the burning building to search for lost husbands. Except for the intervention of employees they would have succeeded. At some point a man looking for a lost relative or friend yelled for him by name. He did so loud enough to be heard above the noise of the fire. He may or may not have succeeded in finding his relative or friend, but he did add immeasurably to the sense of disorder at the back of the building. Others started almost immediately to do the same thing, and soon the noise in the crowd outside the Garden Room matched the roar of the blazing fire inside the club.

The physician moved through the pandemonium of the garden as promptly as possible and headed toward the northeast corner of the building. By the time he reached the grounds outside Exit A the need for his services had grown beyond his anticipation. Near the chapel a woman was stretched out in the grass gasping for breath while her husband held her head in his lap and administered as much comfort as he could. Others in the same vicinity struggled in a variety of ways to rid themselves of the after-affects of smoke inhalation. Most were on their feet getting help from a group of employees and patrons. None seemed to be in serious trouble.

Nearer the exit there was a group lying in the grass that seemed to need more immediate attention: *They were alive but they were just black from the smoke. Their clothes were black, their faces were black, and their mouths were black.* They were coughing and had trouble breathing. None had walked to the outside without help. Rescue workers had dragged them through the service bar and had left them in the grass for others to move away from the building. As he turned his attention to this group the physician noticed that most of his colleagues with whom he had dined just a few minutes earlier were already near the exit trying to help.

The work inside the exit continued at a furious pace. The rescuers carried victim after victim to the outside, ripped open their shirts and removed their ties so they could breathe, and left them a few feet from the building to return for more. The physicians and others moved them as quickly as possible toward the chapel and attended to their medical needs as best they could. To the west of the chapel, in the area outside the Garden Room, a group of employees and patrons tried to help in other ways. They worked to unite families and parties that had gotten separated during evacuation, consoled and calmed the emotionally distressed, and struggled to move the crowd farther away from the building.

Only the last of these endeavors proved to be virtually unmanageable. The crowd in the garden had gotten huge. Word of the problems in the Cabaret Room had reached the throng in the front parking lot. In large numbers people had come to the back of the building to join the large crowd already there. They gathered in small groups near the building, as though partially in a daze, and watched the fire in the Garden Room and the activities near Exit A. Efforts to move them away from the fire were largely unsuccessful until the employees got some unexpected help from developments inside the building.

The glass that constituted most of the north wall of the Garden Room suddenly exploded outward because of the enormous buildup of heat inside the structure. At almost the same moment other loud blasts occurred somewhere inside the building in rapid succession. None of the firefighters at the scene paid much attention to the explosions. They understood the reason for them and knew that such explosions are a common occurrence at a major fire. Gas pockets inside the burning building had suddenly ignited after coming into contact with an oxygen supply. The people at the back of the building, however, reacted much differently to the explosions. Most were sure that the whole structure was ready to explode at any moment. The group working with the injured in the vicinity of the chapel moved them a little farther away from the building, and all of the others moved rapidly away from the fire. A large number hurried to the east side of the building and started over the steep embankment toward the highway, enhancing rumors that served to hamper the work of the physicians and the small army of helpers who had joined them outside Exit A.

Word spread among the people at the back of the building that an underground gas line ran through the garden area from one corner of the club to the other. The crowd reacted immediately to that rumor out of fear of a worse explosion than those they had already heard. A few more moved toward the highway. Those attending to the injured concluded that it was necessary to move them a second time. Toward the end of this effort the crowd had turned its attention to an "imminent disaster" that was the subject of still another rumor. A set of high tension power lines that crossed the property at the back of the building was supposedly about to fall. The injured were moved once again.

During this time additional victims of the fire were being dragged from the service bar and left near the exit. The doctors and paramedics working there were moving from place to place administering aid, issuing instructions to patients and helpers, but gradually feeling overwhelmed by the circumstances developing around them. Darkness was closing in. The injured were now scattered over a wide area around the chapel, and their number continued to grow. Drugs that had been packed for a disaster were on the way to the club in a police car, but for the moment the doctors had very few medical supplies with which to work. Rescue squads had arrived on the hill with additional oxygen, but the need for it had already far outstripped the supply: *People were suffering from smoke inhalation. They needed oxygen. And we had no way to give it to them.*

In addition, those that were being dragged to the outside now were in a worse condition. At first they needed relief mostly from smoke inhalation. Not too many had suffered even minor burns, but as the rescue work inside the exit continued the situation changed drastically:

> *I noticed that these people were burned, twisting and turning, saying please help me. One man was burned on his back; his skin had just rolled up on him. He was burned in the face and bleeding in the forehead.*

> ● ● ●

> *There was a lady burned so bad her hands were black. I thought her legs were black because of colored stockings. But I touched her and discovered that the stockings had burned on her. She was burned so bad she was in total shock, sitting up like a frog, saying nothing, not even moaning.*

> ● ● ●

> *He was burned on his back. I didn't try to take his clothes off; I asked him where he was burned. He said his back. His face was bleeding. He was burned on his face and on his hands. He was saying, "Can't somebody give me something for pain." I said, "Try and keep quiet until we get an ambulance." He said, "Oh God, can't somebody do something."*

Drugs and dressings were desperately needed to treat and relieve the badly burned. Neither was available in ample supply. A couple of nurses used napkins to cover burns. Patrons and employees ripped off their garments—shirts and tee shirts from the men and slips from the women—to be used for the same purpose. The fountain in the garden was used to wet the makeshift dressing before application. There was little else that could be done for the burn victims at the scene of the fire. The physician who had made the initial hospital call located a member of a rescue squad who had a two-way radio. This time he called a police dispatcher: *I am a physician. I'm at the Beverly Hills Supper Club. Call the hospitals in the area and tell them to prepare for casualties.*

5

Firemen arrived at Exit B from the front of the building with air tanks strapped to their backs. They climbed to the landing outside the exit quickly and prepared to enter the smoke-filled hallway on the south side of the Cabaret Room. Below the landing, not too far from the exit, a small group of musicians stood in the grass trying to account for the members of their band. At least six of their friends, each of whom had reacted to the busboy's evacuation order with indifference, had not yet made it to safety. Others in the large crowd on the hillside were engaged in the same endeavor.

John Davidson was still near the exit trying to get sight of his music director. The showroom manager was a little closer to the front driveway looking for hostesses and cocktail waitresses who worked under her supervision in the Cabaret Room. Husbands and wives in various stages of hysteria rushed from place to place trying to locate their lost mates. Scores of others moved frantically through the crowd looking for relatives or friends separated from them. For some there was quick success and exhilaration:

> *I looked and looked but couldn't find her. Then I found her fifteen or twenty feet away. She was on the ground crying, with a girl in a red dress trying to comfort her.*

For others there was only disappointment and more anguish:

> *Finally, I saw this man who had on a blue suit and white shirt like my husband wore that night. I thought, "Oh God, that's him" and I ran up and grabbed him. When he turned around it wasn't him. I backed off. And I thought, "Oh God, I don't know what I'm going to do."*

A man still inside the exit door, and in considerably more distress than this woman, must surely have had the exact same thought flash through his mind. From near the center of the Cabaret Room he had started toward Exit B hand in hand with his wife and four others. Just outside the showroom doors, before fire spread violently down the hallway toward the exit, he had gotten lost in the smoke and separated from his companions. In the near total darkness created by that smoke he had simply maintained a straight course on leaving the showroom and had ended up in the small service bar on the other side of the narrow hallway (see Diagrams No. 1 and 7).

From inside the service bar he had listened for what seemed like an eternity to the distinctive voice of his wife screaming for him from outside the building. He had searched through the small room in darkness and desperation for an avenue of escape. All he had managed to find was a door that couldn't be opened from the inside, because it had no handle, and an ice machine full of ice. The smoke and heat around him had gotten so bad that he had removed his coat, filled it with ice, and put it over his head and face. After that the conditions in the room had grown worse, and he had begun to contemplate putting his whole body in the ice machine. But then from the hallway he had crossed to get to the service bar his thoughts were interrupted by the most welcome inquiry anyone has ever heard: "Is anybody in here? Is anybody in here?"

Between the showroom doors and the exit two firemen with air tanks stood in the smoke trying to locate the position of survivors. Very few of those still alive were able to respond to the inquiry. The man trapped in the service bar strained to let them know of his presence, but the punishing conditions to which his throat had been subjected had reduced his voice to a whisper. He screamed as loud as he could but barely a sound penetrated through the smoke.

He banged with his fists on the walls and the door of the service bar, and the firemen heard. They rescued him from the small room, dragged him to the exit door, and handed him to a police officer for removal to a safe place below the landing.

In a short time the officer located a woman who had earlier denounced him violently under a mistaken belief that he had tried to block the exit opening: *Lady, you said your husband had on a white shirt and a blue suit. I think we may have him over here.* He led her through the frenzied crowd to a spot on a hillside not too far below the building. Barely conscious, her husband was lying in the grass, receiving oxygen from a tank, waiting to be placed in an ambulance, and facing an extended stay in a hospital. Still he was immeasurably more fortunate than those he left inside the exit door.

Near the showroom doors the firemen had encountered a situation not substantially different from the one that existed in the service bar at Exit A:

> *I was covered to my chest, with only my arms and head exposed. The smoke was heavy and it was difficult to breathe. The people to my right were already dead and I couldn't tell about those behind me. But there was no breathing sounds. Neither they nor I could move. At that point two firemen appeared on my left and moved a person to the outside. I raised my left hand to indicate life. They pulled my shoulders with no success. I asked them to free my legs and that was difficult because of the bodies on them. Soon my knees appeared and they carried me to the outside.*

> * * *

> *The fireman kept putting his hand through and saying, "There's someone there, grab hold of my hand and I will pull you out." There was a man on my leg and a girl across my chest. I got to my feet from under the man and somehow hoisted the girl up. She was out but there was still life there, so I pushed her up to the man. After they pulled her out they got me.*

On this side of the Cabaret Room the mass of tangled bodies was a little closer to the outside and smaller than the one near Exit A. The rescue effort at this location should have been much easier and more successful. But it wasn't.

Time was extremely short for rescue of those wedged in the hallway outside the showroom doors. The firemen untangled bodies as rapidly as they could and dragged them to the landing outside the exit. It was obvious that the clock had become an extremely formidable adversary. Earlier the noise level in the narrow hallway had been almost deafening. Now it was quiet enough to hear the sounds of people on the floor trying to secure a breath of fresh air, and there were very few of those sounds to be heard. Under the circumstances there was nothing more the firemen could do to improve the chances for survival of the living. Their effort at the showroom doors was already as furious as it could possibly be.

## 6

By this time the rescue and firefighting operation at Beverly Hills was massive. Additional trucks had arrived on the hill to pump water on the fire, and scores of firemen had come to the scene from surrounding cities and counties. The fire chief had established a command post at the front of the building from which to direct the operation, but he quickly found himself inundated with responsibilities that were growing more burdensome with every moment. Fortunately he got some relief at a crucial point in time from an unexpected source.

His predecessor in office had heard of the fire by news flash and had come to the club as fast as he could. Once on the hill he located the command post and engaged the chief in brief conversation:

*Is there any thing I can do to help?*
*Yes. We've got the damnedest situation you have ever seen in your life. It's really bad.*
*Would it help if I handled your dispatching?*
*Yes. We need extra ambulances and rescue vehicles, and we need them bad. Get what you can.*

The chief had yet had no opportunity for a personal inspection of the situation at the showroom exits. At the end of the conversation with his predecessor he left the command post and headed across the front driveway toward the west side of the club and the garden area at the back of the building.

As he passed the main entrance he noticed that the two water lines that had been dragged through those doors were then in use. Three firemen, only one of which was equipped with an air tank, had penetrated to the edge of the main bar to fight the fire in the front of the club. In that part of the building they had encountered plenty of fire to fight. The main dining room to their left was burning and the area to their right (toward the Zebra Room) was completely engulfed in flames. Ahead of them there was a glow in the Empire Room, clearly visible through the heavy black smoke that had accumulated there, and a roaring fire in the barroom itself. The air in the main bar and the rest of the front area was the hottest in the whole building. Except for a foot or so right on the floor it was not even bearable. Above their heads the three firefighters could hear the ominous sounds of a raging fire on the second floor. But they gave no immediate thoughts to retreat. Lying on their stomachs under the heat and smoke they continued to discharge heavy volumes of water on the circular bar and the burning walls of the barroom.

Outside the building the fire chief turned the southwest corner and hurried along the narrow driveway on the west side of the club. He hesitated outside the kitchen exit long enough to ascertain that he had two men in that room with water lines and then moved on toward the back of the building. As he rounded the northwest corner of the club and entered the west part of the garden area he saw for the first time that the structure was indeed on fire. Before this he had seen only smoke. In the Garden Room he saw what looked like the inside of a furnace. A number of firemen had just penetrated the exit doors with water lines, but the battle against the fire in the big dining room was clearly being lost.

The chief moved on through the garden area toward Exit A to face what he had painfully been expecting to find:

> *By the time I got there, the garden outside the exit was full of people lying in a prone position. They were facing both up and down. Some were covered; they were obviously dead. It was a gruesome scene at best.*

At the exit door firemen and employees were still at the task of dragging patrons from the burning building. Not all of the victims were dead. In the grass near the service bar, doctors and nurses were administering mouth-to-mouth resuscitation and heart massage trying to revive some of those left near the exit by the rescue workers. The fire chief was a man of considerable compassion. He tried hard to control his emotions, but tears dropped from his eyes as he looked for the first time on the sight at the back of the building.

He moved toward the chapel where the physicians and paramedics had established a medical aid station. On the way there he was angered by the sight of people plundering the bodies of the dead for wallets, jewelry, and other valuables. He looked for police help, but the only officer in the vicinity was inside the exit working with the rescue team. At the chapel he found several of the men under his command temporarily out of commission because of smoke inhalation and heat exhaustion. One couldn't remember his name and had his eyes half-closed. Some of the others were acting strange because of lack of oxygen. All were under the watchful eyes of the medical personnel who had directed them to stand aside for awhile. None seemed for the moment in serious jeopardy. So the chief left the chapel, walked quickly to the northeast corner of the club, and entered the building at Exit A.

The smoke inside the exit had lifted a little more but the heat was still terrific. From the service bar he saw fire in the Cabaret Room and observed a rescue effort near the showroom doors that was unorganized but as effective under the circumstances as could be expected:

> Firemen and employees alike were carrying people out, on their shoulders or dragging them feet first or hands first, getting them to the outside as best they could.

Soon after his arrival one of the firemen in the service bar recognized the chief, assured him that things were under reasonable control, and suggested that perhaps he should not run the risk involved in being there.

The chief left the service bar, turned the northeast corner of the building and went to Exit B. The scene outside that exit was similar in appearance to the one outside Exit A except that it was smaller in scale. Fewer rescue workers were dragging patrons to the landing outside the exit. Fewer bodies were lying on the steep embankment below the building, and only two firefighters had suffered the adverse effects of smoke inhalation. One of the two was in serious condition, however. He had been pulled unconscious from the building by other firemen and carried down the steps from the landing feet first by a couple of patrons. In the presence of the chief someone pronounced him dead: *I fell apart. He is a good friend of mine. But I discovered when I checked him that he wasn't dead. We called for an ambulance and in the meantime somebody worked on him, gave him mouth-to-mouth, and he recovered.* Another of the chief's friends, the officer in charge of the rescue work at the exit, was not in much better shape. The heat and smoke to which he had been subjected inside the building had rendered him delirious. The chief ordered him to stand aside for awhile and then departed for the front of the building. He had inspected the whole site. He left the east side of the building in despair: *I just had to leave. I felt like a general in a war must feel. I had to leave.*

At the command post the mayor of the City of Southgate was calling for help from the Kentucky State Police and every other police agency within reach of the club. At the end of his trek around the building, the chief joined him there and assessed the overall situation. The rescue operation at the showroom exits was running as smoothly as possible and still had top priority. Rescue units and ambulances were arriving at the club in substantial numbers. The driveway, though crowded from the highway to the top of the hill, was open for emergency vehicles. Water lines had been laid on all four sides of the building, and fire chiefs from several other departments were directing the work of a force now numbering in the hundreds. Firemen were on the roof and inside nearly every exit with water. The fire had spread to every part of the structure except the extreme front around the foyer and the kitchen. The building was headed for total destruction. There was very little to feel good about. As the chief put it: *The situation was out of control.*

## 7

The clock moved well past ten and ticked toward eleven. The work force inside Exit A was very different from the one that started the rescue there. No longer was it made up mostly of employees. The bartender who had initiated the effort by trying to reach the cocktail waiter trapped at the showroom doors was gone. He had departed the building for the final time after finding the body of the bartender who earlier had helped him direct the evacuation through the service bar:

> *We were getting people from behind the bar when we found Steve. He had waited a couple of seconds too long to try to get out. I dragged his body to the outside and left for home. I couldn't take it anymore.*

Dick Schilling's brother-in-law was no longer involved in the rescue work. He had succumbed to the conditions of the service bar and was on the ground near the chapel awaiting hospitalization. Others from the original band of rescuers had given up the effort for a different reason: *The last person I pulled out was in bad condition. I did not reenter the building again. The ones we were pulling out looked as though they could not recover.* Scott Schilling was still inside the exit doing what he could. So was the bartender who had stood with Scott at the Zebra Room entrance before fire spread to the back of the building. Both were near physical exhaustion but neither had given serious thought to surrendering the building to the fire.

The rescue work here had changed in tone and character. It had ceased to be disorganized and frantic and was now methodical. There was some occasional conversation among the workers, although always pertinent to the rescue, and some noise from a water line brought through the exit door to provide protection against the fire. Otherwise it was quiet in both the service bar and northeast corner of the Cabaret Room. There was a conspicuous absence of noise in the vicinity of the bodies stretched out on the floor beyond the showroom doors.

All of the bodies in the service bar had been removed to the outside, and so had the ones that had blocked the showroom doorway. The rescuers were in the Cabaret Room working to remove the bodies from there. The extreme urgency that had once been attached to their mission was missing. The quiet that had settled over the northeast corner of the showroom was no doubt partially responsible.

The rescue work on the other side of the showroom inside the doorway at Exit B was nearing conclusion. None of the firemen had been able to penetrate into the Cabaret Room from that location because of the fire. So the number of victims beyond the showroom doors was unknown. The rescuers had successfully untangled the bodies stacked in the hallway leading to the exit and had removed most of them to the outside. As they worked to remove the last few, the final rescue operation at Exit B got underway. An assistant fire chief entered the building from the landing outside the exit, turned right in the narrow hallway beyond the exit door, and headed toward the backstage dressing rooms (see Diagram No. 7). None of the other workers had ventured in that direction.

Unlike those workers near the showroom doors, the assistant chief had no equipment for protection against the effects of smoke and toxic gases. He felt, however, that he could move a few feet inside the exit door without undue risk. So he dropped to his belly and crawled to the corridor that ran alongside the dressing rooms in a northerly direction toward the showroom stage (see Diagram No. 7). The conditions in that corridor were as bad as those in the hallway outside the Cabaret Room. Breathing was extremely difficult, even while lying in a prone position, and it was brutally hot almost to the floor. Nonetheless the assistant chief decided to venture a little farther from the exit door, left the corridor still crawling slowly on his belly, and entered the first dressing room off to his right.

Just a few feet inside that small room he found four or five bodies lying on the floor. None seemed to have suffered serious burns but all were apparently dead. From head to toe they were covered with black soot that looked and felt like coal dust. The assistant chief called to the other rescuers for help and started the exhausting job of removing the bodies to the landing outside the exit. Then with a fresh supply of air in his lungs, and the last body on the way to the grass below the landing, he reentered the building and returned to the corridor outside the dressing rooms. There was still no fire in the area but the sounds coming from the Cabaret Room were more threatening than before: *I could hear flames out there; I could hear them cracking.*

This time he moved farther up the corridor toward the stage. In the hallway he found some musical instruments and carrying cases in disarray, pushed them out of his path, and crawled into the second dressing room off to the right. Near the middle of that room he found three or four bodies clad in tuxedoes, members of the band who had reacted slowly to the evacuation order. And then he found not too far away a group of perhaps as many as fifteen people "just stacked one on top of the other"—patrons who had gotten lost no doubt on the way from the showroom exit. As he had done before, he called for help and started for the exit dragging one of the bodies along the floor with him. He knew there was little time left to complete the debilitating work inside the exit. The fire in the Cabaret Room was rapidly closing in on the rescuers.

8

The number of bodies lying in the grass near the chapel and below the landing outside Exit B got larger and larger. As it did the crowd at the back of the building became quieter and more subdued. The physicians and other medical personnel continued to move through the area administering aid to the living and checking for the possibility of heartbeats in the dead. As rapidly as possible the injured and disabled were being loaded into ambulances and other rescue vehicles for removal to hospitals. More and more of the patrons and employees were finding the situation around the showroom exits a little too gruesome to bear:

> *I know some first aid and so I asked a policeman what I could do to help. He said, "Check and see who's alive." I looked down and there*

*wasn't anybody alive. I got a little sick. I went to a woman, and she wasn't breathing either. I just turned and went down the hill. I was numb.*

...

*I saw these people lying on the ground. They looked like they were asleep. They weren't burned or anything, and their faces weren't covered. I almost stepped on them before I realized they didn't look quite natural. I asked a man nearby if they were hurt. He said that they were all dead. I turned and ran.*

At some point hundreds of additional people descended the steep embankment on the east side of the building to get away from the fire. Rope was provided by firefighters to make the difficult trip down the hill a little easier. At about the same time police and fire officials began to ask nonessential personnel to leave the premises. In substantial numbers and in various directions patrons and employees headed toward the highway below the club. The crowd standing around the building dwindled in size, but it did not totally disperse.

Lots of patrons were still trying to find people with whom they had come to the club. Very few were willing to leave the site of the fire. Most of them continued for a while longer to circle the building and crisscross the grounds searching through the darkness for sight of a relative or friend. For some the search ended rather quickly. The thirteen-year-old boys from the barmitzvah party had located their parents within a few minutes of their own evacuation. For others the search extended well into the night:

*All ten of us separated when fire entered the Cabaret Room. Within an hour I had found all of my family except my wife. I thought she was surely dead. But I found her on the highway at about one o'clock.*

For others the painful effort did not end on the night of the fire, nor did it end on the hill surrounding the club. It ended only with the identification of a charred body in a temporary morgue set up in an armory several miles from the site of the disaster.

## 9

During the last phases of the rescue work at the showroom exits, the news media arrived at the scene of the fire in great force. All of the local television stations, the three national networks, and a host of newspaper reporters got there at about the same time. From the moment it started, the media coverage of the disaster at Beverly Hills became to some extent part of the disaster itself. The fire chief was at the command post during this time weighing among other things the advisability of putting more water into the building through the roof. More water would have meant more steam and more steam would have meant additional jeopardy for firefighters, rescue workers, and others still in the building. The mayor of Southgate approached the command post while the chief and others contemplated such matters and informed him that members of the press corps were on the hill and wanted an interview with the person in charge of the fire and rescue operation.

To say the least the fire chief was not very receptive. The building was in full blaze at the time. Firemen were inside nearly every exit with no guaranteed avenue of escape from the building should that become necessary. Ambulances and rescue vans were speeding up the driveway and back down with injured patrons on the way to local hospitals. At neither of the showroom exits was the rescue work complete, and nobody at either one could have known how many people were still trapped inside the structure. Scores of bodies were lying motionless in the grass on two sides of the club, and the number was growing all the time. Under the circumstances the fire chief thought that an interview with the news media was too much to ask, and so he refused.

Before long, however, the powers of the press and the tick of the clock put unbeatable pressures upon him. This time the clock was moving toward late hour newscasts on local television stations all across the eastern half of the United States. The tragic dimensions of the Beverly Hills Supper Club disaster were neither clear nor complete at this moment, but the fire had nonetheless already become a spectacular media event, an electrifying lead story for any news report. And it was recognized and treated as such by the reporters who had managed to get to the scene early. Their normal pursuit of a story and their determination to have questions of importance authoritatively answered led them to pressure the mayor for an interview with the fire chief. That pressure ultimately was felt by the fire chief and had its intended effect. He left the command post in the hands of one of his trusted assistants and headed away from the building to meet the press.

His encounter with the news media started at a station set up in the driveway some distance from the front of the building. For the chief it did not begin on a purely positive note: *I knew exactly what they were trying to do—to make it spectacular of course. They wanted a view of the burning building in the background. And that's what they got.* For the next thirty to forty-five minutes he stood in the driveway with ambulances streaming past him, on camera the whole time, struggling to field questions about the nature and scope of the tragedy. He gave separate interviews to correspondents of each of the three national television networks and then spent considerable time with reporters and cameramen representing local television stations and newspapers.

From its less than propitious beginning, the encounter between the chief and representatives of the media deteriorated steadily:

> *Every one of them tried to put words in my mouth, insofar as four or five or six hundred people being dead. And they kept trying to say, "There are thousands of people left in there, isn't that right?" They didn't want to listen to the truth. They wanted to make it even more spectacular, if it could have been in fact.*

Unhappily, the chief finished the session in the driveway and returned to his command post to attend to matters considered by him to be more important. There he encountered additional members of the press corps waiting with more questions:

> *I told them absolutely not. That's when I had an argument with one of them who was relying on the First Amendment to the Constitution and the public's right to know. What I told him I couldn't repeat here. We had an argument and I walked away from the man.*

Eventually, the fire chief approached the highest police authority he could find to ask that the press be moved as far from the site of the fire as possible. Of course, this was not possible, and the chief returned to his more important responsibilities. He was left, however, with very bad feelings about his experience with the press: *After a time they hampered my ability to think, to work, and to carry out certain required assignments.*

10

The news coverage of the Supper Club fire was of particular interest in two households far from Southgate. In the basement of the governor's mansion in the capitol city of Kentucky a state trooper sat with his eyes glued to a television set tuned to late developing news from the site of the fire. The governor was in an upstairs bedroom preparing to retire for the evening. The governor knew of the fire in the club from television reports he had seen earlier, but knew nothing of the magnitude of the disaster.

As the news from the scene grew progressively worse the trooper picked up a telephone and called upstairs as he had been instructed to do: *The situation at Beverly Hills is a lot worse than first reported.* The governor promptly returned to the basement of the mansion to monitor the news coverage of the fire more closely. Within thirty minutes he knew that a trip to northern Kentucky was essential. He called for a car and prepared to leave as soon as possible.

In Fort Lauderdale, Florida, nearly a thousand miles away, another television set was receiving late news coverage of the fire. Watching that coverage was a man who had earlier received one of the worst telephone calls of his life. The call had come from a private telephone in a small restaurant located on the highway just below the site of the fire:

*Mr. Schilling, there's been a fire. The club is gone.*
*Gone? What do you mean it's gone?*
*I mean gone, burned down!*
*My God! How bad is it?*

*Well, it's bad, really bad.*
*Are the boys all right?*
*Yes.*
*Get them. I want to talk with them.*

The caller had been one of the club's most trusted employees. The conversation with Schilling had been brief and painfully to the point, and it had served to send the employee back up the driveway toward the building looking for Rick and Ron. It had rendered Dick Schilling momentarily senseless. Everything imaginable had flashed through his mind almost instantly, and when he had tried to occupy himself while waiting for a return call from his sons he made a bad choice. He had turned the television set on.

Dick Schilling was not in good health at the time. He was recovering from recent major surgery. The employee who had called about the fire had known of this and had spared him the woeful details of the tragedy at his club, but the news coverage that spilled out into his living room from the scene of the fire was not so considerate. It originated from a driveway that Schilling had used thousands of times in the previous eight years. It purported to provide live coverage. In the background the building was engulfed in flames from front to back and side to side. The words of the news correspondent were utterly and totally devastating: *Scores of patrons and employees are injured. Hundreds are dead. And hundreds of others are still trapped somewhere in the building.*

Dick Schilling no longer needed to talk with his sons. Like the governor of Kentucky, the news report convinced him he was needed at Southgate. *I don't care if I die. I've got to get up there and see what's happening. I can't stay down here.* His physician advised him not to go. He got ready and left at the earliest possible moment.

11

A representative of the governor's office arrived on the hill at some point during the late evening and sought out the mayor of Southgate. The mayor sought out the fire chief. The chief was still stinging from his encounter with the press: *That's your bailiwick. You take care of the governor's office. To hell with them. I've got this building to take care of.* He did have a fire scene to care for but there was very little he could do for the building. He and his assistant had just completed a reassessment of their situation:

> *We can't put out more lines. We don't have any additional water. There are no more doorways to go through with lines. And the fire—it's gotten away from us. It's out of control.*

More than seventy-five firemen and rescue workers were still inside the burning building at "God only knows where." The chief turned his attention to their safety. He left the command post after a brief argument with the representative of the governor's office and headed around the west side of the building: *I think my main aim at that time was to get out of there before I said something to somebody that I would be regretting later on.* He stopped at the kitchen exit to check on his men. They were still inside the building but under no imminent threat, so he moved on to the garden where he found his brother, a Catholic priest, who had come to the site to administer last rites. They exchanged greetings, walked through the garden talking quietly about the situation before them, and separated near Exit A to go about their work.

On his first inspection of the exit, the chief had observed furious activity. The work of the firemen and employees was now much more subdued. By battering a hole through the brick wall behind the showroom stage, a couple of firefighters had pulled a live patron to the outside at approximately 11:00 P.M. Almost instantly that person had died in the grass on the east side of the building. Since then no one had been taken from the building alive. Nothing in sight at Exit A offered the chief much reason to believe that things were very likely to improve there. So he left for the front of the building convinced that no one remained alive inside the club except for the firefighters and rescue workers.

Probably sometime between 11:30 and 12:00 P.M., the head of a fire department from a city adjoining Southgate came to the command post for a conference with the Southgate chief to offer an assessment of the overall situation and some advice:

> *Chief, I think it's out of control. Definitely. And we're not going to do any good inside. We're not pulling anybody out at this point who is alive. And we're going to kill some people. Let's spread the word to the men to get the hell out of the building.*

He was unquestionably right. The Southgate chief knew that. No longer was there even a remote possibility that survivors of the fire remained inside the exits. Still the decision to abandon the building was not an easy one to make.

The rescue work had ended at Exit B but not at Exit A. Flames had filled the hallway on the south side of the Cabaret Room and had forced the firemen there to retreat to the landing outside the building. The fire had moved closer to the double doors leading into the northeast service bar but had not yet made it impossible to enter the showroom there. Scott Schilling, the bartender from the front barroom, a group of firemen, and perhaps a few others were still there trying to remove bodies from the northeast corner of the Cabaret Room. By this time all of them had been exposed to the punishing heat and smoke of the service bar for a long time. Scott and the bartender from the front bar had been there longer than anyone else. Both were very close to collapse: *I was real sick. I went to my knees. I couldn't walk.* And so were all of the others. Most had already pushed themselves well beyond the point of exhaustion.

The Southgate fire chief knew of this fact as he stood at the command post and weighed the advice given to him by his counterpart from the other department. He knew that the risk of being inside the building was steadily getting worse. Both the roof and walls of the structure had been sufficiently weakened by the fire to collapse at any moment. He searched for some reason to continue to expose his men to increasing risk. None could be found. Unquestionably it was time to surrender the building to the fire, so he issued an order for the firefighters and rescue workers to abandon the building as soon as possible.

## 12

The commissioner of the Kentucky State Police arrived on the hill outside the club barely before midnight. Several members of his force had arrived earlier. Most of the patrons and employees who had escaped the fire had moved or been moved off the hill by this time. All of the seriously injured had been taken to hospitals for treatment. The state police had fairly well established control over the site of the disaster. They had impounded all vehicles parked in the Beverly Hills lots and had called for buses to transport healthy people away from the scene. Only a few unauthorized people remained milling around the building, but the media was still there in force. Traffic in the vicinity of the fire was heavy although the highways and roads were open for emergency travel. The driveway in front of the club was lined with vehicles from bottom to top leaving one open lane. As the police commissioner moved up the driveway toward the fire, the last few firemen to comply with the chief's evacuation order were exiting the building through the front door.

At the top of the hill the commissioner left his automobile and headed in the direction of the command post. He located the fire chief without difficulty and soon found himself hearing first hand about the details of the disaster. Before leaving his home in central Kentucky ninety minutes earlier he had been told that the situation at the club was terrible. The facts and figures provided by the fire chief confirmed that report and more. At least seventy people had suffered serious and disabling injuries. Hundreds of others had suffered some degree of smoke inhalation. More than 130 bodies had been recovered from the Cabaret Room. Several of the people sent to local hospitals had been barely alive; some would surely fail to survive. And then of course there was the unknown factor, the number of bodies left behind when the rescue workers abandoned the building. The fire chief thought that there might be as many as two or three hundred additional fatalities in the Cabaret Room alone.

At the end of his conversation with the chief, the commissioner went to his car and called the nearest state police post. He asked that a communications van and additional manpower be sent to the club. Then he had a conversation with the mayor of Southgate in which the mayor asked what the commissioner anticipated: *I want the state police to investigate this matter. We don't have the manpower or authority to do it.* Only the state's chief executive had the authority to respond to the mayor's request. The commissioner discovered by use of his radio that the governor was at that moment on his way to Southgate. He assured the mayor that his request for an investigation would be presented to the governor as soon as possible. Then he left the front driveway for an inspection of the area at the back of the building.

By the time he got to the garden area approximately thirty minutes had elapsed since his arrival. All but thirty to forty of the bodies removed from the Cabaret Room had already been taken to a morgue, and a couple of huge army personnel carriers were then at the rear of the club to get the rest. While the carriers were being loaded a number of firemen continued to pour water on the fire, but it was obvious to the commissioner that the building would suffer total destruction. The exterior walls had already fallen in several places and much of the roof had collapsed. Except for the small section over the northeast service bar all of the roof of the Cabaret Room was down, and toward the front and center of the club the fire was finally burning itself out. As he left the garden area to complete his inspection of the grounds, the commissioner knew that the fire was nearly over.

By 2:00 am the sky was relatively clear over the site and dark. Activity on the hill was minimal by this time and largely insignificant. Those remaining consisted mostly of firemen, police officers, members of the press, and public officials. The commissioner of state police had left to intercept the governor for a meeting on the highway outside Southgate. He wanted to give the chief executive facts and figures about the nature of the tragedy and to tell him about the mayor's request for an investigation.

The fire chief was worried now about only one thing, the bodies lying underneath the ashes and debris of the Cabaret Room. A small blaze or two burned in the building and combustibles were still smoldering, but the fire was finally under control, at least in a sense: *It was under control to the extent that everything had burned up. I mean there was nothing left to burn.*

So in the early hours of the morning he shut down the water lines and organized a meeting of his officers to consider strategy for the recovery of bodies. Both he and his officers knew that the men under their command were near exhaustion. Most had been battling the fire for more than four hours; some had been there longer than five. With no reason to continue working through the night they decided to terminate operations promptly and wait for daybreak to begin the unpleasant task awaiting them in the Cabaret Room.

13

The devastation at Beverly Hills was more clearly visible in the natural light that fell over the club at dawn. The roof had collapsed in every part of the building except the extreme front area, the portion covering the entrance and the foyer, and a small area along the exterior wall of the kitchen. Destruction had been complete in the Cabaret Room, Garden Room, Empire Room, Viennese Room, main dining room, main bar, Zebra Room, and check room. Most of the second floor had also been destroyed. Only the basement of the building had escaped heavy damage, and even there some steel beams had collapsed and allowed the floor above to fall. The people at the site who had known Beverly Hills were stunned. Twelve hours earlier the club had been a beautiful and elegant structure. In the early morning light of May 29, 1977, it was a pile of ashes, rubble, and debris.

At approximately 8:00 AM, the search of the Cabaret Room for additional victims of the fire got underway. It started with the removal of the collapsed roof and the demolition of one of the showroom's exterior walls. In about two hours the recovery team moved through the service bar and entered the northeast corner of the room to begin the actual work of sifting through the debris for bodies. After moving the remnants of tables, chairs, and other objects out of the way, the firemen started a sweep across the showroom floor just inside the service bar.

Very quickly they found thirteen bodies. All had been badly burned. They carried them to the garden area for removal to the morgue and returned to the building to continue the search. A second sweep across the showroom floor, this one a little deeper than the first, produced a total of eight bodies, and a third resulted in the discovery of five more. The location of these bodies, as well as those taken from the Cabaret Room the night before, are shown on a drawing, identified on following page as Diagram No. 9, that was prepared from information given to investigators sometime after the fire. By the end of the third sweep across the search area, the recovery team had moved well into the northeast section of the Cabaret Room. To their great surprise they had found only twenty-six bodies.

After a time they moved to the southeast corner of the room and searched the area near the double doors that led to Exit B. Not a single body was found inside the showroom at that location and none was found in the outer hallway there or in the backstage dressing rooms. After a couple of sweeps across the entire Cabaret Room produced no additional fatalities, the firemen moved into the north-south corridor. They searched that long hallway thoroughly from one end to the other and then made a sweep across part of the Empire Room. The results were the same—no additional victims of the fire.

By this time the rescue team had worked a long day. Only the bodies of the two young women who had died on the second floor of the building had not been found. The firemen left the wreckage of the Empire Room, believing that the casualty list was complete, and headed toward the garden area at the back of the building. Almost twenty-four hours had elapsed since the outbreak of fire at the Zebra Room. Most of the crucial facts about the scope of the tragedy were now a matter of recorded history: more than seventy people seriously injured, hundreds permanently scarred by the trauma of narrow escape, and one hundred sixty-three fatalities.

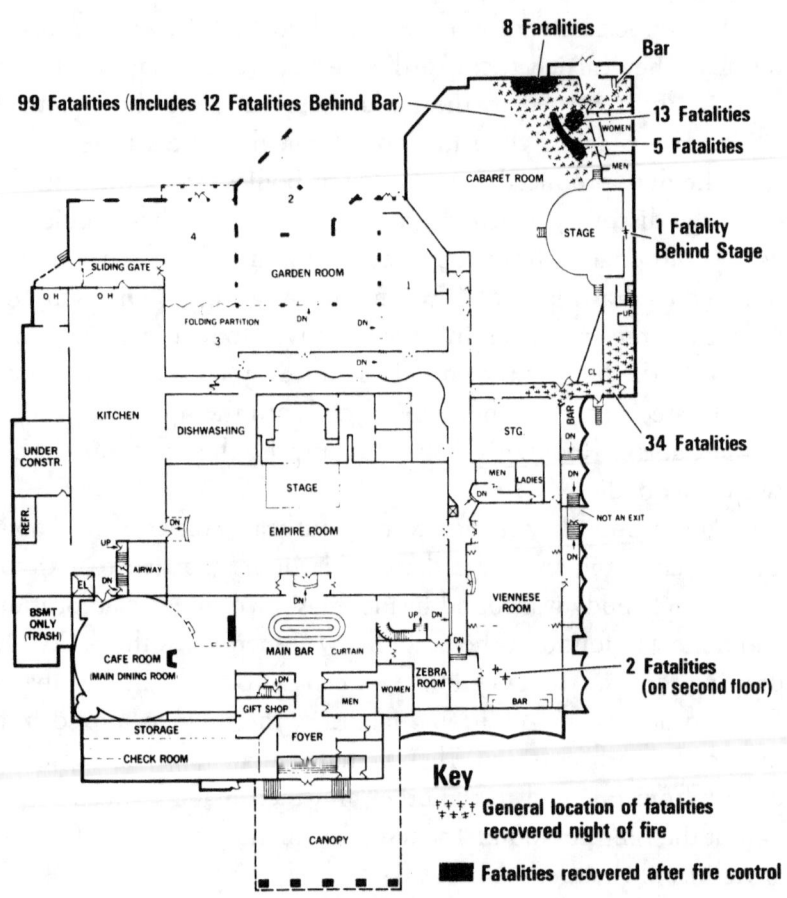

**FATALITIES**

Diagram No. 9

The commissioner of state police spent most of the day after the fire at the site of the disaster. The mayor's request for a state investigation had been approved by the governor, and the commissioner had been assigned a leading role in directing it. He had not yet received control over the premises from the fire chief but he had decided to stay on the grounds during the recovery work to look through the wreckage of the building. As a consequence he put himself in a position at some point before noon to hear the beginning of a most tantalizing conversation.

The state fire marshal had come to the site of the fire early that morning. The Beverly Hills Supper Club was a name with which he was familiar. Apparently he had given the facility some serious thought as he travelled to Southgate in the early morning hours after the fire. Near noon he located the governor in the garden area at the back of the building and gave him some news that he surely would have preferred not to hear: *Governor, we've got a problem with this building.* The commissioner of state police was in the vicinity. He heard the opening of the conversation but not the governor's response. He was told at a later time by another official that the governor had responded rather pointedly: *If there's a problem with this building it's not ours, it's yours.*

# Eight

## The Aftermath

I

The governor wasted no time in acting on the mayor's request. The commissioner of state police and the state fire marshal were ordered to coordinate an investigation. A team of more than thirty detectives from the state police was chosen by the commissioner to work the case. Two fire analysis experts from the United States Department of Commerce and one from the National Fire Protection Association were invited to join the effort. The governor had assembled a complete investigation team by the end of the first full day after the fire. His instructions were brief and simple: Leave no stone unturned in a search for truth about the fire.

The search for answers began in earnest on the morning of the second day. The fire experts arrived at the site of the fire to begin sifting through the ashes and debris of the building's remains. Others on the investigative team established a base of operations at a nearby motel and started the task of identifying and locating people who had been in the club on the night of the fire. The detectives from the state police began the investigation with the witnesses thought to have the more reliable information about the origin and development of the fire. As soon as possible, they questioned the firefighters who had been inside the building at the height of the fire, the sons of Dick Schilling, and the employees who had been most centrally involved in the discovery of the fire. The initial objective of the investigators was to obtain only enough information to formulate some tentative ideas about the origin, cause, and spread of the fire.

At the end of the day they gathered at the motel to compare notes and consolidate impressions. They thought by this time that the deaths had all occurred in the back part of the building. They strongly suspected that the fire had burned for a considerable period of time before discovery, probably in a concealed area around the Zebra Room, and had spread through the building in several directions with incredible speed. More importantly, they suspected even at this early moment that the stunning loss of life still so much on everyone's minds had been more senseless than anyone might have imagined. The fire experts had been inside the remains of the building for only a few hours. They knew nothing yet about the history of Schilling's club, but already they had seen enough to know that the tragedy of Beverly Hills would never be characterized as a freak accident or act of God.

2

For the next few days the investigation moved ahead on two fronts. The experts continued to search through the remains of the building for the cause of the fire and the factors that had contributed to the heavy loss of life. They collected materials from all parts of the structure and sent them to laboratories for analysis of flame spread potential, chemical composition, and identification. They assembled for inspection and scientific evaluation everything from electrical components to samples of support beams. They dissected the remains of the Zebra Room virtually piece by piece in a search for the sources of ignition.

The detectives from the state police simultaneously were working on their part of the investigation. They compiled a list of more than a thousand people with pertinent information about the disaster, interviewed hundreds of witnesses on tape, and began the process of reducing testimony to written form for subsequent use. From the owners of the building they obtained records and documents pertinent to the investigation and scrutinized the activities of state and local agencies that had shouldered responsibility for the safety of the club.

Gradually there emerged from these efforts the outline of an ugly picture. On each succeeding day of the investigation the fire looked more and more like a totally predictable and avoidable act of homicide. In no more than a week the investigators found abundant evidence of carelessness, complacency, and human error. The commissioner of state police and the fire marshal found themselves directing an investigation that seemed headed toward certain engagement with a grand jury. And for one of the two that presented considerable difficulty.

3

From the beginning the fire marshal had limited his involvement in the investigation. He had missed an early meeting without explanation, and during the first days at the site of the fire had been prominent only by his absence. For a while hardly anyone but the commissioner of state police noticed his low profile. But that changed quickly. He became newsworthy enough for mention in a major story in the state's leading newspaper: *To the surprise of some, the state's highest ranking fire official . . . remained behind the scenes yesterday.*[15] And then he was suddenly thrust squarely into the public spotlight by events that occurred more than a hundred miles from the center of the investigation.

A committee of the state legislature convened a public hearing in the state capitol to inquire about the circumstances surrounding the fire. The state senator who had visited the fire marshal's office a few months before the fire appeared before the committee as a star witness. He told of his efforts to sound a warning about fire hazards at Beverly Hills and about his face-to-face encounter with the head of the office. He quoted the fire marshal as having said on that occasion that the club was a known fire risk, that the owner had been particularly uncooperative, and that higher authority had sidetracked his efforts to make the building safe. The fire marshal made no appearance before the committee. For awhile he kept his silence. But ultimately he found himself unable to resist the pressure generated by widespread news coverage of the senator's testimony. He reduced his reaction to writing and released it to the press:

> *Senator Easterly has stated that he discussed the Beverly Hills Supper Club with me in December, 1976. I do not recall this conversation, nor do the log books of my office show that Senator Easterly was in our office during December. . . .*
>
> *If I ever discussed problems of enforcing fire codes with Senator Easterly or anyone else, I would have been referring to problems which existed at the time I was an employee of the Division of Fire Prevention, rather than anything that has occurred since I became Fire Marshal in 1972.*
>
> *Never since I have been Fire Marshal have any of my superiors discussed or communicated with me in any way on enforcement of fire safety at Beverly Hills. . . .*

He concluded his statement with a warning that he would have no more to say about the fire. He understood by this time the seriousness of his predicament and the foolishness of public statements about his conduct. He had delivered to the investigative team the records of his office pertaining to Beverly Hills. He was clearly no longer an investigator of the fire. He was instead one of the targets of the investigation.

4

Constitutional authority to pursue a criminal prosecution in connection with the fire rested in a man who understood immediately the need to be involved in the investigation: *I was concerned about the situation and felt there was a possibility of criminal involvement in one way or another.* He learned early about the mayor's request for an investigation by the state police and was truly pleased about that development. He knew that the state police was the only agency with sufficient manpower to handle the case; and he believed that officers in that agency would be sensitive to his interests and at the right time would invite him to join the investigation.

For a few days after the fire he waited patiently for a call from the commissioner of state police. No one connected with the investigation had given thought to his concerns or interests. A few more days passed before his patience slipped away. Then with the investigation about a week old he called the capitol to complain to the state's attorney general: *I'm the Commonwealth Attorney of Campbell County and solely responsible for criminal prosecutions conducted in this jurisdiction. I have no idea what's going on over there. No one from the state has yet seen fit even to contact my office. And I don't like it.* The attorney general called the governor's office. The governor's office called the investigators.

In less than twenty-four hours the commissioner of state police entered a courthouse near Beverly Hills looking for the office of Commonwealth's Attorney. He was there principally to calm stormy waters. He located the prosecutor without difficulty, briefed him on the status of the investigation, and told him as much as he then knew about the fire. He asked the prosecutor for no assistance and extended to him no invitation to join the investigation. He promised future reports on the development of the case but made no specific arrangements for additional contact. The meeting ended with the investigative team intact and the course of the investigation unchanged. The only man with authority to prosecute crimes committed in the county where the fire occurred was not even on the fringes of the investigation. He was not at all pleased about it.

## 5

The investigators worked at the site of the fire for about two weeks. They relinquished the remains of the building to the owners at the end of that effort and moved their operation to state police headquarters in the state capitol. They continued for several weeks thereafter to interview witnesses and to assemble documentary evidence about the construction of the building and the operation of the club. By early August they had produced more than 10,000 pages of transcribed testimony and a mountain of documents and records about the fire and the building.

By this time a little pressure was being felt by the investigators to move toward a conclusion. No one had urged the investigators to stop the search for information or to rush to judgment about the circumstances surrounding the fire. The pressure was more subtle and more indirect. A federal agency, caught in the midst of an appropriations hearing, had issued a report on the fire. A congressman from Ohio had announced plans to hold a congressional hearing on the tragedy in the city of Cincinnati as soon as possible. In the face of these developments the commissioner of state police felt a need to hasten an investigation that had so far been very thorough and very methodical.

The investigators exhausted their last worthwhile source of information about the fire and reassembled in the state capitol under the direction of the commissioner for the purpose of analyzing the evidence and preparing a report. Scores of questions were ready for final consideration. Where did the fire start? What was the source of ignition? By what route and how quickly did it travel to the showroom? Did the owners and employees issue a timely warning of the need to evacuate? Was the showroom overcrowded on the night of the fire? Did the occupants of that part of the building fail to react promptly and properly to an evacuation order? Did deaths result in the fire because of building and fire code violations? Were state and local officials responsible for the condition of the building?

The investigators moved into the final phase of their work with dispatch. They spent long hours of long weeks organizing and evaluating their evidence, testing theories about the development of the fire, and formulating tentative findings of fact on the crucial issues. Through the month of August they worked no less carefully and meticulously than during their search for information about the fire. But in early September the pressure for an end to the investigation increased.

The congressman from Ohio established a date for his hearing, September 19, 1977, and informed the governor of Kentucky that he intended to proceed on that day with or without the state's participation. The governor wanted to appear before the congressional committee and to submit on that occasion a finished report on the fire. For the first time the investigators confronted a deadline.

The commissioner of state police and the members of his team worked virtually day and night during the first part of September. The deadline was never very far from their thoughts. They drafted their report in segments, without the kind of review and reflection needed, and delivered it to a printer a few pages at a time. The quality of their work slipped considerably. But on September 16, 1977, just three days ahead of the congressional hearing, the commissioner entered the governor's office with a document that was soon to attract almost as much attention as the tragedy itself. It was entitled "Investigative Report to the Governor: Beverly Hills Supper Club Fire."

6

The dynamics of the fire occupied a preeminent role in the state's analysis of the tragedy. In their report to the governor, the investigators identified a concealed area inside the Zebra Room—either above the ceiling or inside one of the walls—as the place where ignition first occurred. Then they provided a description of the manner in which the fire moved from there to other parts of the building:

*The most probable cause of ignition within this [concealed] area was electrical in nature and would have been fed by combustibles located there. Specifically, the presence of concealed, combustible ceiling tile and wood materials used for supports provided a fuel supply for continued spread of the fire through the original and other concealed spaces....*

*The above-mentioned ignition sequence led to an intense heat buildup within the concealed space, which ultimately resulted in the accumulation of smoke and hot gases within the Zebra Room itself. It was at this point when the fire was discovered and attempts were made to extinguish it....*

*During the time attempts were being made to extinguish the fire within the Zebra Room, flashover occurred. In other words, simultaneous ignition of all combustible materials within the room occurred.*

* * *

*When flashover occurred in the Zebra Room, the room resembled a furnace in that all of the combustible furnishings in the room were burning simultaneously. These furnishings included several wood tables, about 20 or more chairs, and the carpet. Under these circumstances the walls of the room, which were covered with 3/16 inch, combustible hardboard paneling applied over wood furring strips, would also have been burning and contributing to the fire. What follows is a most probable scenario for the action of the fire.*

*This furnace-like fire had only one immediate flue or vent available to it, and this was the pair of doors at the north end of the room.... [T]he fire's intensity was of such magnitude that the fire would have quickly consumed the top part of this wooden door.*

*The venting of the fire through this doorway resulted in the passage of smoke, flames, and heat through the upper part of the doorway at relatively high velocities, with an inrush of cold, fresh air, at lower velocities, near the floor. As the smoke, flames, and hot gases left the Zebra Room, they were propelled across the ceiling of the small corridor directly outside the Zebra Room until they hit the far wall, some 20 feet distant. Here, the flames and hot gases split, with part of the flames and hot gases turning down and part turning sideways in both directions. The thin plywood paneling, on the far wall of the small corridor, would have ignited readily under the impact of this flame and hot gas exposure.*

*In the meantime, the fire on the carpet in the Zebra Room would have spread through the doorway also, slower than the flames and hot gases along the ceiling, but sustained by the thermal radiation down onto the carpet by the smoke and hot gas layer at the ceiling. In examination of the Zebra Room, it was found that the carpet and its padding were completely consumed, down to bare concrete, in the door opening, the only location in the Zebra Room with such extensive damage.*

*The flames and hot gases leaving the Zebra Room, in addition to impinging on the plywood paneling of the small corridor wall, also were probably passing up the stairway to the west of the lobby, into the main bar to the west, and through the 15-foot opening into the main corridor to the east [i.e., the one leading to the Cabaret Room].*

*It was apparent, from the on-site investigation, that sufficient heat was present in the stream of hot gases passing through this 15-foot opening into the main corridor to ignite combustibles present in this corridor. These combustibles consisted of the hardboard paneling on the walls and the carpet system on the floor.*

*As the flames and hot gases entered the main corridor, the carpet and the hardboard paneling began to contribute combustible gases to the fire through the driving off of the combustible volatiles in the carpet and the paneling. This resulted in the extension of the burning down the corridor. At about this period of time, sufficient thermal radiation was being directed down on the carpet surface from the smoke and hot gas layer at the ceiling to cause the spread of the fire on the carpet from the small corridor through the 15-foot doorway, into the main corridor. Once this happened, the fire in the corridor was very nearly a self-sustaining fire, feeding on both the carpet and the paneling, with each contributing to the growth and spread of the other. Even so, energy was still being supplied into the main corridor from the fire in the Zebra Room and the small corridor outside. From this point, the fire spread rapidly down the main corridor, with visible fire rolling along underneath the ceiling and a secondary fire traveling along on the carpet face, tailing behind the ceiling fire.*[16]

The investigators identified the probable cause of ignition as "electrical in nature," but stopped far short of blaming electrical system deficiencies for the start of the fire. They had examined the remains of the Zebra Room microscopically during the investigation and knew from that examination that electricity had provided the energy for ignition. But they knew nothing more than this about the cause of the fire and said nothing more in their report. In only this one respect did they leave the governor uninformed about the dynamics of the fire.

7

Probably the most significant part of the Investigative Report, certainly the one of greatest public interest, dealt with the factors thought to have contributed most heavily to the loss of life in the fire. In their treatment of this subject the investigators could hardly have been more uncomplimentary than they were of the individuals responsible for the safety of the building and its occupants. They reported to the governor as follows:

1. For a considerable period of time after the discovery of fire, according to the investigators, the owners and employees of the club tried to control the blaze. No one called the fire department and no one sounded a general alarm inside the building. Not until after "flashover" occurred in the Zebra Room did anyone issue an order for evacuation. Consequently there was a crucial delay in notification to the occupants of the showroom:

> [I]t is the opinion of the Investigating Team that as many as twenty minutes may have elapsed from the time heavy smoke was originally discovered in the Zebra Room until the busboy notified occupants of the Cabaret Room to evacuate.[17]

2. In places of public assembly, of which Beverly Hills was one, the employees are required to know exactly what to do in the event of an emergency. Fire and safety codes applicable to such a facility require an evacuation plan. On the night of May 28, 1977, in Schilling's club, there existed no plan on which to rely:

> Based on statements of many employees, training in emergency evacuation procedures was practically nil. The owner himself stated there was no master plan for evacuation, while at the same time maintaining that supervisory personnel knew what to do in a case of emergency. Analysis indicates there was no common understanding among employees with reference to the emergency evacuation of the building.[18]

Without difficulty the investigators found a link between this failure and the delay of notification to the occupants of the showroom. And just as easily they found a link to the deaths that resulted in the fire: *[T]he Investigative Team has concluded that the lack of training of employees in emergency and evacuation procedures was a direct contributing factor to the loss of life and injury.*[19]

3. The Cabaret Room had a legal occupancy load of 536. A determined effort had been made during the investigation to establish the exact number of people in the room at the time of the fire. The investigators had produced virtually unassailable evidence that 1,011 patrons and employees were there at the crucial time. But because of information provided by a single employee who had barely escaped the fire they believed that the crowd in the showroom had been much bigger than their evidence indicated. So they reported to the governor that the number in the room on the night of the tragedy was 1,360. They described the condition as "gross overcrowding" and concluded that "excess occupant load was a direct contributing factor to the loss of life."[20]

4. The Cabaret Room was short one exit and at least six exit units. The exits that existed were imperfect by design and adversely affected by specific conditions that prevailed at the time of the fire:

> *In addition to the obvious deficiency of exit units . . . certain structural impediments to the egress of occupants of the Cabaret Room were also present The presence of these impediments became particularly critical when the presence of hot gases, smoke, and fire blocked the two main exits from the Cabaret Room. Specifically, both northeast and southeast exits from the Cabaret Room were in part obstructed by the presence of service bars and unused tables and chairs. Further, access to the actual exterior doors at both exits involved multi-level ramps and railings for the occupants actually closest to the exits. Finally, the path of travel to each of these exits was circuitous in that occupants had to pass through various enclosed areas which served auxiliary functions.*[21]

> *In addition to the evidence contained in the questionnaire, there are many statements from occupants of the Cabaret Room which speak of seating in the aisles and on the ramps leading to exits.... Finally photographs which had been taken by two patrons in the Cabaret Room ... immediately prior to and during the initial stages of the fire, bear stark testimony to the obstruction of egress and excessive occupant load.*[22]

The seating of patrons in the aisles and on the ramps was a cause for the loss of life in the fire. But the importance of that factor, according to the investigators, was dwarfed by the significance of exit deficiencies in the showroom: *The magnitude of the loss of life and injury in the Cabaret Room is ... in the opinion of the Investigative Team attributable in large part to inadequate means of egress for occupants of that area.*[23]

5. The fire moved through the main corridor of the building with incredible suddenness. The interior finish in that corridor, its carpeting and paneling, lacked compliance with the flame spread requirements of the law. It facilitated the movement of fire from the Zebra Room to the Cabaret Room and contributed significantly to the deaths that occurred in the showroom:

> *It is the opinion of the Investigative Team that the interior finish directly contributed to the loss of life and injury. First, by increasing the rate of the spread of the fire from the Zebra Room down the 150-foot corridor to the Cabaret Room. Second, by effectively blocking the main north-south corridor of the club which led to the main entrance, and the most generally known exit to patrons.*[24]

The investigators concluded this part of their report without mention of a factor thought by many to be the most important of all. They believed that some occupants of the showroom had failed to respond promptly to an order for evacuation, and that chaos had reigned inside the big room once the fire was visible. They considered the possibility of including both of these factors in the list of things thought responsible for the consequences of the tragedy. But in the end they found themselves unable to justify blaming the victims of the fire for their own deaths. So they conveyed to the governor in explicit terms an unequivocal message. The deaths at Beverly Hills belonged in the category of homicide.

8

The Investigative Report was delivered to the governor on a Friday. For the rest of that day and much of the next he pored over its contents with intense interest. The discussion on the dynamics of the fire and the one involving the factors that contributed most heavily to loss of life were interesting and helpful. But neither of the two captured as much of the governor's attention as a discussion about the responsibility of certain individuals for the most tragic consequences of the fire. Of particular interest to the governor was a part of the report detailing a string of private and public acts of misconduct, deception, and misrepresentation.

Condemnation of the principal owner of the club by the investigative team was unblunted and extreme. His building was described as an "electrician's nightmare,"[25] and he was assigned major responsibility for the condition. He was credited with "culpable acts that created and contributed to maintenance of fire hazards"[26] and with conduct that "constituted a clear violation of the Standards of Safety and perhaps of the Kentucky criminal code."[27] The language chosen by the investigators to describe their feelings about the principal owner was unqualified and harsh:

> *A major factor in keeping Beverly Hills in operation without compliance was the owner and operator's surreptitious behavior and failure to live up to commitments made. First, as to surreptitious activities, frequently construction was going on without a permit and was discovered by accident when almost completed...*
>
> *Second, another significant factor was the matter of unkept promises and misrepresentations. We have already noted that [an electrician] reported that Mr. Schilling indicated he had permission to violate the NEC [National Electrical Code] and use non-metallic cable. It also appears that Mr. Schilling told [a deputy fire marshal] that he would*

> correct all deficiencies noted, including the unenclosed stairway. [The fire marshal] relied on this assurance, as did [the building inspector], and the City of Southgate. The Grand Jury report [of 1971] indicates that the operators of Beverly Hills were going to train their employees, and even form a "fire brigade." None of these assurances were kept. Crucial deficiencies remained and no training of employees was provided. It also appears that Mr. Schilling, did not comply with the architectural plans drawn up by [an architect]. . . [28]

A more unattractive portrait of the owner could hardly have been painted by the investigators. They heaped on his shoulders most of the blame for the consequences of the fire, and they portrayed him as a man uninhibited by requirements of the law and largely unconcerned about the safety of his building.

Not all of the investigators' condemnation was spent on the owner of the building. The officials of Southgate were given a little credit for effort and a load of blame for failure. Their inspections were characterized as superficial, their knowledge and training as suspect, and their capacity to perform the responsibilities of their offices almost non-existant: *It appears that Southgate officials did inspect Beverly Hills but obviously were unable to perceive the existence of hazardous conditions that violated the Standards of Safety and created a high risk of harm to life and property.*[29]

Officials of the fire marshal's office, particularly the two who had occupied the top position during the Schilling period of ownership of Beverly Hills, fared no better in the report:

> The picture that emerges is that the Fire Marshal's Office knew of fire hazard problems at Beverly Hills based on inquiries from Southgate, notations of deficiencies by deputy fire marshals, a complaint by a Kentucky senator, and newspaper publicity (kept in a file in the Fire Marshal's Office). Inspections were not complete or thorough, as admitted by at least three deputy fire marshals. We are compelled to conclude that during the period of time from December 1970 until May 28, 1977, the Fire Marshal's Office did not implement a proper inspection program which would have revealed the code violations. The frequent suggestion in the statements that it was someone else's task to remedy the situation does not reduce the overall obligation of the Fire Marshal's Office to comply with the duties set forth in its own regulations.

*Slicing duties, no matter how thin, does not eliminate them; in fact, it may only compound them.*[30]

Against these individuals the accusations of wrongdoing were more subtle, and the language used to describe their failures not quite so intemperate as that referring to Schilling. But still there was little room for a reader of the report to form a positive impression of the public officials responsible for the safety of the club. Certainly no such impression was formed by the governor. He finished reading the report in a most uncharitable frame of mind:

> *I was appalled that so many died when so many might have been saved had the management of the club done what is obvious—immediately order the evacuation of the facility upon learning of the fire.*
> 
> *I was appalled that so many died when so many lives might have been saved had the nightclub not been packed to twice at least its legally authorized capacity—aisles blocked, exits locked, and routes to safety blocked with people and tables.*
> 
> *I was appalled that so many died when so many might have been saved had the owners provided the required exits, installed the required sprinkler system, provided the required training for their own employees. . . .*
> 
> *How many lives might have been saved had the owners not overtly circumvented the law to what they considered to be their own advantage?*
> 
> *I was deeply distressed that an agency of the Commonwealth had been a party to allowing that overt subversion of the law to continue.*[31]

He consulted with members of his staff, touched base with the commissioner of state police, and found none of them counseling against some kind of prompt action to show his outrage.

So he immediately ordered the suspension of the fire marshal from the performance of further duties and took similar action against the marshal's chief deputy and the field inspector who had done inspections at Beverly Hills. He found no immediate action that could be taken against the owners of the building, but he reserved a prominent place in his thoughts for the Schilling family as he turned attention to some important events that were now approaching, a gubernatorial news conference scheduled for the following evening (Sunday, the 18th) near the site of the fire, a release of the Investigative Report to members of the press, and an early morning appearance on Monday, the 19th before the congressional committee in Cincinnati.

9

About a full day ahead of the time set aside for the news conference, a phone rang in the home of the Campbell County Commonwealth Attorney. He took a call from the commissioner of state police and learned for the first time about the existence of the Investigative Report, about the state's plans to release it to the press on the following day, and about the commissioner's desire to give him a copy beforehand. No one connected with the investigation had contacted him since shortly after the fire despite a promise to the contrary. He agreed to meet with the commissioner at the site of the news conference but was less than happy to find himself four months after the fire still in the dark about the results of an investigation so vital to his interests.

On the following day the prosecutor arrived an hour or so ahead of the news conference and without difficulty located the commissioner. The meeting arranged the night before turned out to be brief and not very cordial:

*He just smiled and handed me the book and said good luck. And that was it.*

• • •

*He made some statements at the time which, if I were in his position, I wouldn't have made: "I'm receiving this report but I'm not endorsing it or indicating in any way that I know what's in it, agree with what's in it, or understand what's in it."*

He chose to stay for neither the release of the report to the press nor the governor's first remarks about the nature of the tragedy. Within a few minutes of arrival, with the Investigative Report in his possession, he headed for home. From the beginning he had believed that a working partnership between his office and the state's investigators was crucial. No such relationship had developed during the course of the investigation. Probably the last real chance for such a development was now gone.

10

The news conference opened with both newspapers and television heavily represented. The governor sought and received a commitment from those present that news coverage of the evening's events would be delayed until after his appearance before the congressional committee on the following day. Copies of the Investigative Report were distributed, and the governor opened his remarks with praise for the work of the investigators. He announced the suspension of the fire marshal and two of his assistants, carefully avoided any implication that the three might have committed criminal acts in connection with the fire, and then proceeded to utter the words of which headlines and lead stories are made.

Surely knowing that his word on the subject would be taken by some as undiluted truth and that his voice would be heard far and wide, he turned his thoughts to the conduct of the owners of the building and that of a former fire marshal (i.e., the predecessor of the suspended fire marshal). He spoke emotionally and without any noticeable degree of reluctance:

> *I tell you, after having [read the report of the fire], I am appalled; I am shocked; I am disturbed at the clear indications it shows of disregard for human life. I believe you will share that emotion with me after you've had an opportunity to read the report yourselves.*
>
> *There are two particular respects that I think bear mentioning initially. In 1971, the then Fire Marshal . . . approved plans and specifications for the construction of a substantial portion of Beverly Hills Club after having taken those plans and specifications from one of the division heads after one of the division heads had told [the fire marshal in 1971] that there were ten violations of codes included in those specifications.*

The Fire Marshal at that time approved those plans and specifications. The construction . . . proceeded and those ten corrections were never made. While he assured the Campbell County Grand Jury that they would be made there is no evidence to support the fact. That Fire Marshal in 1971 participated in a probably illegal act of approving construction at the Country Club in clear violation of the law, and through his own shenanigans never attempted in any way to insure that that construction was made in compliance with all the codes and regulations.

The second major area that shocks me the greatest is the simple fact that just the smallest amount of prompt and responsible action on the part of the owners could well have avoided any loss of life. It is apparent from this investigation that possibly as much as twenty minutes expired from the time the fire was first discovered until the patrons of the Cabaret Room were advised of the existence of that fire, and then not at the direction of the owners, then only at the initiative of one of the employees of Beverly Hills.

There is a shocking amount of complete and total disregard by the owners of Beverly Hills for the safety of the patrons of the Beverly Hills Club. They not only constructed the substantial portion of that club in clear violation of the law using materials that were illegal; they operated it in violation of the law; and even then when a fire broke out, as it did on this disastrous night, failed to even use reasonable care to evacuate the premises.

The evidence shows that one architectural drawing for construction was changed by the owners and the number of exits that were suggested through the architectural drawing were not built; and the architect was surprised to find, upon examination during this investigation, that his plans had been so changed.

Another architect, apparently in a conspiracy with the owners, fraudulently signed a report that certain construction had been made that was totally untrue. . . .

There were only about half as many exits as the law required. The wiring was done in total violation of the code. As a matter of fact, the electrician himself stated that he was instructed by the owners not to use the materials that were in compliance with the code.

Overcrowding was obvious. There were at least twice as many people in the Cabaret Room as the law allowed. There were more people in the total club than the law allowed; and even then, the hallways were cluttered with tables and chairs, and the passageways within the rooms were filled with tables and chairs and people even standing because of

> *the overcrowding condition in the room on that evening.*
>
> *In 1971, in an investigation by the Campbell County Grand Jury concerning that Fire Marshal... approval of those plans and specifications, illegally apparently, the Campbell County Grand Jury instructed the owners to train their personnel for evacuation in the event of such a disaster as this. No such training ever took place by the owners.*
>
> *So a reading of this report shows a shocking and total and complete disregard for human life by the owners of this club...* [32]

His words were neither subtle nor ambiguous. He was asked at the conclusion of his formal statement for an observation about the possibility of criminal charges. He spoke without hesitation or uncertainty: *Indictments will likely be returned by a grand jury and prosecution will be pursued.*

11

The commissioner of state police was surprised by the governor's performance at the news conference: *I couldn't believe it. We had met earlier in the evening with a legislative delegation, to provide them with advance copies of the report, and he had not come on nearly so strong.* His surprise was exceeded by his concern for the potential consequences of the harshly worded accusations against the owners of the building and the former fire marshal. He thought that powder had surely been supplied for a charge that the state had prejudged the case. He feared, especially after the accusations were repeated on the following day for the benefit of the congressional group, that the governor might even have contaminated the case with prejudicial publicity.

Beverly Hills returned to the front page of the newspaper following these events. Coverage of the state's report on the fire, the governor's remarks, and the congressional hearing was massive. The report itself, although nearly two hundred pages long, was printed by area newspapers in its entirety. Hardly a syllable of the governor's remarks was deleted from television and newspaper coverage of his pronouncements about the tragedy. For several days running, the airways and the newsprint of the greater Cincinnati area and the state of Kentucky were literally filled with lead stories, commentary, editorials, and special reports about the fire and its leading figures. And in this massive coverage there was very little to allay the fears of the commissioner of state police.

The biggest headlines in the biggest newspapers captured and preserved the essence of the governor's remarks: "CARROLL RIPS CLUB OWNERS, INSPECTORS,"[33] "EVERYONE KNEW CLUB WAS FIRETRAP."[34] and "BUILT TO BURN."[35] The chief executive had highlighted the most sensational of the state's finding and conclusions about the fire—inexcusable delay of notification, over-crowdedness and lack of exits, "electrician's nightmare," and criminal conspiracy. He had been explicit in his assessment of the conduct of those deemed most responsible for the fire and uncompromising in his condemnation of that conduct. He had made just the right statements to dominate the stories and editorials underneath the headlines.

His accusations against the owners of the building attracted the greatest attention of all:

> *Governor Julian Carroll scathingly condemned Sunday the Beverly Hills owners and several state fire officials for contributing to the May 28 holocaust at the famous Southgate nightspot.*[36]
>
> • • •
>
> *Carroll said he foresees the possibility of criminal indictments against civilians, but not of state officials.*
>
> • • •
>
> *Carroll, an attorney himself, rebuked the Schilling family and the fire officials in extremely strong language. . . .*
>
> • • •
>
> *"There was a shocking, and total, and complete disregard for human life by the owners," Carroll said.*[37]

He served to generate for the state's report on the fire almost as much publicity and notoriety as the fire itself had generated a few months earlier, and for the personal disparagement and condemnation contained in that publicity, the owners of the building held him singularly responsible.

A few days after the news conference and the congressional hearing, members of the press gathered once again near the site of the fire. This time the briefing was called by the owners of the club and conducted by one of their lawyers:

> *We feel that irreparable damage has been done in that a fair trial is now practically impossible....*
>
> *We cannot ignore the impact that the report and statements that have followed the report have had on the Schilling family. It would be a manifest understatement to say that we were shocked at the comments of the Governor (Julian Carroll of Kentucky) at his news conference with the press prior to the release of the report and by his subsequent testimony at the Congressional Subcommittee hearing.*
>
> *His remarks were not only unwarranted, but were also defamatory, scurrilous, irresponsible and unprofessional....*
>
> *Incredibly and without precedent, Governor Carroll has assumed the role of the special prosecutor for Campbell County, judge and jury. His report and remarks carry with them an aura of finality without an opportunity of defense and benefit of trial. Such conclusiveness should not be accepted by the public—certainly it is not accepted by us.*[38]

On this side of the case, as on the other, there was an expectation of indictment and prosecution in connection with the fire. The lawyers prepared a response to the governor's accusations with care and delivered it under circumstances designed to maximize dissemination. Their remarks were brief, their objectives limited. They challenged the conclusiveness of the state's portrayal of its findings and fired a single shot on behalf of their clients: *The Governor has used this report as the stage for politically motivated remarks serving his own political end.*[39]

12

By the end of this storm, the tragedy at Beverly Hills was four months old. The prosecuting attorney had still not entered the picture to any significant degree. He had witnessed the governor's news conference on television and had studied the contents of the state's report with considerable care, but he had seen none of the evidence underneath the state's findings and knew no more about the circumstances surrounding the tragedy than the average man on the street. He had no basis for making a professional judgment about the feasibility of pursuing a prosecution in connection with the fire and no room, he thought, within which to exercise such a judgment:

> *I had carefully avoided prejudging the guilt or innocence of anyone. I had wanted to satisfy myself that the matter should be looked into by a grand jury. But I can say that there was no recourse after the report had been issued and after the governor's statements had been made. I don't think I had any choice after that.*

In early October, after a meeting in the capitol with the commissioner of state police, he finally took delivery of the state's evidence. He promptly relinquished most of his regular duties to an assistant and buried himself in a mountain of sworn statements, documents, charts, photographs, exhibits, and other items of evidence. His first objective was simply to organize the materials and find some point from which to start a process of digestion. By the end of two weeks he had managed to do little more than discover the true nature of his task.

Literally dozens of highly skilled investigators, supported by a substantial staff, had worked three full months accumulating information about the building and the fire. His early efforts for some personal involvement in that work had not been fruitful. And now, almost entirely on his own, he was left to review, absorb, analyze, and understand a truckload of evidence about a possible homicide with 165 victims. The burden on him was staggering. He was apprehensive and doubtful: *In this situation, I knew going in that I was to lose either way. I was a sure loser.*

Through late fall and early winter, with no break even for weekends, he plodded methodically through a mountain of paper, convinced no less than before that events orchestrated by the governor had stripped him of his options. A small room had been set aside for his use in the county courthouse and he worked there most days from early morning until night. He called the commissioner of state police from time to time for clarification of matters contained in the state's report and occasionally consulted with his assistant, but for the most part he worked alone, no one to check his approach, challenge his thoughts, or detect an errant course.

By the end of the year he had worked his way through the evidence only to find himself considerably uncomfortable about the case. A few things about the state's report had bothered him almost from the beginning. It had stressed electrical code violations at Beverly Hills, characterizing the club as an "electrician's nightmare," while practically overlooking the fact that investigators had been unable to find a causal link between the fire and electrical system deficiencies. It had raised the specter of criminal conspiracy, between the owners of the building and public officials, while relying on conspiracy laws that had been repealed long before the fire. While he studied the evidence he had hoped to allay his concerns about the reliability of the report, but he became even more doubtful:

> *In a lot of areas in the report, statements of witnesses were taken out of context, completely out of context. And a lot of investigative conclusions were drawn from the statement of only one person out of fifty who spoke to the matter in question. The statement used was the one the investigators wanted to get in.*

He believed at this moment that indictments were his for the asking: *Had I made up my mind that indictments should have been returned I could have had any number I wanted.* But deep down he felt that the evidence produced by the state simply failed to show the commission of criminal homicide at Beverly Hills. Under ordinary circumstances he would have terminated the prosecution on his own:

> *Q. Would you have screened this case out before the grand jury was impaneled, had you been free of all considerations other than your own impression of the evidence?*
> *A: I don't think that there's any doubt about it.*

But the circumstances, as he saw them at this moment, were not ordinary. A grand jury engagement seemed inescapable. So he gave very little thought to the possibility of terminating the prosecution without a submission of evidence to a grand jury. Instead he began to contemplate some other ways of accommodating his doubts about the strength of the evidence and about the propriety of pushing ahead with a questionable prosecution.

Two things came to mind readily. Ordinarily a grand jury proceeding is one-sided. Jurors hear the prosecution's side of the case and nothing at all from the targets of the investigation. Perhaps in this instance he could offer the witness chair to anyone who desired to appear before the grand jury, even the owners of the building. Also, a grand jury is ordinarily obligated to return indictments upon a finding of probable cause. The proof needed for such a finding is substantially short of that needed for a criminal conviction. Perhaps in this instance he could ask the grand jury to return indictments only if it believed the evidence sufficient to support a conviction. Undoubtedly he could add a substantial measure of protection against the possibility of injustice by doing these two things.

But did he dare, in a case of such enormous interest and importance, depart from standard procedures and do something out of the ordinary that might enhance the likelihood of a termination of the prosecution by the grand jury? Did he dare run the risk of personal blame for what might be widely perceived as a gross miscarriage of justice?

13

On February 23, 1978 a special grand jury was impaneled to investigate the fire. The judge to whom the jurors would ultimately report issued brief instructions: *Determine the cause of the tragedy at Beverly Hills. Ascertain if crimes were committed in connection with the deaths and injuries that occurred there. And return indictments to the court if you so find.* None of the twelve chosen to serve lived very far from the site of the fire. All of them had some knowledge about it and probably a measure of opinion about the guilt or innocence of key figures. They were told to elect a foreman, establish a base of operation that would guarantee secrecy of the proceeding, and engage the prosecuting attorney for aid and direction.

For the better part of a month they had no more than superficial contact with anyone but the prosecutor, meeting in isolation, struggling to acquire an understanding of pertinent requirements of the criminal law and to establish the parameters of their investigation. They spent much of their time buried in an ever expanding mass of written information about the circumstances surrounding the fire. They reached agreement on only one thing during this period. It was that their assignment was not apt to end quickly or easily.

Toward the middle of March, they decided to push their inquiry into a second phase. They had absorbed enough information about the state's investigation to want a live session with the head of the investigation team. So the prosecutor called the state capitol and asked the commissioner of state police to prepare for an appearance before the grand jury. He was to be the first witness.

The commissioner had not been heavily involved with Beverly Hills for a while. But he still knew more about the fire than anyone else, except for the prosecutor perhaps. During the course of the investigation he had not had much time for reflection on the more complex aspects of the tragedy. His thoughts about such things as "culpability" and "blame" were more refined by this time, and his feeling toward those most responsible for the consequences of the fire were more settled. On these subjects he had strong views, very few of which were compatible with those held by the prosecutor.

He believed that the local building inspector and the two fire chiefs who had exercised responsibility for the safety of the club had performed about as well under the circumstances as anyone could have reasonably expected. But he believed otherwise about the officials and employees of the state fire marshal's office. This group had assumed through their actions primary responsibility for the safety of the building. They were better trained than the local officials and much better situated to protect the public against the hazards of fire.

It was reasonable, he thought, to expect of the state officials a higher level of performance and to see in their failures a much greater degree of culpability. They had consistently neglected their official responsibilities—partly, he suspected, because of political considerations—and shortly before the fire had issued an official seal of approval for the club with full knowledge of the existence of safety violations. In their failure to foresee the possibility of disaster at Beverly Hills he saw nothing worse than human imperfection. But in their conscious disregard of risks known to exist there he saw indifference to the value of human life.

Toward the principal owner of the building he harbored even stronger convictions. Dick Schilling, he believed, had not acted with malice or an evil mind: *I don't believe for a minute that any of the Schillings intended to create a deathtrap at Beverly Hills.* But the owner had shown extreme recklessness and a motivation for disregarding safety requirements that the commissioner found particularly unappealing and unacceptable:

> *I think he did whatever was necessary to make a buck. He found people who were willing to prostitute themselves professionally, who were not in touch with current professional standards, and who were willing to take a check and ask no questions. He cut corners in the management of the business and in the construction of the building. There can be no doubt on this.*

A substantial risk of death to patrons and employees of the club had been disregarded by the owner for the sake of profit. This, he believed, made Beverly Hills a case of criminal homicide.

14

The commissioner was scheduled to meet with the jurors one afternoon. He arrived early, located the prosecuting attorney at the county courthouse, and went from there to a country club not far from the site of the fire for some lunch and some talk. Not since the release of the state's report had the two men conversed about the tragedy. They had never exchanged views about the strengths and weaknesses of the case. Their previous encounters had not been cordial and neither was this one: *He [the prosecutor] was still unhappy about the manner in which the investigation had been handled—without him. And I would probably have felt the same way had I been in his position.*

As they talked through lunch they rarely departed from the agenda that had brought them together. There was no light conversation. The prosecutor offered an opinion about the quality of the grand jury, "one of the most representative that could have been assembled." The commissioner identified some of the obstacles to be hurdled on the way to a successful prosecution, "the inherent complexity of the evidence," "the wide distribution of responsibility for the consequences of the fire," and "the failure of the investigators to discover the exact cause of ignition." They talked more candidly about the case than ever before but still there was no unguarded exchange of views.

They finished lunch and headed for the courthouse to meet the grand jury. The prosecutor had been explicit enough in describing his doubts about the case: *My impression was that he didn't think there was much likelihood of any major kind of indictment.* But the commissioner left the country club with his thoughts fixed on something else about which the prosecutor had been even more explicit: *He said it would be easy to get any number of indictments against any number of people. But he had decided to proceed with the case at a higher level to meet a little stiffer test. He said he intended to ask the grand jury not to indict anyone without a belief that conviction would result from the indictment.* The commissioner had long entertained doubts about the capacity of the criminal process to handle a case of the magnitude of Beverly Hills. Not in the slightest did he find his doubts alleviated by his conversation with the prosecutor.

The work of the grand jury extended through the spring and early summer of 1978. Nearly a hundred witnesses, including Dick Schilling and his sons, followed the commissioner of state police into the grand jury room. Between eight hundred and nine hundred written statements about the fire and thousands of records and documents were assembled by the grand jury and analyzed during the course of the investigation. The state's report on the fire as well as a comprehensive report prepared by the National Fire Protection Association were added to the official record and subjected to microscopic examination. Around the first of July the search for information pertinent to the tragedy ended and deliberations began.

On August 2, 1978, after slightly more than five months, the work of the grand jury ended in the courtroom where it had started. The foreman delivered to the judge a report that had been prepared for release to the general public. It was twenty-eight pages in length and contained the jury's analysis of the tragedy. It opened with a preamble reciting the charge under which the jury had worked, proceeded through a lengthy discussion of the circumstances surrounding the disaster and its investigation, and closed with a stunning conclusion about the culpability of those who had contributed to the loss of life in the fire.

In reaching that conclusion the jury seemed to exert little effort to mask its contempt for the state's investigation of the disaster. It raised doubts about the completeness of that inquiry and expressed an unwillingness to rely on the report prepared for the governor:

> *The Grand Jury . . . was able to hear testimony from many witnesses that had never been contacted by the State Police and had access to materials and evidence that was found after the initial investigation was concluded. The Grand Jury also had access to testimony and evidence that was supplied by independent investigators who appeared before this Jury. The Grand Jury tried to obtain information which would be helpful from any source whatever rather than relying completely on the results of any one investigation. The Jury did not accept at face value any reports submitted to it, but reached its conclusions independently after considering all of the evidence.*[40]

More importantly, in reconstructing the circumstances surrounding the fire, the jury adopted findings of fact that were fundamentally at odds with nearly every important conclusion reached by the governor's investigative team.

It found that the showroom had been occupied at the time of the fire by only nine hundred to one thousand people (far short of the 1,360 reported to the governor) and had not been overcrowded. It found that the exit facilities for the Cabaret Room had satisfied the requirements of the building code, at least it so implied through the following statement:

> *Consideration should be given to the enactment of legislation providing for more exits from public buildings than are presently required by law, considering the possibility that some exits that could be utilized in an emergency situation might be blocked or hindered by that particular emergency situation.*[41]

And it concluded that the occupants of the showroom had not been denied timely warning about the existence of fire in the building: "There was no delay in the notification of patrons and employees in the establishment...Time was of the essence and...was treated as such."[42]

Obviously the grand jury and the state's investigators differed greatly over the reasons for the massive loss of life in the fire. Those who died in the showroom, according to the state's report, had perished because of overcrowding, inadequate exits, and untimely warning. Not so said the members of the jury:

> *It seemed there was a sudden surge of the noxious smoke, hot gases and fire that burst into the Cabaret Room from the main corridor...The result of this occurrence was to create panic among those who had not yet exited the room from the exits which were still available. Testimony also indicated that some patrons of the Cabaret Room, even though notified to evacuate failed to react and remained seated until the conditions of the room itself indicated the need to exit. By this time in some instances it was too late.*[43]

Neither the building nor carelessness by the managers of the club had caused the showroom deaths. Occupants of the big room had failed to heed a timely warning to evacuate. They panicked when fire surged into their midst from the main corridor. The tragedy at Beverly Hills, according to the jury, had been caused most of all by the actions of the victims.

The jury found no fault with the efforts exerted by local officials to protect the public against fire hazards in Schilling's club: *It appeared to this Jury that these officials performed admirably under the conditions (under which) they were required to operate.*[44] It condemned the state fire marshal's office for "shoddy record keeping," "a complete breakdown in interdepartmental communicatons," and for being "used as a placement agency for political jobs."[45] But it said absolutely nothing about the many specific contributions made by that office to the fire hazards that existed in the building, and in its only statement about the conduct of the owners of the club, the jury was laudatory: *In regard to the management of the Beverly Hills Supper Club it appears to this Jury that every effort was made to comply with requests made by local and state regulatory agencies.*[46]

The courtroom was packed when the foreman delivered the jury's report to the judge. Most of those present were members of the press who had followed the case from the earliest stages of its development. They had come to the courthouse on this occasion to learn the identity of those who would be subjected to public trial for the homicides at Beverly Hills. Some had come with a list of prime candidates for indictment. Others expected only the principal owner to be charged. Hardly any expected the prosecution to terminate without a trial or to hear the following statement from the foreman of the jury:

> Although the Grand Jury feels there were instances shown where there was negligence involved, it was of the opinion that this negligence was not criminal in nature. The Grand Jury did not find any evidence that would tend to raise the possibility of indictment for criminal negligence and/or conspiratorial conduct indicating such negligence.[47]

## 16

Reaction to the verdict of the jury was overwhelmingly negative. Survivors of the disaster expressed shock over some of the jury's findings. Relatives of the fire's victims felt cheated and voiced anger. Public officials interested in the case bristled over the sudden termination of the prosecution. Newspaper headlines that followed the release of the jury's report were uniformly unfavorable: "JURY REPORT SHOCKS FIRE SURVIVORS,"[48] "BEVERLY REPORT STIRS CONTROVERSY,"[49] "DON'T THINK JUSTICE WAS DONE,"[50] and "JURY REPORT: BLASTED, DEFENDED, REVIEWED."[51] Editorial writers exhumed the state's report on the fire and used it to characterize the jury's verdict as stunning and mystifying.

Pressure for a public explanation of the jury's findings mounted quickly. The foreman of the jury was overwhelmed by telephone calls that reached his home. Reporters stalked members of the group in hopes of an interview. An editorial in one of the area's leading newspapers expressed sentiments widely shared by members of the press.

### An Open Letter to the Grand Jury

*There appears to be a growing feeling that you did not discharge your responsibility adequately....*

*It is the kind of thing that leads some observers to believe that you could have done a much more thorough job sifting the available evidence....*

*We would like to think you are intelligent, responsible people. Certainly, you represent a cross-section of the community....*

*Questions have been raised about your performance that deserve an answer—from you....*

*Your report has raised strong questions about the findings of the official state report on Beverly Hills. The public has a right to know what evidence you relied on.*[52]

Neither the prosecutor nor the jury was in a position to accept this challenge. Grand jury proceedings are conducted behind closed doors, and both jurors and others are legally obligated to protect their secrecy.

At some point the prosecutor attempted nonetheless to explain the jury's failure to indict: *There was insufficient evidence to indicate guilt beyond a reasonable doubt.* In so doing he added fuel to a growing controversy. Reaction to his explanation was sought from one of the most experienced criminal lawyers in the area and subsequently given prominent coverage in the press:

> *That's absurd. I'll accept it as a slip on [his part], but the fact remains that the sole purpose of the grand jury is to determine whether it is more probable than not that a crime has been committed. . . . A grand jury does not determine guilt or innocence at all.*[53]

From this exchange there emerged only one thing of importance—widespread doubt about the grand jury's understanding of its proper role.

The foreman of the grand jury also succumbed to the pressure and consented to an interview with members of the press. The jury had been greatly influenced, he said, by a belief that panic had played a predominant role in the deaths that occurred in the fire. He expressed an opinion that the exits for the showroom had been sufficient to satisfy the requirements of the law. Otherwise, he asked, why would state officials have authorized the club to operate? He restated the jury's conclusion about the number of people in the showroom at the time of the fire but simultaneously confessed that he did not know the legal capacity of the room.[54] He ended his efforts to quiet the controversy without success. His explanation for the sudden termination of the prosecution satisfied very few.

## 17

Within hours of the jury's decision, the governor called the Attorney General of Kentucky to ask for information and advice. He was told that the secrecy of the proceeding could not be stripped away, that the state's evidence could be resubmitted to a second grand jury, and that a special prosecutor could be appointed to handle the case. On the heels of this conversation he asked the commissioner of state police, the new fire marshal, and his own general counsel to review the jury's report and make recommendations.

A few days later, by letter to the governor, the commissioner raised questions about the scope of the grand jury's inquiry. He noted that the state police had interrogated about 630 witnesses during its investigation, that the jury had interviewed only about ninety, and that none of the state's fire analysis experts had been asked to give testimony. He suggested the possibility that "the Grand Jury [had not] had access to all of the evidence collected during the state's investigation." In a separate letter the fire marshal took strong issue with the jury's conclusions "that the facility was not overcrowded, that ample warning was given ... and that ... all individuals involved acted in a rational and responsible manner." He told the governor that the owners had been grossly negligent in the construction and renovation of the building, in failing to provide proper means of egress, and in deliberately overloading the facility to the point of endangering the occupants.

The governor's legal counsel expressed doubt in his letter about the impartiality of the grand jury. He described the jury's report as "an obvious attempt ... to exonerate and commend everyone in Campbell County who played any part in the Beverly Hills fire" and "an equally obvious attempt to cast whatever blame there might be on the various agencies of state government." He expressed the opinion that Beverly Hills was a case of criminal homicide and recommended that the governor ask the attorney general to intervene in the case. He suggested that a second grand jury (if impaneled) be instructed to determine only if there could be found in the evidence "probable cause" to believe that crimes had been committed in connection with the fire.

On August 9, 1978 the governor announced his own views in a letter addressed to the attorney general:

> *Pursuant to KRS 15.200, I hereby request that your office review the actions of the Campbell County Grand Jury in regard to its findings concerning the Beverly Hills fire to determine whether the Grand Jury thoroughly investigated all relevant matters and reached a proper determination as to its legal conclusions. I base this request upon apparent inconsistencies between the findings of the Grand Jury and those made by the special investigative team for this Commonwealth...*
>
> *I feel that it is my duty to make this request to insure a fair, just, and accurate adjudication of the Beverly Hills tragedy, and to maintain the public trust in governmental institutions. The conflicting conclusions concerning the fire make it absolutely essential, in my opinion, that you undertake a review of all evidence and determine if further action should be taken.*

By this time the state was heavily involved in civil litigation over the fire. The attorney general could not conduct a criminal investigation of the tragedy without the appearance of a conflict of interest, so a decision was made to obtain a special prosecutor from outside the government. An appointment to the position was made promptly and a third official investigation of the fire swung into gear.

18

The special prosecutor thought it necessary to retrace the steps of both the governor's investigative team and the grand jury. He examined all of the evidence that had been accumulated about the fire, studied the various reports that had been prepared by agencies of government, and personally interrogated a long list of important witnesses. He interviewed the commissioner of state police, the prosecuting attorney who had handled the case, the experts who had analyzed the fire for the state, and others who had played important roles in the investigation of the disaster. He reviewed the testimony heard by members of the grand jury and engaged in a lengthy conversation with the owners of the building. He exhausted every known source of pertinent information and in the end found himself with essentially the same evidence possessed by earlier investigators and with essentially the same issues.

He concluded his search for answers to those issues in February of 1979 and turned his attention to the preparation of a report. He isolated what he considered to be the most credible evidence available and began the process of making the judgments necessary for a recommendation to the attorney general. Among the most crucial of his findings were the following:

1. About the Circumstances Surrounding the Fire

The crowd in the showroom on the night of the tragedy, though not as large as estimated in the state's report, was almost double the size authorized by the limitations of the law: "[The evidence] establishes beyond doubt that the Cabaret Room was overcrowded at the time of the fire."[55] The exit facilities for that part of the building, he thought, were clearly insufficient to satisfy the requirements of building and fire codes: "Full compliance with safety requirements would have resulted in one additional exit from the Cabaret Room and additional capacity (width) in the exits that did exist."[56] The time it took for notice of the fire to reach the showroom was not the full twenty minutes reported by the state's investigators, but there was a gap of "approximately eight to ten minutes between the discovery of the fire in the Zebra Room and the notification of its existence to occupants of the Cabaret Room."[57]

The victims of the tragedy, he believed, could not properly be blamed for their own deaths:

> *Whether or not the failure of some to heed the warning about the fire might have contributed to the loss of life in the fire is impossible to determine. Until heavy smoke entered the Cabaret Room . . . evacuation proceeded smoothly and without panic. Had everyone proceeded immediately after the fire announcement to move simultaneously toward the exits, it is possible that the evacuation would have been even less successful than it was. . . . The speculation that some of the victims of the*

*fire may have failed to exercise complete care for their own safety can be dismissed as insignificant...*[58]

They lost their lives, he thought, largely because of overcrowded conditions in the showroom, inadequate means of escape to safety, and the time it took for notification of the fire to reach that part of the building.

2. About the Culpability of Public Officials

The firetrap at Beverly Hills was at least in part an official creation. Neither local nor state officials, he thought, could be absolved of blame. The fire chiefs had not familiarized themselves with fire and safety codes and had inspected the building without detecting its worst hazards. The building inspector had improperly issued construction permits and certificates of occupancy, had acquired minimal knowledge of safety standards at best, and had relied on others to make the building safe for use. Officials of the fire marshal's office had conducted grossly inadequate inspections of the building, had failed to order correction of deficiencies known to exist there, had approved the building for use with knowledge of its non-compliance with safety standards, had failed to establish an occupancy load for the showroom, and had failed to heed warning that the club might be a firetrap.

Not all of the blame for these failures, he thought, could fairly be laid on the officials, for none in the group had performed his duties without hindrance or handicap. The fire chiefs and building inspector had worked as part-time public servants performing difficult duties for nominal compensation. None had been adequately trained for the enforcement obligations of his office. The state fire marshal's office had been understaffed, underfunded, and poorly structured. The field inspectors serving that office had been undereducated, undertrained, and overextended. The building and fire codes in effect before and at the time of the fire had been too complex for the people trying to enforce them and in some instances not even available to them, and within the enforcement system there had existed a crippling uncertainty as to the division of responsibility between state and local officials.

A high level of performance under these circumstances could not have been expected or demanded. To disregard this fact after the tragedy, he thought, would be flagrantly unfair and unjust:

> *The crucial issue. . . is not whether the conduct of (the officials) deviated grossly from the manner in which a reasonable person might have acted under ideal circumstances. Instead, it is whether their conduct deviated grossly from the manner in which a reasonable person might have acted under the same circumstances.*[59]

Very few issues in this difficult case, he thought, were susceptible to clearly unassailable solutions. But this one was exceptional. There was little room for doubt in his mind: *When the actual circumstances, as opposed to the ideal ones, are taken into proper account, I find myself unable to conclude that the offense of. . . homicide was committed by any [of the public officials.]*[60]

3. About the Culpability of Dick Schilling

The principal owner of the club, he thought, had not totally disregarded the safety of his building. He had done his damnedest, according to the fire chief of Southgate, "to comply with fire safety standards."[61] He had never refused, according to an inspector from the fire marshal's office, "to comply with any recommendations made about the facility."[62] He had believed his building free of fire hazards and had been told just a few months before the tragedy (by a ranking fire official) that his building was "in substantial compliance with minimum fire safety regulations."[63] He had not on any occasion acted in conscious disregard for the lives of his patrons and employees. But he had, however, made substantial contributions to each of the major factors that led to the loss of life in the fire.

He had employed unlicensed architects to prepare drawings for the Cabaret Room, had failed to submit those drawings to proper authorities for scrutiny, and had supervised construction of that part of the building. Consequently he had no way to escape responsibility for the installation of inadequate exit facilities in the room. He had established the policies and practices under which the showroom operated, the same policies and practices under which the overcrowding had occurred on the night of the fire. He had not fully trained his employees to deal with an emergency in the club and had to suffer blame for the manner in which notice of the fire spread through the building.

The culpability in the owner's conduct, he thought, was greater than that of anyone else. It was sufficiently great to render indictment and ultimate conviction at least thinkable: *After carefully evaluating all of the evidence, both favorable and unfavorable as to this man, I am unable to conclude (as I have done with respect to the criminal liability of others) that the evidence is clearly insufficient to prove the elements of. . . homicide.*[64]

4. About the Grand Jury Probe

The grand jury, he thought, might have been somewhat overwhelmed by the complexity of the case. But it had not been mishandled and it had not been misinformed.

> *The Commonwealth Attorney of Campbell County conducted himself in this case as I would have conducted myself had I been in his place. He presented the evidence to the grand jury in a thorough, objective, and professional manner. He provided its members with necessary legal advice. Consistent with legal and ethical requirements, he gave proper deference to the grand jury's status as an independent legal entity and recognized fully that it was the jurors' responsibility—and not his own—to decide if criminal charges should be brought.*
>
> *The doubt that has surfaced about the thoroughness of the grand jury's inquiry. . . is not well-founded. . . . After carefully reviewing all of the evidence that has been generated from all sources, and comparing it with the evidence received by the grand jury, it is my opinion that the grand jury heard all of the significant evidence that could have been brought to bear on the principal issue before it.*[65]

Under these circumstances, he concluded, "it is not possible to view lightly the end result of this ... proceeding."[66] A grand jury serves as both a sword against those who violate the law and a shield against unwarranted prosecution by the state. Sight must not be lost of the possibility that the grand jury served in this instance to "safeguard against hasty prosecution in an emotionally charged situation."[67]

## 19

The special prosecutor came to the end of the road. He looked for ways to adjust the presentation of the case. Perhaps the issues could be simplified slightly by having the jury focus only on the culpability of the principal owner of the building. Maybe the standards of measurement could be more precisely and sharply defined. Not much else could be changed:

> *The prosecuting attorney would be obligated legally and professionally to perform in relation to the grand jury as [the first prosecutor] performed during the initial submission . . . The resubmission would be made to a group of citizens selected from the same community as the first grand jury; composition of the new jury could not be expected to differ substantially from that of the first one. The resubmission would have to be made on the basis of approximately the same evidence that was heard by the first grand jury; some clarification could be provided but the persuasive force of the total evidentiary product could not be greatly enhanced.*[68]

Only the vital questions were left for his consideration. Is there any substantial reason to believe that a second grand jury would see the case differently? Is there much chance, should indictments be returned, that convictions would ultimately follow? Should a second grand jury be impaneled and a more vigorous prosecution pursued? Would the state's interest best be served by terminating the investigation?

## 20

He traveled to the state capitol for an appointment with the attorney general. He had in his possession a printed report of his impressions of the tragedy and its investigations. In a sense the whole story was on the final page, for there he summarized his conclusions and made his recommendation:

> *1. The evidence of. . . homicide that could be produced against individuals other than the principal owner of the Club is clearly insufficient to warrant further proceedings against them.*
>
> *2. The evidence that could be produced against the principal owner is stronger than that which could be produced against any other individual. In absolute as opposed to relative terms, however, it falls short of making out a good case of criminal liability against him.*
>
> *3. The probability of a grand jury returning indictments against anyone connected with the fire on the basis of presently available evidence is very small. . . The probability of a petit jury convicting someone on the basis of such an indictment (should one be returned) is even smaller. I would say that the latter probability is remote at best.*
>
> *4. The sum of these three factors . . . plus the importance [I attribute to the decision of the grand jury] leads me to my most certain belief about this case. That belief is that nothing is to be gained from additional efforts to pursue criminal prosecution in connection with the fire.*
>
> *5. Thus, it is my recommendation that you not proceed to have a second grand jury impaneled to consider the case.*[69]

He had been told at the outset that his judgment about the case would be honored. He delivered his report to the attorney general and through him to the governor. His word about the fire was officially accepted as the truth. The state ended its effort to pursue prosecution. The file on Beverly Hills closed.

# Conclusion

## I

Circumstances played a big role in the tragedy at Beverly Hills. The location of the fire's origin could not have been worse. The Zebra Room was the only unoccupied area in the whole club when the fire broke out. For a crucial period of time there was no one in sight of the fire to sound an alarm. The Zebra Room was directly underneath the main stairway of the facility which gave the fire immediate access to the second floor of the building. More importantly it was located at the south end of the main corridor of the club which meant that: (1) the fire had an abundant supply of oxygen to fuel the blaze; (2) it had a large "chimney" to serve as a vent; and (3) it had a direct, unobstructed path to the most heavily occupied room in the whole building.

The outbreak of fire was as untimely as it could have been. The club's most popular entertainer was nearing the end of a ten-day engagement. It was Saturday night and the showroom was full, as were all of the major banquet and party rooms in the building. The fire occurred at 9:00 p.m. Had the fire started earlier in the day the building would have been almost totally unoccupied or had the scenario been moved ahead by just thirty minutes the Zebra Room would have been occupied, the fire would have been discovered more quickly, and the time for evacuation of the building would have been enormously increased. Had it been moved ahead by just ten minutes the big crowd in the Cabaret Room would not have been nearly so isolated from the rest of the club as it was.

With the discovery of the fire in the Zebra Room it was logical for the owners and employees to conclude that the greatest threat to life was in the front of the building. Their furious effort to empty that part of the club first was a perfectly normal response to the situation, as was their failure to realize that the occupants of the Cabaret Room—because of the proximity of the Zebra Room to the main corridor— were in as much jeopardy as those nearer the origin of the fire. Much of the big crowd in the showroom, after hearing a warning designed to avoid panic, concluded that the fire was small and on the far side of the building. Not everyone in the group reacted indifferently to the warning, but the ones who did were sufficient in number to deprive the evacuation of some part of its chance for success.

It is clear that these circumstances, and others not mentioned, could easily have been kinder to the victims of the fire. They deserve some measure of consideration in the final analysis of the tragedy, but in according them that consideration it is important that they not be used to obscure the fundamental character of the event. The Southgate disaster was not a freak accident. The building in which it occurred was a firetrap. The loss of life that occurred there was avoidable.

2

The institutions of government responsible for the safety of places of assembly did not protect the public in this instance. The state of Kentucky and the city of Southgate managed in combination to do little more than create a false sense of security about the safety of the building. They started a pattern of neglect and indifference very early. They squandered opportunity after opportunity to enforce safety standards, and through their combined delinquencies provided the victims of the tragedy with very little protection against hazards of fire.

No one factor can be blamed for this massive failure. The list of causes is quite long in fact, but on that list there is a small group that stands out well above all the rest:

1. The law that assigned responsibility for the safety of the building to the agencies of government was ambiguous and deficient. It imposed an obligation on both the state fire marshal and the city of Southgate to enforce fire and safety regulations but did nothing at all to define the respective responsibilities of each. It gave the fire marshal jurisdiction over all property within the territorial boundaries of the state and simultaneously gave the city fire department jurisdiction over all property within the boundaries of the city. It provided a basis for the state to believe that the city, and the city to believe that the state, would look after the safety of the building, and in actual fact nothing less occurred. Both believed, and neither looked.

At every juncture and in nearly every respect the city assumed that the state would bear the burden of protecting the public against the hazards of fire. The building inspector barely perused plans and drawings before granting permits for new construction at Beverly Hills. He and the fire department conducted inspections of the club without the slightest use of building and fire codes. Under the authority of the city he issued certificates of occupancy for new additions on the basis of minimal efforts to ascertain the real condition of the building. Neither he nor the fire department made any effort to fix occupancy limits for the various parts of the club or for the club as a whole. No one from the city ever talked with the owners of the building about this crucial matter.

In the meantime, buried away in the administrative regulations of the state, there existed a provision purporting to impose primary responsibility for the safety of the building on the city. The fire marshal's office responded to occasional specific warnings of danger at Beverly Hills from officials of Southgate. But it engaged in almost no routine inspection of the building at any time, and during a most crucial period, from early 1971 to early 1975, did not enter the club once to enforce the state's standards of safety. Whether deliberately or inadvertently done, the state left the safety of the big nightclub to the good judgment and sound actions of the city.

The combined result of all this was a near total abdication of responsibility for the safety of the building. The city yielded to the state and the state yielded to the city. Each pointed an accusatory finger at the other after the fire, and to some extent each deserved some blame. But neither was as much at fault for this particular condition as the ambiguity and deficiency of the law that attempted to assign responsibility for the safety of the building.

2. The city of Southgate provided almost no resources for fire protection. It left the building inspector without office facilities, gave him no money for essential operating expenses, and paid him nothing from the city treasury for the performance of his duties. It funded the fire department at a level that necessitated the use of a totally volunteer force. Not a single member of the department— not even the chief—received compensation for work done on behalf of the public. It made no effort to provide training or educational programs for its fire officials and failed even to provide them with copies of building and fire codes for the enforcement of which they were responsible. Perhaps there was good reason for this state of affairs. Certainly the city thought it could rely on the state for this service. Undoubtedly it had limited resources at its disposal. There may have been other motivating forces at work but one fact remains undeniable. Fire protection was not high on the city's list of priorities.

As a direct consequence of this, the most significant figures in the regulatory system, those whose responsibilities took them to the building regularly, were not capable of offering much protection against the hazards of fire. Neither the building inspector of Southgate nor the two fire chiefs who served during the Schilling period knew very much about the contents of building and fire codes. On the night of the tragedy, the fire department did not possess a copy of any code, and the building inspector had copies that were obsolete. In neither of these agencies was there anyone who clearly understood the magnitude of the city's enforcement responsibilities under the law. From each there came an effort that was conscientious and dedicated but almost totally ineffective. Failure to protect the occupants of the big club was inevitable.

3. The state's effort at Beverly Hills faltered in many ways for many different reasons. After the mayor of Southgate sounded a warning about the club in 1970, the fire marshal's office discovered that the facility had been reconstructed and expanded without state approval and that the plans and drawings for the construction had contained a long list of deficiencies. It dispatched an inspector to the building, communicated with the owner about the deficiencies, but permitted the club to open for business with fire hazards in place. And then when questions arose about its condition, the state compounded its failure with assurances to the public and to local officials that the facility was safe. Nothing more elaborate than simple human error was at work in this instance, but not very many of the state's failures had such an uncomplicated origin.

The system responsible for enforcement of the state's standards of safety was very poorly structured. Most of the individuals employed to operate it, especially those with front-line duty in the field, were not highly educated. Very few in the group received enough training for their jobs to give them a fair chance of enforcing a body of law that was highly technical and in many instances ambiguous and confusing. The whole system was grossly underfunded and understaffed, particularly the two units of the fire marshal's office, the general inspection and the new construction sections, that shouldered the responsibility for Beverly Hills. The special prosecutor described the situation as follows:

> *The duties of the [general inspection] section were to inspect all existing buildings (excepting private dwellings) in the state of Kentucky other than hospitals, nursing homes, and daycare centers. [The section head] has stated that during part of the period [from 1970 to 1977] his section had 11 men to perform the above-described duties; at the time of the Beverly Hills fire, the section had 21 men. They performed approximately 22,000 inspections per year, restricted mostly to educational buildings, churches, state-owned building, and since 1974*

*some mercantile and industrial plants. According to [the section head] . . . there existed an unwritten policy that other kinds of buildings were inspected only upon receipt of a complaint or request from local officials. During this period of time, the policies of the Fire Marshal's Office served to prevent inspection of buildings after ordinary working hours. (Fiscal constraints were responsible for these policies.) Consequently, inspection of buildings that received heavy use during evening hours was virtually always inadequate. The impact of these policies in relation to the inspection at Beverly Hills was great. The Club was never inspected by the General Inspection Section of the Fire Marshal's Office, and it was never inspected by any section of the office at night when the Club was occupied by patrons and employees.*

*The manpower in the new construction section of the Fire Marshal's Office appears, at the time of the fire, to have been little better. [The section head] . . . had nine inspectors, one of whom was responsible for Northern Kentucky and Campbell County. These inspectors, like those in the General Inspection Section, worked out of their homes, had no fixed offices, and received their assignments by mail. Under this system, which no doubt resulted from the inadequate public funding of this governmental function, supervision of the field inspectors by superiors in the Fire Marshal's Office was difficult, if not impossible.*

*A general, but quite accurate, description of the state inspection apparatus was provided recently by [a man] who once served as state fire marshal:*

> I don't see how it could have been done much better with the lack of personnel you had to operate with, with a state the size that this is and as few field inspectors that you had, inspecting the public school system every year was a frantic operation, just a frantic operation because of being understaffed. It was just a very difficult office to operate with any degree of efficiency. . . . But 25 men roaming this state, my goodness, it was an impossible chore. Just an impossible chore.[70]

Very few, if any, of these weaknesses in the system were without connection to the most lethal conditions that existed at Beverly Hills. Illustrative of this fact are the events of a particularly crucial period of time.

From early 1971 to early 1975 no one from the fire marshal's office entered the big nightclub on official business. Neglect of the building by the state was total for the full four years. During the period the structure was altered in highly significant ways, and it was subjected to considerable expansion. Most importantly the Cabaret Room was added to the back of the building. The fire marshal's office reviewed no plans or drawings for this part of the structure and conducted no inspections of the showroom before it was opened to the public for occupancy and use. Routine inspection of facilities other than schools during this period of time was a rarity for the fire marshal's office. As a consequence the state lost its best chance to discover the firetrap in the building and to avert the disaster.

4. In addition there was an overwhelming, intangible factor at work. In no part of the enforcement system was there a firm belief that applicable building and fire codes could be enforced to the letter of the law. Those responsible for enforcement of the codes, at both levels of government, sought to obtain as much compliance as possible, treated the regulatory system as one needing constant pragmatic manipulation, and expected never to make public buildings as safe as the law required. For reasons that are very difficult to pinpoint, violation of the state's regulatory procedures and of its standards of safety was accepted by officials of government as an intrinsic part of the system. Nothing contributed as much to the development of the firetrap at Beverly Hills as this.

The impact of this factor was felt early and extended through to the very eve of the tragedy. On numerous occasions the building inspector of Southgate accepted plans and drawings for construction of the building without requiring the seal of office of a licensed architect. He issued permits authorizing construction without any real basis for concluding that the plans and drawings had been checked against the requirements of building and fire codes. The fire marshal's office learned repeatedly of construction completed or underway without the necessary prior approval of the state. Indeed most of the facility was so constructed. For good reason the owner concluded quickly that these important requirements of the law would not be enforced with vigor and consistency, and for equally good reason he came to view them as technicalities of the law to be honored only in the breach and with impunity.

In the history of the club's construction there are numerous specific illustrations of this institutionalized willingness to accept less than perfection in compliance with the law. In 1970, for example, the owner installed in his building a stairway that constituted a major fire hazard because it was not enclosed. This stairway was undoubtedly one of the club's most attractive features and at the same time one of its most dangerous conditions. It was identified as a violation of safety standards even before the club opened for business, was scrutinized by inspectors repeatedly over a six-year period, and was left intact to threaten the lives and safety of the bulding's occupants.

Perhaps a more revealing illustration of this characteristic of the regulatory system occurred just a few months before the fire. Additional construction at Beverly Hills had taken the fire marshal's field inspector to the building on several occasions. He had inspected the facility from corner to corner and more than once had seen the fire hazards that would prove so decisive on the night of the fire. He concluded his effort with an official report to his superiors in the state capitol. The building, he said, "is probably as good as we can expect although it does not come into complete compliance." Within a few days of this report the owner received a letter from the fire marshal's chief deputy. It mentioned no violations of the law, sounded no warning about the condition of the club, and demanded nothing of the owner. Instead it declared the building to be in "substantial compliance" with standards of safety. More significantly, it painted a vivid picture of the most telling characteristic of the regulatory system. Violation of the law was acceptable even to those at the highest levels of authority. With benefit of hindsight, it is very easy to see how the Beverly Hills club became a firetrap with an official seal of government approval.

3

Only the owner of a place of public assembly has the power to employ individuals to design and construct his facility. The state's attempt to influence the owner in this regard is limited to a requirement that plans and drawings for construction contain the seal of a licensed architect. In 1970 Richard Schilling obtained the services of an architect not licensed in the state of Kentucky and simultaneously assumed personal responsibility for construction of the building in accordance with the plans and drawings provided by the architect. Ultimately he managed to obtain the seal of office of a licensed architect for his plans, but never did he get what he needed and what was contemplated by the spirit of the law, a careful review of the plans and drawings in the light of applicable building and fire codes.

In subsequent years, with other construction projects, he repeated this practice. Then in 1974, when adding the Cabaret Room to this club, he increased the dangerousness of the practice by neglecting to obtain approval from the state fire marshal's office for his construction. This part of the building, where 163 people died on the night of the fire, was designed by an architectural student, constructed without any scrutiny of the plans and drawings against appropriate building and fire codes, and opened for occupancy without inspection by anyone familiar with the state's standards of safety. In 1976 he added the Zebra Room to his building without obtaining plans and drawings for the construction, without seeking a building permit from the city, and without obtaining approval of the state fire marshal's office. So the part of the buiding where the fire started and the part where all but two of the victims died were constructed without compliance with important requirements of the law.

Undoubtedly these failures of the principal owner were blamable in part on weaknesses in the regulatory system. At least it is clear that he did not act in the dark of night out of the sight of officials responsible for the safety of places of public assembly. On the other hand, the weaknesses of the system and the failure of the government to enforce the law against him do not in any sense render him blameless for the lethal condition of his club on the night of the fire. More cautious and foresightful action on his part could have rendered the failures of the government harmless. But he did not act with caution and foresight. He took substantial risks in the construction of important parts of his building.

In two other ways he added to the risk involved in the occupancy of his club. He failed to provide his employees with adequate training for an emergency in the building and did not provide them with plans for an evacuation in the event of fire. In addition he established for the operation of the Cabaret Room the policies and practices under which it was filled with twice the number of occupants authorized by the provisions of building and fire codes. While institutions of state and local government contributed to this condition, by failing to establish an occupancy load for the room, the owner of the building was undoubtedly in the best position to control the size of the showroom crowd on the night of the fire.

In the aftermath of the fire Dick Schilling was accused of having shown a complete and total disregard for human life. Victims of the fire, employees of the club, and public officials joined in harsh condemnation of his conduct. But no one was ever able to produce evidence to show that he acted in conscious disregard for the safety of his patrons and employees. In fact the evidence was all to the contrary. He believed his building to be safe. To deny him the benefit of this fact is to lay on his shoulders more blame than he deserves. More importantly, to deny him this fact is to obscure the most important lesson that can be learned from the tragedy. Beverly Hills was not the product of a malevolent mind. There was no political favor involved in the creation of the Southgate firetrap, no conspiracy between public officials and owners of the club, and no wickedness in the actions of the principal owner or anyone else. The tragedy was a product of the most common of all human errors—carelessness and lack of foresight. One hundred sixty-five lives were lost on the night of the fire because of a failure of ordinary individuals to measure and recognize extraordinary risk of death to other people. In this last simple fact is the real lesson of Beverly Hills.

# Epilogue

## I

The similarity between the Cocoanut Grove fire in Boston in 1942 and the one that occurred in Southgate in 1977 is striking. On a Saturday evening during a very busy season, the building was filled over capacity for an occasion which included dinner, cocktails, and entertainment. The sole owner of the facility was in bad health and absent for the evening. A brother and a trusted employee had been left to operate the club under established policies and practices.[71]

The fire started at about 10:00 P.M. in a lounge area and moved through the building with incredible speed, aided by finish materials that facilitated the spread of fire. Occupants from all parts of the club moved in mass toward exits whose locations were difficult to find and known only to employees. The lights inside the building went out, further terrifying the crowd. Nearly a thousand people pushed wildly through the facility in all directions, looking for avenues of escape and struggling with each other for survival. The evacuation attempt ended in total panic, and a rescue effort initiated by firefighters met with limited success. No more than half the crowd made it to safety; almost five hundred victims were claimed by the fire.[72]

Investigation of the tragedy quickly produced evidence of safety code violations equivalent in magnitude to those found at Beverly Hills. Within a few days of the fire, investigators reported that defective wiring had been installed in the building by an unlicensed electrician, that inflammable decorations had been widely used in the club, that means of escape had been improperly maintained, that exits from the building had not been adequate for an emergency evacuation, and that the facility had been overcrowded at the time of the fire. It was also discovered that the City Fire Department had inspected the club only a few days before the tragedy and after the inspection had described the condition of the building as "good" and the avenues of escape as sufficient to meet the needs of an emergency.[73]

In the days and weeks following the fire, as details of the tragedy came to light, a public expression of horror and outrage was directed at those thought to be responsible for the catastrophe. Accusations were leveled against the fire department, the principal inspector of that department, and the city's fire commissioner. Police officials were assailed for failure to enforce the laws against overcrowding, and governing authorities of the city (the mayor and city council) were condemned for delaying the adoption of a proposed new building code. The operators of the club, particularly the owner, were subjected to merciless condemnation for their part in the tragedy and accused of willful violation of the law for the sake of profit. And underneath all of the condemnation and outrage there was an expectation that the victims of the fire would be avenged through swift and firm application of the law.[74]

Barely a month after the fire, New Year's Eve 1942, indictments for multiple counts of manslaughter were returned against the owner of the building, his brother, and the employee who had helped manage the club on the night of the tragedy. Two of the three were subsequently acquitted of all charges, but the owner of the club was convicted of nineteen counts of manslaughter and sentenced to imprisonment for a term of not less than twelve nor more than fifteen years on each count. The convictions were affirmed on appeal and the sentences were imposed on the owner.[75]

In 1946, after three years of incarceration, the owner of the club was moved from prison to a state hospital for treatment of incurable lung cancer. Expecting to live no more than a year, he petitioned for a pardon of his crimes and release from further imprisonment. The attorney who had prosecuted the case objected ("The defendant ... deliberately failed to care for the safety of his patrons"), as did relatives, of those who had died in the fire ("I bitterly and irrevocably insist that even the suggestion of pardon or parole is unthinkable"). The Attorney General of Massachusetts, supporting the petition, declared that the sentence imposed on the owner had been excessive and that on the merits of the case he deserved a full and complete pardon. The Governor agreed and on November 26, 1946, the only man punished for the massive loss of life that occurred in the fire was pardoned of his crimes, fully and completely.[76]

2

After the Southgate fire, the Commonwealth of Kentucky found it difficult to level accusations of wrongdoing against anyone. Its own contributions to the disaster left it deserving of a generous share of responsibility for the consequences of the tragedy. As a result there was no pardon to be granted in connection with the fire at Beverly Hills. The principal players in the tragedy lived for almost two years under a serious and debilitating threat of criminal prosecution. But in the end no one was imprisoned or even indicted.

No one from the state fire marshal's office or from the city of Southgate was ever held civilly liable for the consequences of the fire. The local building inspector retained his office during the investigation of the fire and beyond its completion. The fire marshal who was relieved of duty by the Governor before the grand jury inquiry returned to service in the fire marshal's office after a thirty day suspension, though not as head of the agency. In a subsequent reorganization of the office he accepted an assignment as assistant director to the fire marshal with responsibility for electrical inspections. The other two employees of that office, upon whom suspensions had been imposed by the Governor, returned to employment in a different department of state government.

The owners of Beverly Hills emerged from the immediate aftermath of the tragedy facing millions of dollars in damage claims against the family business. Settlement was their only viable alternative. Insurance proceeds from the fire and all other assets of the business, including the land left vacant by the fire, were relinquished to the victims of the fire in return for release from further liability. The remains of the family business was the cost of freedom to start anew. And start anew they did. Within a short time of the settlement the family opened a couple of small establishments in Cincinnati and not long after that laid plans for a new club to be located somewhere in northern Kentucky or southern Ohio.

3

Institutional reform is a natural consequence of a tragedy as appalling as Beverly Hills, and both the need and demand for it in this instance were extraordinary. Within a few months of the fire the Commonwealth of Kentucky adopted a new building code, created a new department of government to regulate the construction and use of buildings, and allocated new resources for protection of the public against the hazards of fire. A substantial effort was made to identify and address the problems that had caused the institutions of government to perform so poorly at Beverly Hills. Major changes were made in organization, approach, and personnel.

The fire marshal's office became a division of a new department, called Housing, Building, and Construction, with substantially reduced responsibility limited largely to the safety of existing buildings. A new division on building code enforcement was created and was assigned responsibility for the regulation of all new construction in the state. A staff of attorneys was added to the department for the purpose of giving inspectors and other officials easy access to the court system and other enforcement agencies. A licensed architect was installed as head of the department and was given assurances that political influence and manipulation would not be permitted to affect his efforts to protect the public.

A system of operations was developed to guarantee regular inspection of buildings designed for high-risk use. Places of assembly were added to the very top of a priority list along with schools and health care facilities. A computer system was installed to provide better control of the inspection process and also improved supervision of field inspectors. An educational program was implemented to provide everyone in the system with an adequate understanding of the law and the enforcement responsibilities of institutions of government. Legislation was enacted to require every fire official in the state, even those working exclusively for local government, to demonstrate substantial competence by passing a comprehensive examination. Inspectors were ordered to insist on strict compliance with the law and to use the legal staff of the department to bring recalcitrant owners in line as an effort to change long standing attitudes and expectations of both staff and private individuals.

A system of political patronage that had played a significant role in the staffing of the old fire marshal's office was replaced with a system based on merit and educational achievement. Old positions were upgraded and compensation levels improved across the system. For the first time the state was able to attract highly qualified professionals to look after the general safety of the public—a graduate architect to head the department, a professional engineer to fill the position of fire marshal, another engineer to head the section of new construction, and a number of individuals with associate degrees in technical fields to fill other important positions. The overall size of the staff was increased substantially with a special effort made to provide an adequate number of inspectors for work in the field.

Rarely is institutional reform complete, and certainly that was true in this instance. Responsibility for electrical inspections, which are crucial to the safety of buildings, was left in the hands of private inspectors and remained largely beyond effective control by the state. Old buildings, where the threat of life is greatest, were left uncovered by the more rigorous standards of safety of the new building code. Significant responsibility for the protection of the public against the hazards of fire was left to local government where competence to provide the protection is most questionable. In other ways the regulatory system emerged from the aftermath of the tragedy with flaws and shortcomings, but in comparison to the one that existed before 1977, it seemed to have only trivial deficiencies.

4

Memories fade with time. Very few owners of buildings dared to question the judgment of a fire inspector immediately after the Southgate fire. Even fewer inspectors hesitated before insisting on full compliance with recommendations for greater safety. The possibility of disaster seemed not so remote as before. As time passed, however, the fear generated by Beverly Hills began to moderate. For awhile after the fire, the lawyers in the new fire protection agency of state government had a full load of enforcement cases. By the end of the year following the fifth anniversary of the fire, the enforcement activity of the legal staff of the agency had diminished drastically. In fact the lawyers of the department had no enforcement cases on their calendars. Perhaps the natural recalcitrance of owners had permanently vanished. Perhaps not.

For a period of time after the fire, officials in high places in state government had no difficulty seeing the need for greater resources for the protection of the public against the hazards of fire. The staff involved in such activity grew from one hundred ten at the time of the fire to almost one hundred sixty. The number of inspectors for the field, where the real battle for safety is waged, increased during the same period from sixty-five to almost one hundred. But the sensitivity generated by Beverly Hills gradually disappeared under the pressure of tough economic conditions, and so did the commitment for greater resources for the protection of the public against the hazards of fire. By the end of 1982 the total staff of the new agency had slipped back to one hundred twenty-one and the number of field inspectors had dwindled to seventy-four.

5

Memories do indeed fade. More than anything else the fires at the Cocoanut Grove and Beverly Hills were the result of complacency, carelessness, and human error. A period of thirty-five years elapsed between the two disasters that are presently recorded as the country's worst. Undoubtedly another tragedy of comparable magnitude is waiting to take its proper place in recorded history. The next interval may be longer than the last. At least it is more realistic to hope for this than it is to believe that the lessons of Beverly Hills have altered in some permanent way the basic flaws of human character that led to the catastrophe of May 28, 1977.

1. City of Southgate Ordinance No. 75-5, Sec. II (1947).
2. *Id.* at Sec. III.
3. City of Southgate, Volunteer Fire Department, *Fire Report*, p. 2, undated.
4. Kentucky Revised Statutes 227.370.
5. Kentucky Department of Public Safety, *Memorandum to State Fire Marshal from Plans & Specifications Bureau*, December 7, 1970.
6. Cincinnati Enquirer, February 26, 1971.
7. *Id.*
8. "Chief Backs Beverly Safety," *Kentucky Post*, February 26, 1971.
9. "Beverly and Bluffs 'all clear,'" *Kentucky Post & Times Star*, March 4, 1971.
10. Commonwealth of Kentucky, Campbell Circuit Court, *Report of Grand Jury*, March 6, 1971.
11. National Fire Protection Association, Reconstruction of a Tragedy— The Beverly Hills Supper Club Fire, [hereinafter NFPA Report] pp. 63-64 (1977); Dunn, *Report of the Special Prosecutor—The Beverly Hills Supper Club Fire*, [hereinafter Special Prosecutor's Report] pp. 103-04 (1979).
12. NFPA Report, pp. 64-65; Special Prosecutor's Report, pp. 102-03.
13. NFPA Report, p. 66; Special Prosecutor's Report, p. 103.
14. NFPA Report, Appendix C, by Richard G. Bright, Center for Fire Research, National Bureau of Standards, p. 100.

15. "Dining Area is Thought to be Origin of Club Fire," *The Courier Journal*, June 2, 1977.
16. *Investigative Report to the Governor—Beverly Hills Supper Club Fire*, pp. F-18, F-19, E-7 through E-9 (September 16, 1977).
17. *Id.* at F-3.
18. *Id.* at F-14.
19. *Ibid.*
20. *Id.* at F-5.
21. *Id.* at F-15.
22. *Id.* at F-13.
23. *Id.* at F-14, F-15.
24. *Id.* at F-20.
25. *Id.* at H-1.
26. *Id.* at H-15.
27. *Id.* at H-16.
28. *Id.* at H-17.
29. *Id.* at H-33.
30. *Id.* at H-23.
31. U.S. Congress, House of Representatives, Committee on Interstate and Foreign Commerce, Subcommittee on Consumer Protection and Finance, *Fire Prevention Study Act of 1977*, Ninety-Fifth Congress, 1st Session, H.R. 7684 Serial No. 95-76, p. 128.
32. Statement of Julian Carroll, Governor of Kentucky, News Conference, Ft. Mitchell, Ky., September 18, 1977.
33. *Kentucky Post*, September 19, 1977.
34. *Cincinnati Post*, September 19, 1977.
35. *Cincinnati Post*, September 20, 1977.
36. "Carroll Rips Club Owners, Inspectors," *Kentucky Post*, September 19, 1977.
37. "Report Says Indictments Are Possible," *Kentucky Post*, September 19, 1977.
38. " 'Fair Trial Impossible'—Beverly Lawyer," *Cincinnati Post*, September 21, 1977.
39. "Schillings Break Silence, Rip Carroll's Fire Charges," *Kentucky Post*, September 21, 1977.
40. Commonwealth of Kentucky, Campbell Circuit Court, *Report of Special Grand Jury*, p. 5, August 2, 1978.
41. *Id.* at pp. 25-26.
42. *Id.* at p. 6.
43. *Id.* at p. 10.
44. *Id.* at p. 15.

45. *Id.* at pp. 11-12.
46. *Id.* at p. 19.
47. *Id.* at p. 27.
48. *The Courier Journal*, August 4, 1978.
49. *Kentucky Post*, August 3, 1978.
50. *Kentucky Post*, August 3, 1978.
51. *Kentucky Post*, August 4, 1978.
52. Editorial, "An Open Letter to the Grand Jury," Kentucky Post, August 4, 1978.
53. "Gilday Wants Fresh Beverly Probe," *Kentucky Post*, August 7, 1978.
54. "Jury Foreman Says: Panic Killed Them," *Kentucky Post*, August 5, 1978.
55. Dunn, *Report of the Special Prosecutor— The Beverly Hills Supper Club Fire*, p. 105 (February 1979).
56. *Id.* at p. 103.
57. *Id.* at p. 38.
58. *Id.* at p. 39.
59. *Id.* at p. 90.
60. *Ibid.*
61. *Id.* at p. 107.
62. *Ibid.*
63. *Id.* at p. 112.
64. *Ibid.*
65. *Id.* at p. 115.
66. *Id.* at p. 116.
67. *Id.* at p. 119.
68. *Ibid.*
69. *Id.* at pp. 121-22.
70. *Id.* at pp. 81-82.
71. See *Commonwealth v. Welansky*, 55 North Eastern Reporter 902 (Sup. Jud. Ct. of Mass., 1944).
72. *Id.*
73. See Goldstein, Dershowitz, & Schwartz, *Criminal Law: Theory and Process*, pp. 829-833 (1974).
74. *Id.*
75. *Commonwealth v. Welansky, supra* note 71.
76. Goldstein, Dershowitz, & Schwartz, *supra* note 73.

ROBERT G. LAWSON served as a consultant to the special prosecutor for the state of Kentucky on the Beverly Hills Supper Club fire. He was a law professor at the University of Kentucky for 50 years and served two terms as dean of the College of Law. He was the principal drafter of the Kentucky Penal Code as well as the Kentucky Rules of Evidence, is the author of an important book on Kentucky evidence law, was twice awarded the University of Kentucky Great Teacher Award, was nominated by President Jimmy Carter for appointment to both the U.S. District Court and the U.S. Court of Appeals for the Sixth Circuit, received the Kentucky Bar Association Outstanding Lawyer of the Year Award for his service to the state's legal profession, and has received numerous awards for his work in criminal law (such as the Department of Public Advocacy's Nelson Mandela Lifetime Achievement Award and the Judge Charles Mengle Allen Advocate for Fair Criminal Justice Award.

www.ingramcontent.com/pod-product-compliance
Lightning Source LLC
Chambersburg PA
CBHW070757020526
44118CB00036B/1826